IT CAME FROM
SOMETHING AWFUL

IT CAME FROM SOMETHING AWFUL

How a Toxic Troll Army Accidentally Memed Donald Trump into Office

DALE BERAN

ALL
POINTS
BOOKS
New York

First published in the United States by All Points Books, an imprint of St. Martin's
Publishing Group.

IT CAME FROM SOMETHING AWFUL. Copyright © 2019 by Dale Beran. All rights reserved.
Printed in the United States of America. For information, address St. Martin's
Publishing Group, 120 Broadway, New York, NY 10271.

www.allpointsbooks.com

The Library of Congress Cataloging-in-Publication Data is available upon request.

ISBN 978-1-250-18974-5 (hardcover)
ISBN 978-1-250-21947-3 (ebook)

Our books may be purchased in bulk for promotional, educational, or business use. Please
contact your local bookseller or the Macmillan Corporate and Premium Sales Department at
1-800-221-7945, extension 5442, or by email at MacmillanSpecialMarkets@macmillan.com.

First Edition: July 2019

10 9 8 7 6 5 4 3 2 1

O God, I could be bounded in a nutshell and count myself a king of infinite space, were it not that I have bad dreams.

—*Hamlet*, act II, scene ii

To those
who remain
crescent fresh

Contents

Introduction:
The Garbage Fire Eternal

On a warm summer day some thirteen years ago, I found myself in the frigid air of Baltimore's convention center attending Otakon, a gathering of "otaku," super-fans of Japanese media, namely anime and manga.

I didn't particularly like anime. And I felt I was a little too old for the event. I had attended a few times when I was in high school in the late 90s. Back then it had been held in a set of hotel conference rooms darkened to play obscure animation taped off Japanese TV. But in recent years, the crowds had grown big enough to require the city's largest venue. And the event had evolved too into an elaborate festival where otherwise isolated suburban kids came to bond over their favorite TV shows.

The convention was held next to the city's famous Inner Harbor, an outdoor shopping mall with a tall clipper ship drifting in the black water beside a dreary set of chain restaurants. And the meeting hall, like the mall, was brutalist and modern, made of hard right angles, truncated geometric shapes, and whirling, structural triangles, which teens employed as a science-fiction backdrop for their costumed photo shoots.

I was there with an old high school friend. We had both just graduated from college and wanted to be professional artists. I was particularly interested in becoming a writer, though I had no idea how to do it. So we had started making a short online comic, mostly about ourselves, called *A Lesson Is Learned But the Damage Is Irreversible*. To our surprise, people were reading it. And we had gone down to Otakon to hand out flyers to promote it.

Besides the webcomic, it hadn't been all that great of a year. Just after I graduated, my father had died suddenly of a heart attack. I had spent the previous months winding up the complicated affairs of his finances and psychiatry practice, badly. When the dust settled, there wasn't really an inheritance when split among my siblings, more of a series of minor tax problems. As a child, I had willfully shut myself up in the abstract realm of books. And so the transition out of childhood, into an adult realm I didn't quite understand, full of stultifying tasks and bureaucratic forms, was painful. It mingled with the absence of my father, who had been both a source of whimsy in my life and, somewhat contradictorily, intellectual rigor.

For this reason, entering into the cool, safe bubble of Otakon, where adolescents attempted to commune with the comforting kids' fantasy on the other side of the screen felt slightly unsettling to me, though I couldn't put my finger on why.

And at a certain point, wandering the triangle-shaped halls lined with wooden ships trapped in bottles handing out flyers for my webcomic to teens dressed as rubber monsters, things started to get weird.

Not for me, then—I hardly knew what I was seeing then. But for all of us, now.

Years later, I realized I had become an indifferent witness to a turning point in history, a vast secret hinge upon which world events would swing.

What did I see? Well, more of the same: kids in costumes. At the front of one room, there was a fifteen-year-old boy with a sharp chin, golden locks, and a baseball cap, going through a PowerPoint presentation that was a mixture of website statistics and lewd jokes mocking various types of cartoon pornography.

These included many fan-drawn images of the boy himself depicted as a curvaceous pink cartoon cat-girl wearing white panties. As the increasingly silly Photoshopped drawings slid by, the raucous crowd shouted words of encouragement, gearing up for the late-night techno dance party that would follow.

Despite all the adulation, the boy seemed slightly ill at ease. The cap was slung a little too low, as if to disguise his eyes. And he let his friends at the table do most of the talking.

This was one of the first meetings of a now-infamous online message board, 4chan.org. The boy in the cap was the site's founder, Christopher "moot" Poole. In October 2003, "bored and in need of porno," he had programmed 4chan on a whim to trade pictures of anime girls with his friends, but soon discovered thousands, and eventually millions, of other people wanted to use it.

It seems ridiculous to say the site was important. But even more ridiculously, its importance is already documented in the history books. In *Alt-America*, David Neiwert wrote that the Nazi-worshipping alt-right "began" with 4chan, "with people talking online about Japanese anime."[1]

Few of these books, including Neiwert's, offer an explanation for how this could have possibly happened. How we got from anime otaku to the anime Nazis of 2016 and onward. How all of this resulted in internet weirdos marching with tiki torches and similar fantasy-themed costumes in Charlottesville in 2017.

Of course, the kids in that room weren't Nazis. Far from it. The last thing they wanted to discuss was politics. And at that moment, I certainly didn't feel as though I was present for some great turning point in history. In fact, it seemed like I was confronting yet another moment of anti-history as the vast landscape of the American suburban nowhereland was imported into the convention center, a place that, in its expanses of smooth, clean carpeting, model ships, and big tumbling geometric shapes, felt a little like an infinite kids' rec room. The teens weren't trying to make a mark on the world; they were trying to escape from it by pantomiming discarded scraps of fiction.

However, looking back, it all reads like some crazy premonition.

As the microphone was passed from rubber dinosaur to trench-coat mafia kid to sea witch to ask their curly-headed leader questions, the teens/monsters kept debating and joking about things called "memes" and "trolls."

In the mid-2000s, these terms were meaningless to anyone outside that room. But later they broke out of it and saturated every inch of the world.

And stranger still, from 2016 onward memes and trolls became central concepts that obsessed political commentators. Almost overnight, the terms invaded the domain of world leaders and redefined the contests between them. Now there are Russian trolls, Facebook trolls, and of course, the original 4chan trolls all jiggling through the ether.

Back then, I was surprised to find that I knew what these terms meant.

Before I had encountered 4chan at Otakon, the site constantly popped up in my webcomic's referral logs (the data that shows where people came from when they visit your site).

When 4chan began it wasn't all that different from other online message boards; it was a place to post content and talk to people on the internet. At the time, it imported a few innovations from Japanese sites, which accounted for some of its popularity. It was easy to post images. And following a Japanese custom, it didn't require the user to sign up for an account. Anyone could post under a default name, which eventually became the name of all 4chan users, "Anonymous."

But this hardly explained why it ballooned so rapidly. Why, almost as soon as it appeared, people began gathering to celebrate it. Each year, the 4chan meeting at Otakon doubled in number, until finally, the hordes flowed out of the room and 4chan stopped holding meetings. By 2010, 4chan was one of the most popular websites ever.

How did all of this mutate into the alt-right? Into Donald Trump and trolls and memes? To borrow a phrase, what happened, not just to the election, but to politics, culture, and counterculture as it was heaped into the "garbage fire" that was 2016 and onward, as old ideas and norms burned away into a bleak, odd future? The garbage fire, as we now understand it, Eternal?

To put a finer point on it: How did a pornographic anime website transform from a postcultural garbage heap into the postcultural garbage heap upon which the great events of our age stood?

That story is the story of this book.

Strangely, when I began to write it, many of the disasters in it had not yet occurred. The manifestation of internet Nazis in Charlottesville, Trump's defense of their cause, and the 2017 street battles between the alt-right and antifa all still lay in the future.

The mystical realm of fake news and trolls was not yet ascendant. The *Washington Post* did not yet run articles reporting on 4chan posts. The *New York Times* was not yet putting out calls on its tip line for plots on 4chan to disrupt elections. Though, to be fair, Trump had already adopted 4chan's meme, Pepe the Frog, as his symbol during the campaign. And Richard Spencer, the infamous neo-Nazi, had just been socked during Trump's inauguration as he pointed to his Pepe pin. And all of this was not 4chan's first entrée into politics. Many fake 4chan conspiracy theories had turned into political causes: gamergate in 2014 and pizzagate in 2016. And just a few years prior to that, 4chan had spawned an international *far-left* hacktivist collective called Anonymous, which had played a role in Occupy Wall Street and the Arab Spring.

As the Trump presidency progressed, my friends delighted in forwarding me the increasingly bizarre stories that appeared on the front pages of major publications, as if to say, "How's that going to fit?" Since Trump-era events were so preposterous, the joke was, of course, they wouldn't fit into my scheme or any others. They were, by definition, totally random, designed to attack reason itself and our ability to make sense of the world.

Strangers would gasp when I explained that the subject of my book was the alt-right. "Very timely," they would reply. But then another thought would occur to them: "How? It must be *so difficult*," they would add sympathetically. "Every week it changes."

What they meant by this was that media reports, Trump, fake news, late-night TV, and talking-head pundits on twenty-four-hour cable news, all tangled into the heap of social media, were the font of confusion, the great source of chaos. What they were saying to me was, "How can you ever understand the font of confusion? It's where confusion comes from!"

Well, this book attempts to provide an answer. The idea is to trace the way culture and counterculture, the internet and reality, and politics and entertainment came to reflect one another in a sort of hall of mirrors. One that seems to have terminated with the manifestation of a once-unimaginable entity—a reality-TV president.

New language has been invented to describe all this uncanny mirroring. We are in the political era of "echo chambers" as messages bounce in and out of social media through TV personalities who were once politicians and vice versa. Close up, contemporary events appear like that dim recursive haze that manifests when you point a video camera back at the monitor displaying what it's filming. Meaning, and even the message itself, gets lost in infinite replication. This work aspires to draw far enough back we can look at how the system was wired up in the first place, to provide clarity by widening the historical frame.

The key to understanding what happened will be 4chan itself. And indeed, this book details how Trump's 2016 campaign was intimately wrapped up with the site's userbase. But why this occurred is part of a larger narrative, that of youth counterculture. 4chan was ultimately so influential on mainstream culture because it was the center of a counterculture. And stranger still, the site became the place where counterculture catastrophically split into left and right camps in 2017.

The first section of this book traces the history of countercultures prior to 4chan. It describes how all countercultures from the 60s onward suffered a similar fate—they got eaten by the screen.

It's a sad but now familiar tale: as late-60s counterculture struggled with the burden of infinite choice in postwar plenty, manufacturers were struggling with the same problem: If all the basic needs of human beings were met, yet the factories were still running, how would they get people to buy their products? The solution they came up with was to manufacture need. As American capitalism transitioned from selling products as practical necessities to products as gateways into ideals, aspirations, and joys, counterculture was employed as the advertisers' most powerful tool.

What followed, from the 70s to the 90s, was a game of predator and prey, in which new countercultures would emerge to combat the forces of materialism and marketing only to be swallowed whole by marketing campaigns that adored selling transcendence and rebellion. By the 80s, counterculture after defeated counterculture were used to bludgeon and skin next season's counterculture. (The hippie label sold fine food, anti-glamour punks sold filthy glamour, etc.) As a result, countercultures hoping to resist co-optation in the 90s employed nihilism as a survival strategy. They became about nothing, about having no value system, leaving the house of their mind, morals, and desires empty so there was nothing to steal. And this numb indifference complemented a numb indifference to politics, a response to the so-called end of history. In the wake of the collapse of the Soviet Union, the then neoconservative political philosopher Francis Fukuyama defined the pervading political idea of the period: perhaps the leftist utopian projects of other eras would never emerge and we had already reached the "end" of historical progress. In other words, American-style capitalism would endure for all eternity, no radical reconfiguring needed.

This seemed, then, to be the natural terminus of counterculture. But by the late 90s, the advent of the web had produced new dissonance in the void beyond: Gen Xers became otaku. Ironically, half-ironically, or genuinely—by this point it hardly mattered—younger generations were migrating out of real life and into the screen. Still contemptuous, they now celebrated escapism. But even as they embraced this lifestyle, something even wonkier happened: they squeezed it so hard they broke it.

The 90s contest to outpace co-optation by diving into nihilism de-generated into a race to the bottom to see who could be more screwed up, offensive, and grotesque.

The second part of this book details how 4chan won. It became the place where people achieved new lows. Prior to the internet, screen worlds had flowed one way: from manufacturer to subject. Computers reversed that process, allowing new generations to vomit up all the colorful gar-bage shoved down their gullets since they were born, telling them who and how to be. With the advent of the web, all the discarded pieces of pop culture, entertainment fiction, advertising, and video games that manufacturers had sold to youth to tell them who and how to be began to rise in their gorge as a spout of sliced-up, digitized chunks. And once ejected, they could be refashioned, snippet by snippet, into a homemade culture of jokes—memes. The new youth culture was created based on this gag reflex.

4chan.org became a hub world for this existence, the number-one psy-chic garbage dump into which young people discarded their misery and creativity into a pile of old art, cartoons, ads, video games, movies, TV shows, comic books, and toys.

And, as it turned out, everyone needed what 4chan had created—everyone needed memes to feel a sense of agency over the stream of nonsense gushing from the screen, not only for fiction, but "nonfiction" as well.

In 2008, 4chan saw its creations drift out into the world and take root. It spawned hacker/trolling collectives that propagated joke narra-tives in mainstream media to parody efforts to manufacture consent. And to the surprise of everyone, what started as a joke transformed into something unseen since the 1960s: a sincere countercultural political movement.

Absurdly, 4chan's ultra-nihilistic, ultra-apathetic culture of post-90s indifference went through a black hole and emerged on the other side as a genuine political force. For a brief few years between 2008 and 2011, 4chan denizens no longer believed they were powerlessly trapped behind their screens. They felt that they could effect great change through their screens.

During this period, Anonymous, 4chan's anarchic userbase of trolls, metamorphosed into Anonymous, an anti-corporate, anti–power struc-ture, pro-democracy hacker collective, which went on to play a key role in international protests and revolutions. However, by 2012, the movement had collapsed, its principal members arrested by the FBI.

The last part of this book details how, in the wake of this collapse, 4chan spawned the alt-right.

With the dissolution of 4chan's newfound agency, its userbase and counterculture sank to previously undreamed-of lows. A new generation of young people, somehow even more immersed in screen worlds than the last, flooded onto the site, while older Gen-X users found their prospects in life diminishing after the 2008 economic crash. Scores of young people, young men in particular, retreated from work and the world and never returned.

It was in this environment that the alt-right formed. These new groups coalesced around a resurgent otaku lifestyle celebrated on the chans like it was 2005, except this new version was even sadder than the last.

4chan was populated by a group of declassed individuals set so far apart from society and so wholly lacking in identity that they began to obsess over it. They clung to race as a means of self-definition. These new fascist movements emerged much as the first ones had, out of decontextualized people thrust from society by the mercurial throes of modern economics. Degraded and superfluous, convinced life was nothing but a cruel power struggle (because they were constantly losing it), they fashioned their own context out of absurd medieval power fantasies.

By 2014, many of 4chan's new and old otaku had converted to this ideology. And in 2015, they teamed up with Steve Bannon and Milo Yiannopoulos to back the candidacy of Trump, who promised America's losers that he would make them win so much they would get sick of winning.

Meanwhile, the youth counterculture that had remained on the left orbited around another popular image-sharing website, 4chan's rival, tumblr.com. On Tumblr, youth were so deeply steeped in screen worlds, memes, and fantasies, they created a new counterculture to match, a redux of 90s identity politics in which the old countercultural/marketer obsession with self-definition seamlessly mingled with fantasy products and entertainment fiction.

As the two political factions emerged, Bannon and Yiannopoulos precipitated (partly by design, but mostly by accident) a catastrophic clash that snowballed into street demonstrations, then brawls, and finally the violence of Charlottesville.

The result was that, in the wake of Trump's rise to power, something broke in youth culture and politics in general. At first it appeared as though we were finally lost for good in the mirrored maze of the screen, helplessly watching events transpire behind glass. But on another level, a clear pattern was emerging.

Politics, long constrained in a narrow band of debate between liberal capitalism and slightly more liberal capitalism, began sorting itself into youth battles that were a century or two old—between socialism and fascism, democracy and oppression. Broader themes from the nineteenth and twentieth centuries reemerged as the cracks in American-style capitalism grew larger.

By 2018, even the *New York Times* was running op-eds such as "American Capitalism Isn't Working," and the author of *The End of the History and the Last Man*, Francis Fukuyama, whose big idea was that American capitalism might last forever, suggested that perhaps socialism "should come back" because "at this juncture, it seems to me that certain things Karl Marx said are turning out to be true."[2]

Where exactly does that leave us?

After I encountered baby 4chan in the flesh in the mid-2000s, I started to read and document the site. This was partly because I needed something to write about. But it was also because 4chan attracted people like me—idle young men. The first ten years of my adult life weren't all that different from the second. I spent most of it unemployed or unemployable, drifting from gig to gig in the service economy, quitting jobs that somehow paid less from sitting at home selling virtual items on the internet. Even now, I own almost nothing outside of my school debt.

It's hard to tell how much of this came from, as another quite successful artist friend of mine put it, "ruining your life by becoming an artist." But I think I was luckier than most. I had the benefit of an education. As I struggled, I suspected there was a teeming mass of people out there who knew with fatalistic certainty that there was no way out. Others my age and younger, shuffled behind cash registers and into cubicles, saw even less on the horizon. Not just economically but, for lack of a better word, spiritually, on whatever plane art and hope were made. So instead, they preferred to live their life through the screen.

Ridiculously, as soon as I entered adult society, it attempted to convince me to never join it, to instead root for its rotten collapse. How else does one interpret negative assets? Owning less than nothing, compounding and replicating, somehow, into even more lessness? Is it any surprise my peers were even more convinced?

Why wasn't I among them? In costume at Otakon, locking myself in the glass orb of fantasy as a teen, or an even sadder gray cubicle as a young adult? And later, why wasn't I on the streets drawing blood? Why did I choose to stalk sad nerds and watch them, from a great distance, slowly transform into Nazis?

It took me years to realize this, but the reason my father's affairs were such a mess when he died, partly the reason why he died, was totalitarianism.

When my father was in his early twenties, he escaped from behind the Iron Curtain hidden beneath camping gear in the back seat of a Morris Mini Minor, a Nazi Luger pressed against his chest. When he reached the freedom of the West without having to fire it, his first act as a Westerner was to dismantle the gun and throw the pieces into a lake. He always ended the tale that way, proudly concluding that "the pieces are probably still there, rusting away at the bottom of that lake."

He never told me who helped him cross the border into the West. He had a companion next to him. I never learned who that was either. In my childhood imagination, the pieces of the gun seemed to embody this unsourceable mystery. What my father said about them, that they were still there, lying inaccessible at the bottom of an unnamed lake, resonated with the unfathomable.

And after he died and was reduced to nothing but a memory, strangely enough, that was one of the memories he became—not as I knew him, but as I used to imagine him in the story: twenty-two years old, hiding under sleeping bags next to this unknown companion, with the Luger pressed against his chest. I knew how he felt then because he expressed those same emotions throughout the rest of his life: anger and resentment.

He remained furious that he had been placed in such an absurd position, that he might have been forced to use the Nazi gun to shoot his way to freedom, that he almost had to employ the tactics of idiots, bullies, and evil men to escape another set of them.

That was what the pieces at the bottom of the lake meant to him: that happily he was not forced to use the gun, that he could abandon it all for life in the United States. Except those pieces did not quite abandon him. They were still dissolving in the story, never dissolved.

He did tell me how he got the gun. It started when thousands of Nazi soldiers surrounded his village in what was then Czechoslovakia some seventeen years earlier, in 1945, when he was five years old.

They lined their tanks up on a ridge and told the town to evacuate because the next morning they were going to shell it into oblivion. But the next morning came and the town was still there, and so were the tanks. Only the men had disappeared.

Instead of leveling his village, they had shed the burden of their ordnance, hundreds of tons of it, and walked away with nothing but their coats and hats, hoping to surrender to the Americans before the Soviets got them.

He never forgot how ridiculous it all seemed. How the vaporous substance of ideas can compel millions of men to madness before dissolving in the blink of an eye. How in an instant, the nightmarish dream of the men, the Reich, the war, simply ended. The world appeared to him then as he always insisted it was: a joke, a thin sheen of rationality covering an ocean of human stupidity.

He used the same language to describe the world order and the political order of the United States—a dream that could whorl away in an instant. He had seen it happen.

"It could happen here," he would say. "Americans don't know catastrophe. It seems unthinkable to them. But it could happen anywhere."

He kept our passports up to date. He stored canned food and bought many new guns to replace the one rusting in the lake—guns in the house, guns in the car, guns buried with emergency camping gear.

I wasn't supposed to tell these stories. The Nazis, the Communist partisans, Stalin's spies, the SS—the men had all died, but they weren't dead, only sleeping. The factions would come again, and angry that he had bested them, take revenge for old grievances.

When he returned to his village in the early 90s after the fall of the Iron Curtain, people blanched, he said. They thought they were seeing a ghost. When a person mysteriously vanished during Communism, it generally meant the regime had made them disappear. He laughed when he said this. And for a while, I really thought it was a joke.

The way he talked about it, with nations simply melting away and all of Europe going mad, was in a lighthearted sort of way, as a grand farce. It was part of the Czech national style. Just before Hitler rose to power, the Czech author Karel Capek wrote a science-fiction novel in which Czechoslovakia is absentmindedly destroyed when the world decides to go to war with a subhuman species of newt.

That, too, took me years to realize, in my stupidity, that I had received the child's version: the fable, when in the adventure, no one got hurt or killed.

When I was younger, we lived an ordinary, upper-middle-class life. My father adored the comfortable existence a traumatized postwar America had created in the suburbs, the Barnes & Nobles and the Starbuckses. He delighted in how Americans consciously crafted a meaningless, empty experience, totally bereft of culture—the same comfortable emptiness that was imported into the halls of Otakon. Culture, after all, had been the sticking point that Europe had almost choked and died on.

But as he got older the trauma came bubbling back up, along with the paranoia. As we cruised in the largest Cadillac he could possibly buy, from Bob's Big Boy to Walmart to SuperFresh (more American to him than the skyscrapers and the Cadillacs were the superstores), he began to pile on top of the apocalypse guns, food, and camping supplies a heap of other items—furniture, computers, exercise equipment, sporting goods, cars, VCRs, entertainment centers—all the consumerist baby boomer nonsense of the previous decades.

Inch by inch, I was slowly learning what was happening. He was suffering and dying from the myth of the clean break, the gun rusting at the bottom of the lake, as we coasted toward the end of history, post-Communism, post-Fascism, toward the products of America forever, the so-called end of history. In other words, a mirage.

When he died, the house was filled to the brim with purchases. We lived in several American households layered on top of one another in an absurd parody of overproduction. When I visited Otakon, I was in the process of throwing it all away.

The Nazis would return one day, he insisted, even in America. Not dead, only sleeping. I never believed him.

In 2015, a resurgent Nazi-themed youth movement in the United States seemed unthinkable, let alone one aligned with a sitting U.S. president. In 2016, it was a reality. And more absurdly, it was largely composed of young men my age, in their thirties and forties, on the fringes of a society they hated dearly.

If only my father had lived to see it! How the movement arose, of all places, from that ridiculous room in Otakon, with little kids and sad adults dressed as cartoons. He would have laughed so hard.

History repeats itself, first as tragedy, then as farce, Karl Marx wrote, correcting Hegel.[3] But what's next? There's no word for a farce of a farce.

Well, reader, here you are. Time to pick up the pieces. The story of anime to anime Nazi. Internet utopia to dystopia. Reality TV to reality. America to Trump. I hope you laugh too.

PART I

COUNTERCULTURE AND THE SCREEN

Countering Counterculture

Well, whatever, nevermind.
—Kurt Cobain

When I was young, I assumed the way the American landscape was changing around me was somehow temporary. The buildings, after all, looked temporary; ramshackle strip malls, Pizza Huts, and 7-Elevens thrown up chockablock—all of it devoted to a transient purpose, meeting a momentary need in the marketplace.

As my parents' generation replaced forest and farmland with pavement and a multitude of stores selling ever more elaborate and specific items, I wondered, naively, what would come next: What would replace these things that were built to disappear? Would my generation drastically alter the landscape of America as the previous one had? The answer, of course, was no. What would replace these stores was more stores, piled on top of one another in a mad jumble. Odder still, many people seemed unhappy with this development. The vast parking lots, for example, were friendly to shopping but inimical to human beings. And this is to say nothing of what economists label the "externalities," all the hidden costs that go into production, like the pollution in the air and the destruction of the environment—once a mere tragedy, now an existential threat in the form of global warming.

The American countercultural revolution, the spirit of '68 that started with the baby boomers then swept the globe, intended to remake the world into a more equitable and human-centered place. But whatever it did manage to do, it wasn't quite that.

What happened?

In her 1983 book *The Hearts of Men*, Barbara Ehrenreich described how, prior to the 60s countercultural revolution, men were constrained into the ideological role of breadwinner. If a man didn't marry in his early twenties and begin earning a wage to support his family, he was considered abnormal and, in some ways, not really a man. To 1950s American society, a bachelor in his late twenties was either immature or a latent homosexual. And oddly, the first escape out of these oppressive expectations didn't come from the counterculture, but from Hugh Hefner and *Playboy* magazine.[1]

When Hefner abandoned his own domestic, wage-earning existence and created the image of the single playboy, he fashioned an alternative masculine role. Instead of becoming a breadwinner, a man could use his salary to maintain a negative space defined by the absence of a wife and children called a bachelor pad. Properly adorned with the latest stereos, liquors, and the rest of the items advertised in the magazine, the pad was supposed to attract an endless procession of pretty young girls.

However, this Hefnerian vision of manhood was still tied to economic achievement. Like the breadwinner version of manhood, it encouraged conformity and merely changed the system of rewards.

When the first modern American counterculture emerged in the form of the Beats, it challenged both the breadwinner and playboy archetypes by attempting to disassociate masculinity from wage earning. The Beats styled themselves wandering "dharma bums" who slept with women and men as they pleased, and they were as contemptuous of settling down as they were of acquiring material possessions. For this reason, their cultural movement was condemned by both mainstream breadwinning society and *Playboy*. The Beats were dismissed as insubstantial "Beatniks," vibing out on nothing, just as the Beats accused the conformist "squares" of doing.

Hippies, following on the heels of the Beats, were also opposed to consumerist society and were equally interested in transcendence. Like the European Romantic artists of the nineteenth century, they were fascinated by the boundless capacity for human experience, achievement, and connection. In this spirit, they created novels, paintings, and music that celebrated the infinite worlds contained within the self.

However, as the new wave of hippie counterculture spread across the country, society responded in a novel way. Mainstream capitalist culture, including *Playboy*, did not try and push it back. Rather, it got on top and began to surf.

Why was the reaction to hippie counterculture so different?

Un-coincidentally, one of the books that sparked the countercultural revolution, Herbert Marcuse's 1964 *One-Dimensional Man*, happened to be on the subject of societal expectations and calibrating one's own sense of inner gratification. In his best-selling treatise, Marcuse observed that America had begun weaving sex into every aspect of society in the 50s and 60s, transforming it into a dangling reward for conformity.[2] Sex became commodified as both an aspect of work and compensation. Many of the cultural victories of the late 60s came so easily because capitalism was hardly opposed to blending work and pleasure. Marcuse noted how employers were encouraging the mingling of public and private life in order to exert a singular form of control. Shops, apartments, and offices were all exposing themselves with huge, transparent windows, and clothes were shrinking to trace the body. All of this dovetailed with the use of sex in the workplace as *Playboy* had modeled it: as a way to sell status, pleasure, and permission. The oppressive hierarchy of the workaday world, the daily grind of bosses and obligation, was combined, weirdly, with its opposite, the frequent promises of the modern world for adventure and stimulation. Indulgence and toil, personal and private, self-actualization and company loyalty were all to become one.

Now, this is simply an acknowledged part of our reality. Contemporary socialist philosopher Slavoj Zizek often uses the example of the word "Enjoy!" stamped on cans of Coke.[3] At first glance, "Enjoy!" reads as an invitation to indulge. But beneath this surface meaning there is a secret assumption. The advertisement has surreptitiously rested its hand on the spigot of our enjoyment, telling us when and when not to enjoy, assuming the burden of answering a difficult philosophical question: What do I enjoy and how long do I go about enjoying? (Coke's answer: If you have bought a Coke, then go ahead and enjoy! If not, then don't enjoy.) And we are all used to experiencing the sort of mindless joy (which secretly conceals an abysmal emptiness) that accompanies buying anything; when pleasure, permission, and happiness are, for a fleeting moment, determined not by our own mind, but mediated by the purchase.[4]

Likewise, we know the same trick can be performed with sexual gratification. It can be reduced to a commodity, in which gazing at an objectified starlet in a film is part of "enjoying" the film. Unconsciously, we have *bought* permission to leer. Just as acquiring all the commodities in a bachelor pad earns the playboy the right to impress women and therefore the reward of sex.

But Marcuse's insight was that this system of commodification and permission is not limited to sex or even enjoyment, but expands to what he called "the conquest of transcendence," in which all that is sublime— one's personal dreams and the boundless horizon of self-actualization and experience—is circumscribed and applied as rewards for conforming to society.

Why did all of these advertising and entertainment shifts occur in the mid-twentieth century and increase so wildly that today they dominate almost every aspect of our lives? Why have cable channels, movies, and marketing, of all things, multiplied?

This too was articulated by many postwar writers who inspired the counterculture revolution. Many argued the same point: the industrialized economies of wealthy nations like the United States, having fulfilled the basic needs of their citizens, have now turned from manufacturing things they didn't need to, in effect, manufacturing need.[5]

These critiques came from leftist cultural critics like Charles Reich and Marcuse, but also conservatives such as Catholic political commentator Reinhold Niebuhr and liberal economist John Kenneth Galbraith. All warned that if America did not stop producing tremendous waste and absurd new visions of what was considered affluent to sell, the country would eventually become a nightmarish version of itself, in which the fabric of its values and communities (not to mention its public services) would tear under the weight of industrial marketing.

As Marcuse put it, after "true needs" such as "nourishment, clothing, [and] lodging at the attainable level of culture" were met, the industrial engines that generated these goods didn't simply shutter their factories and declare their jobs done. Instead, they discovered it was far more profitable to simply generate false needs by convincing people "to relax, to have fun, to behave and consume in accordance with the advertisements, to love and hate what others love and hate." These items could be sold again and again because they created a "euphoria in unhappiness."[6]

To this end, manufacturers hit upon a method that Reich called "substitution," in which false needs were generated by a denial of true needs. If, for example, your modern life lacks adventure, you can experience adventure on TV. If you're unable to wander through the beauty of un-despoiled nature, you can do so in a video game. And if you are isolated, you can participate in the ersatz interaction of virtual communities, such as message boards and social media.

By denying true need, the false need is generated. And it carries all the satisfaction of scratching a mosquito bite. As false, it is encoded with a sort of planned obsolescence, so that, ultimately unsatisfied, you seek out the same inadequate remedy again to achieve momentary relief. In other words, the more unsatisfying the substitution (for example, processed food for fresh), the more profitable the enterprise. So when the intricately duplicative art of mass media nests in the soul like a cuckoo, replacing real experience with simulation, it is not so much a flaw as a feature. The manufactured impostor not only thrives on what once fed the real need, but attempts to murder its rivals by extinguishing desires for genuine experience.

This meant that after the countercultural revolution of the late 60s, the hippies' message of boundless enjoyment free from the authority of a Big Other, who told you when and how to live your life, was ironically usurped by corporate marketers looking for ways to pretend that their products gave the consumer access to a world of limitless pleasure unregulated by any authority. They neatly fenced off what were in fact free possibilities for happiness, and separated pleasure into discrete chunks limited by how much the consumer could spend.

Hippies were opposed to the isolating competition of capitalism and the shallow material world of commodification and consumption. But this is exactly where we find their image today, plastered on packaging in the health food aisle, invoking the idealism of a better world to sell unadulterated chicken, refined ice cream, home-brewed drinks, and balms and oils you can buy by the ounce to make you feel better.[7] When we enter high-end, hippie-themed stores like Whole Foods, we hear a pastiche of counterculture anthems—The Doors, The Ramones, The Clash, disembodied voices from different eras all growling angrily about the way society is structured—piped in to convince us to let loose and enjoy ten-dollar teas. Even the hippies' boundless transcendence is chopped up and sold by the hour as meditative yoga sessions.

The hippies' demands for a new power structure and a new way of existing in society were not met, but the smaller items on their list, those that had to do with individual lifestyle pleasures, were granted almost immediately. The Beats and their predecessors, men writhing away locked in breadwinning gray flannel suits, got what they asked for: new outfits. Casual bell bottoms and jeans became appropriate, as did long hair. The reinvention of music through the medium of technology, electric rock 'n' roll, became a new commodity market. And to appeal to the hippies' interest in exploring nature and the body, industry and marketing produced expanding waves of workout gear, cosmetics, and outdoor equipment. Obscure sports came into vogue, and with them new industries: surfing, rock climbing, parasailing.[8] The hippies became a "me generation" who explored their new horizons, literally, with new commodities.

This co-optation didn't end with the hippies, but rather inaugurated a mad half century in which an ever-expanding mainstream consumer culture chased down and trapped the countercultures that harassed it. Each time a counterculture was snagged, it was then transformed, like a vampire, into a soulless husk that served the enemy.

The contest resembled something out of a Cold War computer simulation. The two forces, consumer culture and counterculture, were locked in a struggle for survival, constantly adapting in an attempt to digest the other. Strains of counterculture perished, and new mutations were born with adaptive counterstrategies to avoid being immediately devoured.

When punk emerged in the 1970s, it was a porcupine, literally armored and covered in spikes. Unlike the welcoming hippies, it appeared to be designed to resist being swallowed up. It embraced everything mainstream culture wasn't: anything ragged, filthy, offensive, brutal, disgusting, or weird. For this purpose—just as 4chan would later—it adopted Nazi imagery in an attempt to shrug off co-optation.

And though punk today is mostly remembered as a fashion statement and some albums you can buy, beneath the outfits were the far-left ideas and political aspirations of the 68 Paris uprising of antiauthoritarian Marxists who aspired to resist American imperialism, capitalism, and consumerism.

But in the succeeding years, capitalist marketing seized upon punk with eager relish, bisecting and chopping it up into bite-size segments. Just a few years after punk died, Madonna was prancing onstage in the same studs and spikes, singing about how "we are living in a material world and I am a material girl," flirting with the same duality of pleasure and permission that existed at the center of marketing.

In response, counterculture dropped its world-changing aspirations. Hippies had wanted to reinvent society. The punk aesthetic reveled in its crumbling urban decline. Artists did not reach outside art, but inward toward fantasy and self-reflection, only able to produce Romantic art: proof that there was more to the world than what it was, that it could be imaginatively reinvented. Though the work quickly became infected with the despair of being used by the forces it despised.

> Re-issue! Re-package! . . .
> Satiate the need
> Slip them into different sleeves!
> Buy both, and feel deceived

So sang the post-punk The Smiths in "Paint a Vulgar Picture" in 1987 just before breaking up their band for good.

As corporate culture, commodification, materialism, and advertising became increasingly dominant in the 80s, punk morphed into L.A. glam rock, which was then destroyed almost overnight by the surprise counterattack of grunge in the early 90s, a new anti-corporate, anti-commodification, anti-materialism movement, which adopted punk's obsession with filth and old clothes in the hope that it would not be immediately hoovered up by marketers interested in selling the next trend.

As a gag response to having their own youth culture spoon-fed back to them, teens turned the screams of punk into disaffected, shrugging disinterest. The result was that by the late 80s and continuing into the 90s, counterculture fell into a deep confusion. Who was friend and foe? People kept switching uniforms. What exactly was counterculture asserting? All of this was exacerbated by the stranglehold of corporations that were fusing into vast conglomerates that held the keys to all media channels. Nirvana is a sad example of this nouveau punk. The band's front man, Kurt Cobain, wore ratty sweaters and never washed his hair. He told his fans he hated his life as a rock star, the TV that promoted him, and the record label that sold his music. His breakout album depicted a baby swimming after a dollar baited onto a fishhook on its cover and struck a chord with how kids felt, innocents tugged in all directions by consumerist desires. Promised a commodified, transcendent nirvana, this new generation instead felt indifferent, as the album's wobbly title *Nevermind* asserted. Eventually, Cobain blew his brains out, a final insistent act to prove that he was genuine, that he truly did despise his role in the whole affair.

Soon, the period of time it took for youth counterculture to be snatched up and devoured by mainstream corporate culture diminished to milliseconds. The border between the two blurred in a strange state of quantum uncertainty. The hunted counterculture of the 90s became an otherworldly dance of signifiers. How do you signal to your allies that you've been infiltrated by the enemy when at every instant your code is being broken?

And so, in all this nihilism, another strategy evolved to evade capture by the marketers—irony. Counterculture began to play a shell game with those hunting down their enthusiasm: they claimed to never be truly serious or enthusiastic about anything. Coolness, after all, was indifference. As marketers snatched up what they imagined to be cool to profit off it until they made it lame, irony became a defense mechanism in which marketers would abscond with a cultural artifact youth pretended was cool, only to find themselves selling something that was secretly uncool. It also made it increasingly difficult for marketers to read the motivations of young people. The youth's desires and interests were encoded in layers of winking, disingenuous joking, which, if torn away, revealed nearly indistinguishable shades of confused, unhappy indifference.

Naturally, this produced a counterculture of helpless, sullen, shrugging vacuity. Marketers continued to search for the next big thing that would get youth excited, so youth decided that the next big thing was being excited about nothing, becoming listlessly dead to all desires and trends.

Rap music went through similar cycles and epicycles. The lighthearted party music of the 80s was replaced almost overnight by furious "gangsta rap," speaking to deep-seated inequities in American society. But rap, too, experienced a Hefner-style reworking from art that critiqued society to art that sold a lifestyle. That is to say, it fooled the consumer into buying commodities as a ticket to imagined pleasure. By the late 90s, the biggest rap stars were spouting their lyrics from the decks of yachts, displaying wealth, women, and capitalist achievement as outward signs of their masculinity.

So 90s art and culture expressed a fizzling out, an ennui, a longing for the revolutionary spirit of the 60s undercut by a feeling that it was impossible to achieve. The material gains and wealth of consumerism made capitalism seem unassailable. In rock there was a constant note of complaint, vague discontent with cozy, middle-class life bleeding away into spiritual voids and material acquisition, feeling just okay, but no better. The expansive promise of life itself seemed to be on life support.

The hit rock band that followed the grunge wave, Radiohead (its name evoking the new theme of media dictating your own mind to you), captured this glitched-out feeling in *The Bends*. "Where do we go from here?" the title track of the album began,

> Just lying in the bar with my drip feed on
> Talking to my girlfriend, waiting for something to happen
> I wish it was the sixties, I wish I could be happy
> I wish, I wish, I wish that something would happen

The infamous catastrophe of Woodstock 99, in which the symbol of 60s peace and love turned into a fiery riot as greedy corporate marketers trapped concertgoers in a place where water cost eight dollars, seemed to encapsulate the disaster.

Meanwhile, technology was producing a new element that only exacerbated this hyper-saturation of marketing and indifference, a hyper-saturation of screens.

In the early 80s, the first VCRs and PCs began to be sold with yet another innovation in marketing: corporations found they could aim their advertisements at very young children. Cartoons, computer games, films, TV shows, and other media were produced to sell the new material plastic, which, if imprinted with the fantasy of intellectual property, could be moved at a tremendous markup. The number of television channels grew from five or six to several hundred. And so here too, my generation became soaked in something new, a flood of elaborate fantasy worlds, each rendered slightly more real than the last as the screen worlds multiplied. Many of these worlds were beautiful, genuine reflections of the complexities of human nature. That is to say, they were art and so heirs to the revolutionary Romantic movement that plumbed the unreal depths of individuality with stories of things that never were, that existed only in the heart, castles in clouds, princes and princesses, myths and gods.

Or they were direct descendants of the equally optimistic genre of postwar science fiction, depicting possibilities of things that might be. Though there was an equal amount of bad art, through which it was easier to glimpse the gossamer strings that tugged at even the best of it—the nihilistic purpose at its center—which was not lost on us children. In fact, we absorbed the lesson better than the adults: the delicately constructed worlds that spoke directly to our emotions existed to briefly convince us to buy a product. It was a cruel perversion of Romantic art, to use the magic hand that could reach inside a person not to soothe in comity but to manipulate.

And so, between the failures of counterculture and the multiplication of screens, by the time my generation reached adolescence, everything felt slightly unreal or illegitimate. Genuine sentiment, our own and others', was difficult to hunt down. Sentiment itself seemed corrupted in a vague way by the vast forces constantly tugging on our emotions and values, insisting some product or way of living was important while often simultaneously selling a virtual fantasy world to escape into; a simulation that approximated the real thing and, in many ways, transcended it. The exciting world of film, the power fantasies in video games, commercials on TV, and articles in magazines all worked vigorously to calibrate our value systems, to tell us what was cool and uncool. The competing signals transmitted a sense of unreality to 90s Radiohead kids, Gen Xers ("X" meaning, in this case, a mystery substance, a nothingness). Meanwhile, the hyper-real fantasies of film and the constant objectification of desire washed out landscapes of cluttered strip malls and shopping centers, anti-places that were built to be nowhere in particular. Meaning moments, significance, were hidden elsewhere too, in the romanticized world of media. By the early 2000s, youth movements like those at Otakon formed, dedicated to escaping reality and re-creating screen worlds.

And thus a bizarre, undreamed-of population appeared on Earth, one brutalized by the transcendent—taught not so much a system of values as a confusing multiplicity of value systems, each competing for a petty, selfish purpose. And this new wave of teenagers formed the cynical opinion that although they despised things as they were, they could never be different.

By the time I reached Otakon to witness the birth of 4chan, counterculture had been turned on its head. It was not optimistic but deeply pessimistic. It was not interested in building any new worlds but in finding a retreat into fake ones.

In 2014, internet cultural critic Mark Fisher argued that there had been "a slow cancellation of the future."[9] Fisher suggested that the generations born in the 70s and 80s had witnessed the promise of progress grind to a halt. Society did not admit that it had stopped moving forward into an improved and radically different future; it still *pretended* it was when in fact it was spinning in circles, like a scrolling backdrop behind a stationary car in an old film presents the illusion of motion until the loop on the scroll begins to repeat.

Of course, technological innovations still occur every day, but they often seem more menacing than helpful. Most inventions are no longer regarded as a step toward some better world. Rather, they are often read as yet another minor herald of inequality and apocalyptic disasters (via global warming, new wars, etc.). Even the most prominent examples of "progress," like smartphones, are generally employed as ways to disappear, to distract and remove ourselves from an increasingly unhappy reality.

The phrase "slow cancellation of the future" expressed how progress had slowed and halted. The modern postwar world of strip malls and highways that sprang up before our parents' eyes seemed to freeze and age. Nothing replaced them but more strip malls and highways, piled on top of one another in an increasingly frantic heap. The hippies produced cultural "victories" like long hair and casual office environments, but their larger goal of using new technology to radically alter the structure of postwar capitalist society was never realized.

Where did counterculture go after 2000? Backward and into the screen. Fisher looked at how even counterculture's most prominent achievements—art and music—seemed, as time progressed, to no longer move forward, but bend around in nostalgic loops of "retrofuturism" that played air guitar over hopes of a future that never came to pass. By the early 2000s, music had become endless techno remixes of past genres. Film evoked 80s and 90s vibes, and the future, whatever it was, resembled the digital loops of film and music, old styles, old clothes, old feelings on shuffled repeat.

The notion that we had experienced sometime in the 80s the "end of history" had also been the central thesis of Fukuyama's 1989 article, then his best-selling book *The End of History and the Last Man*, which suggested that U.S.-style capitalism was perhaps the best way human beings could ever organize themselves. After the 80s, this attitude only hardened under decades of "capitalist realism" that asserted, as Fukuyama did, that the best we were going to get was already here, a point that was strengthened by the collapse of the Soviet Union, which had endured for decades as a nightmarish parody of its ideals.

And so, by the 90s, it seemed to many that time had gone off track somewhere. This was the theme of leftist philosopher Jean Baudrillard's 1991 riposte to Fukuyama, *The Illusion of the End*, and Jacques Derrida's 1993 *Specters of Marx*. The latter used the young bohemian Hamlet's statement that "time is out of joint" as the central phrase of the book.[10] The "specter" for Derrida was the strange, haunting way Marx had been declared dead in 1989, but of course, was still alive in his death, haunting the West as something that needed to be explicitly declared unimportant because he was still secretly very important. Or as Baudrillard put it in *Illusion*, "The end of history is, alas, also the end of the dustbins of history . . . Where are we going to throw Marxism, which actually invented the dustbins of history?"[11]

Sixties counterculture had imagined that the emancipatory potential of technology, particularly that of networked computers, was going to create a radically more equitable world. But in *Illusion*, Baudrillard describes how technology has also continued to be a countervailing force to emancipatory projects. Screens function as mechanisms of control to maintain the status quo as virtual worlds undermine a sense of reality.

> History, meaning, and progress are no longer able to reach their escape velocity. They are no longer able to pull away from this overdense body which slows their trajectory, which slows time to the point where right now the perception and imagination of the future are beyond us . . . [P]olitical events already lack sufficient energy of their own to move us: so they run on like a silent film for which we bear collective irresponsibility . . . These societies, these generations, which no longer expect anything from some future "coming," and have less and less confidence in history, which dig in behind their futuristic technologies, behind their stores of information and inside the beehive networks of communication where time at last wiped out by pure circulation, will perhaps never reawaken.[12]

The vague notion that "at some point in the 1980s, history took a turn in the opposite direction," he wrote, implies a linear narrative. When, in fact, we've fallen out of linear space and into the realm of the screen, "where normal time, normal ideas of action and progress no longer apply." Progress and forward movement died in the cascading virtual worlds of screens, where radical young people find not only their coalitions but themselves and their sense of reality fragmented in a hall of mirrors.

Growing up, my generation expected the bright and prosperous future of the baby boomer era. Instead, Gen Xers and millennials inherited a world shrugging toward ecological, economic, and political disaster and drowning in the detritus of entertainment culture welling up from the past in the sewer of the internet, casting everything in the eerie screen glow of unreality Baudrillard first described as a sense of "collective irresponsibility." There was no second postwar *Trente Glorieuse*. Instead, wealth inequality reached heights surpassing that of the era of the 1920s, the previous modern record, mostly at the expense of the young.[13]

Gen Xers and millennials entered a society more dominated than ever by vast, immortal institutions. Yet, despite being born at the foot of institutional giants, most Gen Xers and millennials lack even the stability of serving these institutions. Instead, we found ourselves thrust into an economy of networking that emerged in the 90s. As Zizek pointed out, this soon had people regarding themselves as (mostly failing) minicorporations, amortizing our future by taking on massive school debt, then drawing business from various gigs as 1099-R subcontractors.[14] Thus, in a rootless world of constant competition and pressure to succeed, much of today's youth culture, when it is not sifting through the memeified scraps of media, became focused on the issue of their own intense anxiety and depression.

In *The Unbearable Lightness of Being*, Milan Kundera uses the metaphor of history looping over and over—what Friedrich Nietzsche called "eternal return"—to describe the static political world behind the Iron Curtain and its facade of insoluble stability. If eternal return were true, Kundera reasoned, we would all be as helpless as if we were frozen in a block of ice. History would "become a solid mass, permanently protuberant, its inanity irreparable."[15]

This absurd end-of-history feeling—that the status quo would last forever—endured in counterculture until this decade.

One of the most popular memes of 2014 was the saying "time is a flat circle." The phrase came from the popular TV show *True Detective*, which reworked familiar cheery stars from the 80s and 90s into gritty old police officers fighting America's decline. Repeating the phrase "time is a flat circle" not only expressed a certain flattened cynical helpless-ness, but the ridiculous way screen fantasy was attacking reality and gen-uine sentiment, how all events would eventually become pre-scripted and reenacted like a stupid TV repeat starring old actors.

Likewise, the remixing and looping of music described by Fisher had reached a crescendo, or rather, the ultimate drowsy decrescendo, in 2015. The newest cutting-edge "wave" posted anonymously on YouTube was called "vaporwave." It took snippets of utopian 70s muzak (once pumped into elevators as a way to improve society) and other facile "relaxing" clips and looped them relentlessly, and sometimes sloppily, over a gauzy nest of nostalgic VHS images, old cartoons, news clips, and credit se-quences.[16] The result was like nestling the soul in packing peanuts, es-cape by post-commodity time loop. Here were, as Baudrillard wrote, new generations "dig[ging] behind their futuristic technologies," no longer "expecting anything from some future 'coming,'" rather vibing off the failed dreams for the future from days past as a means to escape the present.[17]

Then all of this shattered.

An old 80s entertainment icon *really did* ascend to the top of world events. It was a retro future, social media noted, that had already come to pass in the 1989 film *Back to the Future II*. In the movie, an evil char-acter based on Donald Trump rules over a dystopian 2015. The symbol of helpless indifference, TV time loops, had become real.

A new meme called the "Mandela Effect" joked that perhaps we really had "skipped timelines" and time was literally out of joint. Message boards became obsessed with the idea that misremembered childhood memories (such as the commonly held but erroneous belief that revolu-tionary South African emancipator Nelson Mandela had died in jail in the 90s) meant that a time traveler had fiddled with the past and we were living in a glitch. All at once, youth seemed to copy Hamlet's lament, "The time is out of joint / O curs'd spite / That ever I was born to set it right!"

By 2017, youth culture would split into warring camps of radical Marxists and fascists. Memes about comfort in the face of anxiety and depression were remixed into pop-culture jams in which Pikachu advised socialist revolution. And internet fascists attempted to co-opt vaporwave into hyper-political "fashwave."

What precipitated this dramatic change?

The start of the 2016 U.S. presidential election.

Years before the election got under way, corporate media told us who the two front-runners would be: Hillary Clinton and Jeb Bush. To "realistic" network pundits, this was a sure thing because of the two candidates' cash and connections. Weirdly, what had once been a running cynical joke, that presidential elections only presented the illusion of choice determined by special interests, was being reported as reality. There was nothing more undemocratic than a small family of elites running a country. Yet the two candidates were to be second- and third-tier relatives of political dynasties anointed by corporate media.

Weirder still, no one felt any great need to hide it anymore. Jeb hardly bothered to distinguish his platform from the disastrous reign of his brother Bush II. And Clinton, as comically wooden and uncharismatic as Jeb, explained that she thought her husband did a good job and eight more years like the Clinton administration in the 90s would be just fine, essentially running on a platform of replicating an era twenty-five years prior.

Half-realizing her mistake, Clinton eventually sought to conceal her weakness by advertising it as her strength, marketing her campaign around the word "forward." She was a progressive, she insisted, working with the status quo to change things, just very, perhaps imperceptibly, slowly.

Had we indeed reached some sort of eternal capitalist power structure at the end of history? As static as the seemingly immortal feudal order that the Enlightenment had smashed? With sleepy aristocratic "dynasties" sending out their third best to rule? And all other grander political hopes shuffled away into dustbins? Were new better worlds confined to entertainment media, where we could at least watch revolutionary superheroes righting great wrongs?

Of course, we now know that the comically lackluster offerings of the status quo only laid the groundwork for candidates dismissed as ridiculous jokes by the establishment media: the socialist Bernie Sanders and the populist Donald Trump.

As both Sanders and Zizek pointed out at the time, left and right were outdated categories.[18] Now, left and right were competing to see which party would be pro globalized status quo and which against it. And after Sanders' defeat, it appeared as if the right was winning. Or, as Trump's young supporters put it on 4chan, he was "breaking the conditioning."[19]

Lost in the unprecedented events of the 2016 campaign and the spectacle of Trump's ascension was another extraordinary new first: youth counterculture, that old guardian of societal progress, broke catastrophically in two. Though buried in layers of cynicism, escapism, and indifference, the core of counterculture was still dedicated to the Enlightenment dream of a radically different and better future. In 2015, no party offered this. Conservatism, of course, represented preserving the societal patterns of the past. And much of the establishment left, like the neoliberal, centrist Clinton, advertised progress but in fact were interested in preserving the existing power structure.

Since the 1960s, U.S. counterculture had been firmly on the far left. But when Trump appeared to represent radical, wrecking-ball-style change, a vast portion of youth counterculture snapped off and drifted to the right.

The cracks had been growing on the internet since 2012, but during the election they widened into fissures. Afterward, they opened up into a vast chasm.

Predicted by no one, the two broken halves left their computers to draw blood on the streets in a series of brawls that echoed the conflicts between socialists and fascists in Europe in the 1930s.

And to explain how they sprang off the internet, we must first look a little closer at the relationship between counterculture, the internet, and technology.

The Two Sprouls

It is as though history were rifling through its own dustbins and looking for redemption in the rubbish.
—Jean Baudrillard, *The Illusion of the End*

Shortly after Trump ascended to the presidency, the conservative blogger Milo Yiannopoulos attempted to visit Berkeley's Sproul Hall to give a speech. The talk was part of what he labeled his "Dangerous Faggot Tour," an allusion to his homosexuality, but also the font of his rhetoric, 4chan, whose users referred to each other as "faggots." Though no one knew it at the time, the tour had been organized by Yiannopoulos' former boss at *Breitbart News*, Steve Bannon, and the richest man in the world, an eccentric computer programmer named Robert Mercer. The tour had been a campaign stunt. But Bannon likely had weightier matters on his mind now. He had just entered the White House with Trump, and Yiannopoulos, ever the self-promoter, continued on his merry way from college to college to speak about how, in a phrase he also borrowed from 4chan, "feminism is cancer."

The performance Yiannopoulos offered wasn't all that cogent—a sort of Falstaffian vaudeville with a lot of motley costumes (leopard print mixed with pearls and gold, or, as Bannon described the look, "gay hooker"). But the act enraged the left. In fact, that was one of the stated goals of the tour, "triggering SJWs" (Social Justice Warriors).[1] And now that Trump had taken office, tensions boiled over. At his previous speech at the University of Washington, one of Yiannopoulos' supporters had attempted to murder a counterprotester, possibly in response to the clashes that had occurred between far-right and far-left protesters on inauguration day. And so, as Yiannopoulos approached Berkeley, hundreds of faculty, staff, and students sought to bar him from entering. Soon, what began as a peaceful demonstration disintegrated into a riot as black-clad anti-fascists started fires, smashed windows, and attacked Yiannopoulos' supporters.

A few weeks later, Yiannopoulos' star power faded when videos of him seemingly condoning sexual relations with minors surfaced. But the "Battles of Berkeley" continued on without him. For the rest of 2017, alt-right and anti-fascist groups met to brawl, first at Berkeley, then around the country, organizing on the internet and uploading their footage afterward, cutting it up into memes. What had once been a long-standing online cultural war between the male-dominated 4chan and the primarily female image-sharing website tumblr.com solidified into a literal physical conflict.

"The whole world is now a message board," wrote Max Read in *New York Magazine* after another mad Berkeley clash on April 15, 2017, in which six people were hospitalized, one of them stabbed. "For most of last year, it was hard to avoid the sensation that something had broken somewhere and the internet was leaking into real life."[2]

Indeed, the central image of Yiannopoulos' philosophy, "taking the red pill," expressed this strange collision of reality, fantasy, technology, and politics. The phrase had been borrowed from 4chan, which in turn had taken it from the 1999 film *The Matrix*, in which a revolutionary hacker named Neo (Keanu Reeves) is offered the choice between taking a blue or red pill. The blue pill would have allowed Neo to lead an ordinary workaday life. The red pill, by contrast, casts the scales from the hacker's eyes, revealing that the entire world is a computer simulation constructed to maintain control over the populace.

The Matrix was inspired by the works of Jean Baudrillard. (In an early scene, Neo stores his hacking materials in a hollowed-out copy of Baudrillard's *Simulacra and Simulation*.) But Baudrillard condemned the film, saying, "*The Matrix* is the sort of movie the Matrix would make." By this he meant that *The Matrix* exploited the longing of a generation to liberate themselves from the paralysis of the screen to sell yet another escapist screen illusion, a kung fu action movie. *The Matrix* expressed a duality: On the surface it conveyed Baudrillard's revolutionary message of using technology to shatter the oppressive technological control systems. But secretly, it proclaimed the opposite, suggesting that people dive further into screen illusions. The underlying ideology of the film was that reality was fake and the screen was real. In other words, it used people's longing to be effective in the real world to advocate escapism.

Yiannopoulos' gospel of the red pill also held these contradictory concepts. On the surface, his philosophy appeared to be an emancipatory idea, a way to dissolve the oppressive control of ideology. But he was really suggesting layering a false ideal version of reality over how things actually are, just like movies and the internet often did. He considered himself more of an entertainer than a political activist. He told the press he was a nihilist, interested most of all in advancing his career. And his message of red pilling also contained this duality of embracing performance as reality and illusion as legitimate. His audience was a vast population of idle young men on 4chan and related sites who had already dropped out of real life and retreated into the realm of the screen. Immersed in video games and the internet, they celebrated defining their own reality any way they pleased on message boards. Rather than suggesting they get out of the house to meet people, Yiannopoulos encouraged them to wait until advances in virtual reality created better pornography.

Yiannopoulos' red-pilled fans imagined retreating online would liberate them, but after they did, they were frustrated that they were trapped behind their screens watching, as Baudrillard wrote in 1991, events "run on like a silent film for which we bear collective irresponsibility."[3]

This new gush of confused political sentiment, what many perceived as the bilge water of the internet leaking into real life, flows from a source that we need to examine more closely: the idea that technology will be the means of creating a radically improved future. Since the 60s, this belief has mingled with its opposite—that if technology does not succeed in liberating us, it will surely be our destructive oppressor.

Yiannopoulos later relabeled his tour a "free speech" campaign, a reference to the free speech movement that had begun with a sit-in at Sproul Hall fifty years before.

In 1964, a student leader named Mario Savio had stood on the steps of Sproul Hall and told protesters to throw their "bodies upon the gears and upon the wheels, upon the levers, upon all the apparatus" of an "odious machine."[4]

As described in Fred Turner's *From Counterculture to Cyberculture*, the "odious machine" was the university and by extension society.[5] But it was also the computer. As the 1964 protests progressed, students hung computer punch cards around their necks to symbolize how they were being fed into the mechanized maw of Moloch, holding up signs that read "don't spindle or mutilate me." They had noticed how corporate-built computers in the schools were sorting them for their use value, just as they had sorted soldiers, car parts, and scenarios for nuclear annihilation. The students resented being forced to contribute their own work to the absurd logic of the Cold War. The computerized pipeline from academic to cold warrior was exemplified and partially invented by Robert McNamara. Called the "IBM machine with legs," the Berkeley grad had pioneered standardized computer testing and computer analysis for bombing runs in World War II. After a brief stint as president of the Ford Motor Company, he then orchestrated the Vietnam War as secretary of defense in much the same way, routing human beings and bombs according to the calculating logic of punch cards and Cold War necessity.[6]

Theorists from across the ideological spectrum whose thinking laid the foundation for the counterculture—sociologist C. Wright Mills, conservative Catholic theorist Jacques Ellul, liberal economist John Galbraith, and socialist philosopher Herbert Marcuse—had all argued a similar point to the one taken up by the student protesters. The logic of doing things the most efficient way had produced an ironic result: technology was not serving us, but following its own logic, and in many ways, creating a world inhospitable, if not destructive, to human life.[7] The solution, as both the theorists and protesters saw it, was not to eliminate technology but to use it in a way that better served human needs, as a tool for personal and political emancipation.

As Marcuse articulated in *One-Dimensional Man*,

Freedom of enterprise was from the beginning not altogether a blessing. As the liberty to work or to starve, it spelled toil, insecurity, and fear for the vast majority of the population. If the individual were no longer compelled to prove himself on the market, as a free economic subject, the disappearance of this kind of freedom would be one of the greatest achievements of civilization. The technological processes of mechanization and standardization might release individual energy into a yet uncharted realm of freedom beyond necessity. The very structure of human existence would be altered.[8]

The idea that the "process of mechanization . . . might release individual energy into a yet uncharted realm of freedom beyond necessity" was not original to Marcuse. It was the central aspiration of optimistic countercultures that had endured since the Enlightenment.

The notion was first articulated in the late eighteenth century by inventors like Thomas Jefferson and Benjamin Franklin, whose attempt to refashion a society with these ideals (at least partially) succeeded when they created the United States. Their ideas were reworked by nineteenth-century Romantics in Europe, profoundly interested in the new experiments of democracy and social justice. Today we take it for granted (or perhaps used to) that society will improve, that there will be progress, both political and technological. But prior to the American, French, and Industrial Revolutions, most civilizations believed their societies were static and eternal.

In the early twentieth century, this precept of progress still endured in mainstream Western society. For example, in H. G. Wells' 1914 novel *The World Set Free* the future is imagined as a utopia "set free" from labor by technology, in which all of Earth's population pursue intellectual and artistic endeavors.[9]

Why was the idea of a world set free picked back up on the steps of Sproul Hall in 1964? And why did it echo across the United States in '68 and '69 and eventually, by the early 70s, the world?

Partly this was because postwar advances made a future like Wells described seem imminent. In the 1960s, the world finally appeared, as Tom Wolfe put it in *The Electric Kool-Aid Acid Test*, "beyond catastrophe," and so the new counterculture devoted itself to "some incredible breakthrough . . . what to do in that scary void *beyond catastrophe* where all supposedly will be possible."[10]

Indeed, Wells' imagined utopia had emerged in the wake of a world war and was powered by nuclear energy. Some, like the New Deal economist Galbraith, imagined the real, new-and-improved society might be effected by a form of liberal capitalism, which would rein in corporations and use the wealth they generated to invest in public projects. However, most of the new counterculture moved left of this sort of economic liberalism. As was evident in the '64 protests, the collusion of corporate and government interests had created a troubling postwar power structure.

In another book that defined 60s counterculture, the 1970 *Greening of America*, a Yale Law School professor named Charles Reich argued that technological advances were not generating increasing autonomy and individual freedom.[11] Instead, they were creating a vast cooperative power hierarchy split between corporations and government bureaucracies. Even the people at the top, the politicians and CEOs of companies, had little power to change the interlinked, hyper-logical system. Reich called this the "Corporate State."

Academic degrees, he argued, had become a form of "new property" that bought postwar students a right to a certain ranking status in the technocratic machine. The counterculture, he suggested, rejected both the Republican Party's conservatism, which limited Enlightenment progress to "freedom of enterprise," and the Democratic Party's economic liberalism, which by definition helped corporations grow to enormous proportions and "reduced [Americans] to the impotent 'little man' of today, dominated by public and private power."[12] Instead, counterculture sought a third way, which would dissolve both these forms of outdated politics by reinventing culture and human interaction to create a new, more liberating mode of existence.

To this end, several of those at the Sproul Hall sit-ins went home and invented the world's earliest computerized message boards. The first such device was installed in a Berkeley record shop in 1973. It was as a teletype machine enclosed in a cabinet like a jukebox, and connected to a university computer via a phone line. Instead of posting or reading the messages on the real tack board above it, a record shop–goer could drop a quarter into the machine and search or post to a much larger database of messages stored on the computer.[13]

It was created by a computer scientist named Lee Felsenstein, who had been arrested at Sproul Hall, and fellow countercultural programmers, many of whom had also been present for the protests. The group called themselves Loving Grace Cybernetics, and the machine was labeled Community Memory. "Cybernetics" was a reference to a mathematical theory used to calculate bomber runs during World War II, which considered human pilots as part of the machine-system of the planes.[14] Hippies, enamored of this idea, adopted the term to imagine a new form of harmony that might exist between man and machine. Likewise, "loving grace" was a reference to Richard Brautigan's poem "All Watched Over by Machines of Loving Grace," which imagined a cybernetic utopia in which technology served the needs of people rather than people serving the merciless logic of technology.[15]

In the mid-70s, Loving Grace Cybernetics transitioned into the Homebrew Computer Club, an effort by Felsenstein and others to make computers and communications networks "personal," out of which the first PCs and modems emerged, most notably Steve Jobs and Steve Wozniak's Apple computer.

When Apple's declaration of mass empowerment arrived in 1984, its outward appearance evoked the themes of Reich, the Homebrew Computer Club, and hippie counterculture. In one of the most famous TV ads of all time, created by the director of *Alien*, a buxom blond woman hurls a sledgehammer at an immense screen depicting a drab dictator droning on to fixated masses. She is dressed in brightly colored nylon athletic gear—the new outfit of baby boomer personal liberation. Because of the new Apple computer, the ad declared, 1984 "won't be like '1984.'" The outward message was clear: the computer would break the old world order of rigid hierarchy and the totalitarian stranglehold on information. It would prevent a technological dystopia ruled by screens—as Cold War America imagined it—in the form of the restrictive Soviet Union.

Stewart Brand, one of the original hippie Merry Pranksters from Wolfe's *The Electric Kool-Aid Acid Test*, was described in the opening pages as "a thin blond guy with a blazing disk on his forehead too, and whole necktie full of Indian beads. No shirt however." By the early 70s he was keenly interested in computers. In 1972, he wrote an article in *Rolling Stone* about a new computer user he called a "hacker," as opposed to a Cold War planner. Planners used computers to run war games. Hackers made games out of war. They reworked computers to make new art, like video games. Computers were the new acid, he declared, a mind-altering portal to novel worlds that would transform how people thought and interacted. They would, like drugs, make people more playful, creative, vulnerable, human, and fun, and in doing so, usher in a new consciousness. "We are as gods," his own publication, *The Whole Earth Catalog*, frequently declared, a message that resonated with Bay Area hackers. (Steve Jobs called the catalog the "bible of my generation.") A godlike feeling flowed from technology, which the hippies were going to use to remake the world.[16]

By the mid-80s, Brand had transitioned from countercultural utopian

homesteader to businessman, whose world-changing ventures would occur in the corporate sphere. Much of the over-the-horizon experiences
the hippies had longed for had in fact been made possible by the liberal
state. A rising tide of wealth meant many of those middle-class radicals
could spend their leisure money on new products that promised a fuller
existence in tune with one's body and the outdoors. Yippies turned into
yuppies and utopians became a me generation increasingly interested in
consumer spending as a passport to a fuller life.

During the 70s, the internet was a network of university research
computers called ARPANET, on which personal discussions were forbidden. But running parallel to the hippie hacker scene in the Bay Area,
corporations like Xerox, universities, and quasi-government corporate
institutions like Bell Labs were also developing PCs and network proto-
cols. And in 1979, two young academics working in this field, Tom
Truscott and Jim Ellis, invented a "poor man's ARPANET" called
Usenet, which could be accessed via a modem and the new PCs. Soon,
Usenet looked much like the message boards of today, except they
were, of course, text-based. Users subscribed to different news groups
and commented on threads on topics ranging from cooking to space
exploration.[17]

In 1985, Brand adapted some of this early message board software
to create a new digital offshoot of the *Whole Earth Catalog*, the Whole
Earth 'Lectronic Link (The Well), which became a prominent early online community.

As a business hippie who was still anti-hierarchy, Brand championed
a freelance networking approach to work as opposed to the old cradle-
to-grave service to a large institution. To this end, he cultivated relationships with screenwriters, scientists, computer experts, and radicals alike.
And so, when The Well began, it was populated by influential thinkers
from many different fields. Membership cost hundreds of dollars per
month, but journalists were often given access for free or at a discount.
In this way, The Well generated not only one of the first virtual communities, but many of the ideas that would come to define cyberspace as a
new digital frontier for individuals to wander like free-roaming cowboys.[18]

But under the nose of older baby boomers who, cozy in economic
security, felt like things were heading in just the right direction, the first
generation of unhappy, disaffected teens moved onto the internet and re-

invented Brand's vision of hackers. The new hackers were not creative poets generating a transcendent reality; they were scrabbling, ratty resistance fighters who were profoundly anti-corporate and interested in infiltrating systems and combating the immense forces that used the internet not to liberate society, but to entrench it in unfair power hierarchies.

This new hacker ethos had always been part of the old. Famously, Steve Jobs and Steve Wozniak had been part of the phone phreaks hacker scene in San Francisco and acquaintances of Don "Captain Crunch" Draper, who had discovered that the toy whistle in cereal boxes replicated the exact tone that convinced a payphone a line was open (2,600 MHz), thus earning the whistleblower free access to the phone company's network. Draper had also been part of the Homebrew Computer Club. In fact, in 1977, he had built one of the first modems for the Apple PC, though it was never used, possibly because it granted the user unlimited free calls by routing the communication through toll-free lines. It's hard to imagine it now, but at the time, the massive institution that the counterculture suspected of invading everyone's privacy and perpetuating a state of warfare was the quasi-governmental, quasi-private monopoly of the phone company. Draper, the legend goes, once phreaked his way up the lines to the top of the pyramid, calling the wiretapping President Nixon himself.

But by the late 80s, infiltrating large institutions had become the defining activity of a new generation of hackers. And in 1989, representatives from this group of young hackers were invited to participate in a *Harper's*/The Well debate, "Is Computer Hacking a Crime?"

The participants included the old guard of hippie hackers, Felsenstein and Brand, as well as John Perry Barlow, a former Grateful Dead lyricist and libertarian rancher who had become a spokesperson for the new cyberculture through his associations on The Well.

It also included a new generation of practicing hackers who defined themselves by their capacity to understand systems and break into them: Eric Corley, under his pseudonym "Emmanuel Goldstein" (the name of the radical enemy of the government in *1984*), who published *2600: The Hacker Quarterly* (named after Draper's 2,600 MHz), and two teenage members of a New York City–based hacking group, Mark "Phiber Optik" Abene and Elias "Acid Phreak" Ladopoulos.

To Felsenstein, quoting Ginsberg, hackers were "burning for the ancient heavenly connection." They went "where artists go," to the "Epsilon-wide crack between What Is and What Could Be."[19] And they had largely accomplished their goal. They had liberated computers from large institutions and turned them into tools for creative expression. "We cracked the egg out from under the Computer Priesthood," he wrote, "and now everyone can have omelets."

But the young, practicing hackers weren't chasing the sublime. Rather, they saw themselves as fighting a war with institutional forces who were using the burgeoning internet to establish a stranglehold on society. For the new hackers, breaking into systems wasn't a criminal lark, but a means to show how entities like banks and governments were secretly collecting a "mountain of data" on every individual.[20]

The new, pessimistic counterculture imagined themselves fighting a war that had already been lost. Technology's capacity to oppress was overwhelming its capacity to liberate. "There is nothing magical about computers that causes a user to undergo religious conversion and devote himself to the public good," a hacker in the debate calling himself "Adelaide" wrote. "Early automobile inventors were hackers too. At first the elite drove in luxury. Later practically everyone had a car. Now we have traffic jams, drunk drivers, air pollution, and suburban sprawl."[21]

The new hackers were so frustrated with the older generation's refusal to see how much control institutions had already taken on the internet, they began hacking the older hackers during the conversation. Barlow, who had taken a particularly strong stance, insisted young hackers were simply engaging in adolescent mischief, equivalent to breaking into someone's house. As a riposte, Phiber Optik hacked Barlow and published his credit history, the idea being, it was not *really* his own, but rather, the property of his bank. The libertarian Barlow was soon convinced. "No one has ever put the spook in me quite as Phiber Optik did at that moment," he later wrote. "To a middle-class American, one's credit rating has become nearly identical to his freedom."[22]

Remarkably, this starker vision of what the internet was to become had been predicted in science fiction, which was growing increasingly bleak. The term "cyberspace" was coined by William Gibson in his 1984 book *Neuromancer*, the first in a burgeoning cyberpunk genre. In the novel, cyberspace was a three-dimensional virtual reality experience that was half internet, half acid trip. But there was a flip side to *Neuromancer*'s cyberspace, what Gibson called "the sprawl," the endless, cluttered tangle of shopping strips and highways that comprised the East Coast of the United States.

In *Neuromancer*, hackers call themselves "cowboys," evoking Brand's digital frontier. But the characters in the book are young people who feel they have no escape, who are born into the fulsome mass of the sprawl and postmodernist consumerism. Suicidally nihilistic and unhappy, they long to escape it by dipping into cyberspace, where they are employed by all-powerful, cruel-minded corporate-governmental conglomerates to steal secrets from one another in the vast reaches of data that comprise the net. In the course of a few decades, society's view of technology went from progress to doomsday. From optimism to nihilism. The message boards created a half century ago as "machines of loving grace" had been reshaped into cyberpunk form: 4chan, Yiannopoulos, and angry riots.

And how this fiction became a reality begins, like *Neuromancer*, in the weird virtual worlds of postwar Japan, where the first and second channels that preceded 4chan (the fourth channel) coalesced in a totally new dimension.

It Came from Something Awful

Seriously though, sister death is no reason for you to plan a mass murder at your origami club on Youtube . . . the folders and students at Gay Ass 'Gami dont want to die by your bombs or guns because youre a depressed outraged loner quiet guy second amendment columbine how do i make bombs making bombs making explosives building explosives exploding school killing all classmates guns bombs homemade bombs columbine plan blueprints origami club plant bombs police response time revenge against jocks gunpowder anarchist's cookbook wikipedia dead sisters.

—Something Awful member FATSEX responds to reports that a young user had killed himself after relentless cyberbullying about his origami club from other forum members,[2] from the "Fuck You and Die Criterion Collection" (2010)

Also present in the infamous *Harper's* hacker debate on The Well was Kevin Kelly. Kelly would soon release another successor to the *Whole Earth Catalog*, *Wired* magazine, touted as the new publication for cyberspace.

In March 1993, just as web pages were starting to pop up on the internet, the first issue of *Wired* premiered on newsstands. Like the *Whole Earth Catalog* from which it derived, it was bursting at the seams with countercultural optimism about tech's role in expanding freedom, choice, and even world peace.

The feature story was a conversation between Well founder Stewart Brand and scholar Camille Paglia discussing Brand's intellectual idol, media philosopher Marshall McLuhan. While Brand waxed optimistic about how McLuhan's vision of a new techno-community would come about, Paglia struck a different tone.

"What the heck happened?" she asked. "It wasn't just a conservative administration in the '70s and '80s. That's not it. It was a failure on the part of the '60s generation itself . . . What we have is total domination by the pop culture matrix, by the mass media matrix. That's the future of the world."[3]

And indeed, right next to the feature was another article about "total domination by the pop culture matrix," a piece by Karl Greenfeld titled "The Incredibly Strange Mutant Creatures Who Rule the Universe of Alienated Japanese Zombie Computer Nerds."[4]

It was one of the first mentions in a major U.S. publication of the Japanese "otaku-zoku," people who had retreated into the ever-widening world of commercial fantasies: manga, anime, TV, video games, and cyberspace. And they were often associated with a related group in Japan, the *hikikomori*. "Hikikomori" literally meant "pulling inward," and it describes the sociological phenomenon of older children refusing to abandon the comfort of their parents' home or seeking extreme isolation in apartments because of economic downturns or their own numb unwillingness to face society.

At the time, otaku seemed like a grotesque subculture, but *Wired* had found what would become a new type of man (and they were mostly men, at least at first) in Japan and then the United States who aspired to subsume themselves completely in the media matrix, to get as close as possible to their screens and eventually dissolve into the upside-down dream, of stepping like Alice through the looking glass. Rather than creating a global village of social comfort and intimacy, as internet enthusiasts like Brand had imagined, the network was creating a generation of atomized individuals who adored retreating into increasingly intricate and solipsistic fantasy worlds.

Two factors had created the otaku. The first was the same expansion of leisure marketing to children that had occurred in the United States. In the early 80s, Japanese homes filled with VCRs and TVs. Previous generations had faced the austerity and deprivation of war, but postwar consumers found themselves with disposable income for an ever-expanding market of recreation and entertainment products. As in the United States, fantasy worlds designed to enthrall children and convince them to acquire a set of plastic toys and tapes flooded the market. (In Japan, it began with a giant robot craze.) Many children learned to gratify their existence through self-centered consumption of commercialized media. And as they grew older, their worldview and habits grew with them.

The second factor was unique to Japan, though eventually similar dynamics would spread to the United States. Japanese children of the 80s were called "the bean sprout generation" because they grew quickly and tall in postwar prosperity, like bean sprouts, but were strangely substanceless. As the American model of the postwar Corporate State was imported to Japan, Japanese kids fell into the machine Savio and the counterculture had protested in 1964. They were flattened out into machine parts, reduced to facts and figures, ranked by computerized tests, and then assigned a place in the hierarchy according to their usefulness, represented by the degrees they received. This way of operating was not all that different from the preceding fascist system in which individuals subsumed themselves in the greater collective hierarchy of the state. It also dovetailed with the Japanese belief that hard work, difficult experiences, and sometimes even suffering (often administered by an authority figure) were good for the soul. And so parents and schools pushed students to succeed in ways that were considered extreme to Americans in the 80s, though eventually, as competition increased, such practices would be imported to the United States.

Ridiculously, the idea that the Japanese would out-America America through their willingness to sacrifice their entire beings to the American corporate model became a point of cultural anxiety in the United States in the 90s, finding its highest point of expression in the Michael Crichton potboiler *Rising Sun*. But the by-product of all those efficient cars, cameras, and microchips was a blanched generation of children.

A 1984 article in the *New York Times* about the bean sprout generation reads like something out of *A Clockwork Orange*. It reported how students had been juiced, their spirits crushed by the time they had reached middle school. Young kids were able to grind through tables of equations but then stood listlessly at recess, not comprehending play, asking their teachers what they were supposed to do with themselves. Various studies showed how many of the kids harbored sociopathic thoughts, focused on destroying the system that oppressed them.

In the fifth and sixth grades, when students are near the age of serious test taking, the desires became sinister. One boy said he would "drop atomic bombs all over the world." Another wanted to beat his father. This is what one sixth-grade boy wrote: "I would go to a bank and rob it. I would burn all the money I stole. I want to cut apart a human body with a kitchen knife. I want to set fire to a house. I want to run over about 300 people with a car. If I could do all these, I would have no regrets before dying."[5]

The *Wired* article described how this same generation raised to do nothing but compete and relax by consuming had, by their twenties, withdrawn deeply inward:

Now in their late teens and twenties, most are either cramming for college exams or stuck in cramming mode. They relax with sexy manga or violent computer games. They shun society's complex web of social obligations and loyalties. The result: a burgeoning young generation of at least 100,000 hard-core otaku (estimates of up to 1 million have been bandied about in the Tokyo press).

A subset of these men were "idol otaku," who defined themselves by an intense emotional bond to fictional characters, generally cartoons of adolescent girls. This practice was mixed into Japan's idol culture, in which actual young girls are made into pop icons in magazines. And indeed, the first *New York Times* article to mention otaku a few years later, in 1996, was about the phenomenon of "dating sims," computer games that created an intense romantic bond with fictional, computer-generated characters. The phenomenon had a Japanese name of its own, later imported to the United States: "*moe*." As a result, an antisocial symmetry emerged in which young, emotionally stunted men interpreted intimacy as robotically memorizing a set of fake facts about a fake person (or a real, commodified one, in the case of an idol) in the fantasy of games and bulletin boards on the internet.

It wasn't lost on anybody that otaku were the "apotheosis of consumerism and an ideal workforce for contemporary capitalism." They had embraced the commodification of desire, of, in fact, human spirit. All their pleasures and fantasies—romantic, social, or otherwise—had been redirected toward products they could buy and enjoy alone, most of which had been purchased as a brief but ultimately ineffective respite from their intense loneliness.

The otaku phenomenon was an uncanny mirror universe of the

counterculture homesteaders of the 1960s. Like the hippie homesteaders, otaku rejected climbing the ladder of the competitive hierarchy generated by capitalism. However, otaku did not move outward to use technology to seek independence, greener pastures, and expanding horizons. Rather, they retreated inward. They were not "unto gods," as the preface to every *Whole Earth Catalog* characterized its readers. They didn't employ emerging technologies to radically change their society or landscape. Brutalized by both marketing and years of preparation to ascend the hierarchy, they used new technology to retreat into escapism. Nor were these private products of their thoughts even their own. The otaku were passive participants in their own imaginations, receiving rather than generating intricately crafted fantasies from commercial enterprises. They were consumers who pushed consuming to its radical limits. They did not run away from the one-dimensional desires on the screen, they embraced them. *The Whole Earth Catalog* had obsessed over listing "tools" people could use to change their world. Otaku, by contrast, were interested in never touching the world at all, instead using the computers as a means to be acted upon by other people's instruments.

When the *Wired* article ran, otaku had just entered public discourse in Japan in the wake of the so-called otaku murderer. In the early 90s, Tsutomu Miyazaki, a twenty-six-year-old loner who lived in the suburbs of Tokyo, had kidnapped four little girls, murdered them, sexually violated their dismembered corpses, and, on some occasions, ate their flesh.

After Miyazaki was apprehended, he told the police he transformed into a comic book character he called "Rat Man," which he often tried to draw. To the public, it seemed as if he had mingled reality with the thousands of comics, cartoons, and gory films found in his home.[6]

It was later disputed whether Miyazaki was a true otaku. Miyazaki was disabled (his hands were fused to his wrists) and he had spent his life as an outcast. But it was hard to deny that there were a disturbing number of digitized violent sexual fantasies at the center of otaku culture. The antisocial anger of the bean sprout generation hadn't so much dissolved as been reissued and repackaged in new screen worlds.

The debate that followed Miyazaki's arrest was similar to those that would take place in the United States after the Columbine massacre in 1999. Was violent media desensitizing youth and turning them into psycho killers? Mass shooters, after all, often acted out the homicidal fantasies depicted in increasingly violent movies and video games.

The Columbine killers, for example, maintained a website where they posted modified levels to the first-person shooter game *Doom*, which digitally replicated and rewarded the experience of wandering through hallways shooting everyone you could. Even weirder, the events at Columbine mirrored a scene in *The Matrix* in which Neo and a companion, recognizing that the world and all the people in it are unreal, go on a cartwheeling killing spree, lovingly rendered by the film's directors as an exultant, slo-mo ballet. *The Matrix* had been released only twenty days prior to the shooting. Investigators alleged the killers had copied the film. But it was unclear whether art seemed to be tracing life or the other way around.

Of course, the majority of media consumers don't become homicidal maniacs. Most otaku were defeated nerds who only harmed themselves by retreating into their screens. And today, in some sense we are all otaku, partially withdrawing throughout our day into various screens and escapist fantasies.

The more relevant question is, why was there an ever-expanding market for such nightmarishly violent fantasies? Why was there so much manga and anime available to Miyazaki about sexualizing young girls, chopping them up into bits, and eating them? Why was so much of the creative content of video games—what Brand had heralded as the new, transcendent art—now about blowing people's heads off?

It was same reason why the young otaku, the brutalized grade-school bean sprouts, daydreamed about annihilating everyone around them. Frustration with being on the bottom and constantly being told what to do was sublimated into angry power fantasies. Moreover, as Herbert Marcuse and Charles Reich had described, the invention of inventing needs rather than satisfying real needs had evolved into an art of manufacturing products that not only sold people's dissatisfaction back to them but generated long-term discontent along with short-term satiety. In this case, virtual intimacy and virtual power, which could be bought in gratifying increments, were substituted for real intimacy and real autonomy. And it didn't take long for the two to become twisted, so that sexual fantasies became opportunities to prey on the helpless. The figure of a powerless child often became not only the otaku's identity and a source of shame, but also their choice of victim in the fantasies they consumed.

The Matrix reflected the Columbine shooting so completely because Hollywood was tracing the discontent in its audiences' hearts and projecting it onto the screen. The deranged Columbine killers dreamed of escaping their misery by acting out violent media fantasies. In a similar manner, *The Matrix*'s muse, Baudrillard, pointed out, Hollywood had acted out 9/11 on the screen in countless action films before it occurred in real life. One of these films was *The Matrix*. Neo's Columbine-style massacre takes place in the lobby of a skyscraper. And his adventure begins when he narrowly escapes his cubicle in the high-rise in which he works. The destruction of the seemingly indestructible corporate hierarchy, symbolized by the twin towers, was repeated ad nauseam in fiction until it finally occurred in real life. After 9/11, there was a brief moratorium on skyscraper destruction in movies (famously, a scene from *Spider-Man* in which a helicopter is flung at the towers had to be cut). But soon superheroes were bounding above the confining grid of the workaday world of skyscrapers (and destroying them in the process), like Neo in the last shot of *The Matrix*.

A weird spiral of unhappiness that began in films and TV was drawn directly onto the internet. The new communities that dominated the web largely derived their habits, style, and culture from otaku culture. People interacted on the web as collectives of isolated individuals, immersed in fantasy products, cruel-minded gore, and self-obsession, all a means of escape from the multiplying anxieties and dissatisfactions of real life. And at the center of this, the quivering, vulnerable, and pale underbelly of the internet that would digest it all, would be the chans.

The 1993 *Wired* article centered around a certain otaku named "Kojack" as he courted his virtual girlfriend by hacking rivals on Nifty Serve, the Japanese network of anarchic bulletin board systems (BBSs) that predated the web. And it was the Nifty Serve network that would, a few years later, spawn the first and second chans.

The earliest such site was created by an otaku named Shiba Masayuki, who went by the handle "Shiba" online. In August 1996, he started a Japanese BBS called Ayashii's World (*Ayashii Warudo*, meaning strange, suspicious, or dubious world) on the Nifty Serve network. Ayashii's World was dedicated to porn, games, *warez* (stolen software), and file sharing,[7] though reportedly, at its beginnings, it specialized in child pornography. By some accounts, it had first been created to replace a BBS called Japan

Lolita Complex Graphics, run by someone calling himself *"Pedo Koushaku"* ("Duke Pedophile").[8]

By 1997, Ayashii's World had become the center of a larger web of copycat sites, collectively referred to as *Nanashii Warudo* ("The Nameless World"). "Nameless" expressed the obscure nature of the board's content, but it also referenced a unique sociological phenomenon.[9] Japanese society was based on a strict hierarchy. How you addressed a person depended on their status and your own in the community. Indeed, the word "otaku" derived from this confusion of terms. The word was close to a phrase that meant "someone else's house," referencing the otaku's insider lifestyle. But it is derived from a formal way of saying "you." Otaku employed this formal mode of address as they were groping for the proper way to speak to people who shared their interests. There was no word for that sort of relationship.

As the otaku spread online, the last thing they wanted was to replicate the world from which they were escaping: a complex hierarchy of identity and status. American forum users, of course, were doing just that, creating usernames and cultivating reputations in their online communities. For most American bulletin boards, in order to post you had to sign up for an account and create a name. In the Nameless World things were different. Users could leave the name field blank, and all that appeared for each user's identity was the default term *"nanashii"* ("nameless"). This allowed otaku to discard not only the hierarchy, but the sad fact of themselves, and roam not simply without their bodies but without their souls in a ghostly Saturnalia where all laws, prohibitions, and even human identity dematerialized into a catalog of interests, desires, and self-gratification.

When Ayashii's World shut down a year later, a smaller BBS in the Nameless World network ballooned to fill the void. It was called Amezou ("First Channel"), and it was run by someone calling themselves *"Amezou-shi"* ("Mr. Amezou"). Amezou-shi modified how posting worked to create a "floating" system that later became the key to 4chan's success, and eventually sites like Reddit's and Facebook's, in which popular content is voted to the top of the site.

Amezou also lasted for about a year before folding amid hacker feuds. And one of the readers who filled the vacant market niche (because he was one of the rivals spamming the site) was a twenty-one-year-old

Japanese exchange student named Hiroyuki Nishimura (the present owner of 4chan) studying at the University of Arkansas. According to Nishimura, he was bored because his fellow students had all left for summer break. So he decided to take Mr. Amezou's BBS code and adapt it into a web-based forum. On May 30, 1999, he launched what would become one of the most successful sites ever in Japan, 2channel (*Ni channeru*) at 2ch.net.

The name was a literal one-upping reference to Amezou, but it was also an allusion to old-school video game consoles, which broadcast video games through the default second channel of Japanese TVs (channel 3 was used in the United States).

2channel imported many of Amezou's features, the floating threads, the default nameless username, and also all the acrimony, chaos, and running jokes. Though the site began life as a successor to Amezou, it quickly began to attract a broader userbase. Otaku were extremists. But their culture, obsessive fan interest in products and escapist fantasy worlds, was growing in the hearts of the broader population. In addition, many Japanese visiting the web for the first time reveled in the anonymity. They too found relief in escaping Japan's strict hierarchy of polite deference. Unlike the hyper-polite real world, people found they could be rude to one another with impunity. 2channel's most popular replies were "*omae mo na!*" ("you too, asshole") and "*itteyoshi*" (meaning either "please leave" or "please die").

```
     ∧ ＿ ∧／
    (  ´∀｀ ) ＜  オマエモナー
    (      )  ＼ ＿ ＿ ＿ ＿ ＿
     |  |  |
    ( ＿_)＿ )
```

A 2channel character-art cat telling you to "please die!"

For years, 2channel was an open secret in Japan. However, as it grew into a cultural force, it became accepted by mainstream society and incorporated into the entertainment complex. Nishimura evolved into a web celebrity. Cast as a tech entrepreneur and entertainment expert, he

appeared frequently on TV and in magazines. However, at the center of all
of this was a certain cultural negation that characterized his generation,
one that would soon be replicated on parallel sites in the United States.

In appearance, 2channel is remarkable not for its chic elegance, but
for a messiness that characterizes its design. It's a set of maddeningly un-
aligned pastel boxes with plain text interspersed and other items piled
up chockablock in the corners of the screen. Nishimura, like his design
sensibility, was shockingly breezy, sloppy, and indifferent in a society that
prized none of those things, or at least, not previously. He was not quite
an otaku. But like his 90s American counterculture counterparts, he was
a slacker, jaded and nihilistic about everything. He attributed his success
to luck and discouraged others who wanted to follow in his footsteps.[10]
He was neither polite nor interested in what most people had to say.
When other parties threatened him with lawsuits, he didn't even bother
to show up. In interviews, he was as terse and vague as the replies on
2channel. He wasn't quite a bean sprout, or at least the frustrated,
homicidal variety; he resembled the strain that was filling the pages of
2channel.

Meanwhile, in the United States, sites reflecting similar youth trends
were appearing.

Shortly after *Wired* premiered in 1993, the advent of the World Wide
Web fueled a wild period of unprecedented speculation on Wall Street,
which, after its inevitable crash in 1999, became known as the dotcom
bubble. The wide-eyed optimism of the Wellians and *Wired* filled it with
hot air.

As described in *The Electric Kool-Aid Acid Test*, Stewart Brand had
become obsessed with the first photograph of the earth from space during an acid trip in the 60s. So the premiere issue of the *Whole Earth
Catalog* had run the image on its cover as a symbol of how technology
would bring about a new era of unity. In 1997, a *Wired* cover, in homage,
featured a picture of the earth depicted as the hippie smiley face, a daisy
hanging out of its mouth. "The Long Boom," it declared at the height of
the bubble. "We're facing 25 years of prosperity, freedom, and better environment for the whole world. You got a problem with that?"[11] Was
the new era arriving? Not with post-capitalism, but within capitalism?
This was at least what the techno-utopian *Wired* imagined. And such
ideas were reflected in 90s politics, with the hippie-ish Clintons, students
of Reich's, swinging the liberal party to the right rather than the left.

Former hippies had lived lives of unprecedented generational wealth. Now many were getting richer off tech. Maybe all that talk of radical revolution had been a little extreme. It would be a velvet revolution. Change would come softly, slowly, and surely.

There was no better symbol of the counterculture selling the web as a corporate utopia than *Wired* itself.[12] At the height of the speculative tech craze, Goldman Sachs helped *Wired* go public with an initial IPO of $447 million.[13] There were no takers. And when the boom ended, *Wired* had to be restructured through bankruptcy.

Adrift in these wild throes was a young 90s Gen Xer who was pretty sure the web was going to be more weird than great. Richard "Lowtax" Kyanka had dropped out of engineering school in his early twenties and taken a job as a systems administrator at a large institution in Kentucky, where he spent most of his time playing the *Doom*-style first-person shooter *Quake II* on his PC. Tall, with dark kinky hair and a perpetual five o'clock shadow, he didn't appear particularly nerdy, though much of his life was centered around his computer.

Like the young otaku in Japan, Lowtax occupied a cubicle in a vast, impersonal bureaucracy. Unhappy, he retreated to games and online networks. But unlike the otaku, Lowtax did not aspire to enter the game and lose himself in the experience. His attitude typified the American response to the same problem, informed by a counterculture that had spent decades battling corporate co-optation. He knew the fantasy worlds sucked too. And the best defense he could muster against them was unrelenting mockery.

He recognized that a life of sitting around playing games on your PC and looking at the internet all day was, well, awful. But, he reasoned, so was the rest of culture. Ridiculously, his derisive *Quake* playing eventually attracted the attention of those in the business of promoting the game. Right before the dotcom bubble popped, Lowtax was invited out to California by *GameSpy* magazine and paid a salary of $24,000 a year to promote what was, in his words, "just a standard first-person shooter where you kill demons or whatever" for planetquake.com. Even before the job, the office, and the corporation evaporated almost overnight, the absurdity of it all was not lost on him.

GameSpy had hired a self-hating gamer to promote games to other gamers by mocking them mercilessly. And when it all collapsed in financial puffery, this confirmed his suspicion that the web was not so much human communion, but the nihilistic void of accumulation. "To imagine that a company that made a USB drive that emitted different smells was going to make you a millionaire," Lowtax told me over the phone in 2018. "Yeah, it was that kind of time. It was obvious that was gonna work out great for everybody."

As a young man in the shadow of corporate culture, he did not see the internet as a network that would bring about a transcendent way of doing business and communicating. Rather, he intuited the common truth of his generation: that he was living in a psychic garbage dump. The world was filling up, invisibly but inevitably, with the discarded wrappers of corporations and entrepreneurs trying to find a niche or invent a need—of marketing and pop culture, of fantasy worlds and screen illusions. And it was the internet that would hold it all.

Around the same time that Nishimura created 2channel in Japan, Lowtax founded a site he called Something Awful (SA). It was a name he plucked out of nothing, specifically the nothing of the fast food–littered suburbs, a phrase he simply uttered all the time, as in "that Del Taco burrito sure is something awful."

SA was (and still is) a humor site, mostly full of the sort of cultural mockery that *GameSpy* paid Lowtax for, but freed from having to write about (and somehow promote) games by mocking them. Users on SA commented on the entirety of internet culture, or, as Lowtax put it, "crappy internet things." Today, SA's post-everything, nonsense humor style defines Twitter, after some of its most prolific posters (most notably @dril, who has 1.2 million followers) migrated there in a campaign they called Weird Twitter.

But in 1999, the internet was just beginning to fill up with this cultural detritus. Discarded TV shows and products now languished in the psychic space of millions of kids who had grown up awash in a sea of solicitous products. The hyper-saturation of commodified fantasy realms invited many people to dive into them in totally new ways. For example, the otaku had popularized body pillows, a human-size pillow imprinted with the image of one's *waifu* ("wife") or *husbando* ("husband"), the anime girl or boy to which the otaku imagines he or she is married. As Lowtax explained to *Vice* magazine in 2017,

I would find a page on horrible, scary dolls and I would review the dolls. Parodies of wonks who were saying the internet was the future without saying, "Well there could be a possible downside to the internet." I'm obviously not a visionary, but I predicted that the internet would be shitty back in 1999. Everybody was talking about how the internet was going to revolutionize everything and everything was going to be great, but nobody ever talked about how shitty the internet could also be.

A long time ago, if somebody said they really wanted to fuck a pillow with anime on it, if they went out in public and said that, they would be laughed at. There would be some element of shame. They would keep that inside and say, "Well, I want to fuck a pillow with anime on it but I can't tell anybody." But then the internet came along and they could get on a webring or whatever it was back in the day. Go to rec/all/fuckanimepillow or whatever. Then other people would say "I want to fuck anime pillows, too." You had this community of people who were very intent on fucking anime pillows. The typical person does not want to fuck a pillow with anime on it. This, of course, was back when fucking anime pillows was fresh and new.

I found it to be very interesting that these subcommunities would sprout up and their numbers would grow and pretty soon it's Pillowfuckers United, Inc. And I found that whole process back then—it was even happening in the usegroup days—I found that whole process incredibly interesting, how the groupthink would manifest itself and increase exponentially over time.[14]

In some ways, SA fit into the genre of nihilistic 90s web pages that celebrated the transgressive. Early on, some of the most popular sites on the web were dark shock sites, which showed images that would never have appeared in print (rotten.com, for example). Several other internet writers, most notably George "Maddox" Ouzonunian of the Best Page of the Universe and Jay Stile of Stile Project, mixed dark humor, cynicism, crass language, and pop culture into streams of popular content.

But what soon distinguished SA was the odd growth of its forums. Since the advent of the web in the early 90s, text-based BBSs were slowly migrating to web-based versions, which functioned in more or less the same way, though they were now framed in a graphic user interface rather than just text. And as was typical at the time, Lowtax added a web-based bulletin board to accompany his site. To do this, he employed freely available software. As a result, SA's forums hardly differed from thousands of others. Each page appeared as a set of vertically stacked blocks, each block a new topic. One of the few things that was easy to customize was the color scheme. Lowtax chose dark grays highlighted by hot pink, fitting for the boards' mix of dark humor and chopped-up pieces of pop culture. Image posting was limited, but unlike on 2channel, possible. The threads did not "float," like on 2channel or a modern social media feed; whatever thread received the most recent comment (as opposed to the most comments) was at the top. And likewise, like almost all Western boards at the time, a user had to sign up for an account.

SA's nerdy content quickly attracted the cynical, pop-culture-obsessed 90s adolescents who were clambering onto the web. All forums suffered from the same systemic problems since the days of Usenet: flame wars, obsessive users, and rude comments. This behavior seemed to come more easily when people were safely separated by their computers. But what set SA's forums apart was its attitude toward all of this. Rather than strip out all the bizarre aggression that inevitably accompanied forums, SA simply let it grow as a grotesque experiment, cultivated it even. SA forums encouraged exactly what moderators elsewhere took great care to eradicate: bile, cynicism, cruelty, mockery, and vulgarity.

There had been a few places like SA—most notably the Temple of the Screaming Electron (TOTSE), a text-based BBS started in 1989 by Jeff Hunter in San Francisco dedicated to *Anarchist Cookbook*–style adolescent mischief, bad ideas, drugs, weapons, bomb-making, and hacking—but never on the scale of SA. (Many of TOTSE's members eventually migrated to SA and 4chan.)

SA's approach was so radical, no one knew quite what was on the other side. By steering into what everyone else avoided, it emerged into a strange terra nova. And as the community swelled to hundreds of thousands, the moderators started treating SA like what it was—an unexplainable growth—poking, prodding, and trimming it on a whim, then waiting to see the result. There wasn't a forum like it, and it quickly eclipsed the main site.

Ostensibly, the forum was also dedicated to humor and users were supposed to be funny. But what occurred was a wild free-for-all of adolescents acting crass and weird. As users were banned for offense after offense, Lowtax eventually instituted a paywall and charged "goons" (as the users of the SA now identified themselves) ten dollars for an account.

This led to the absurd result that those who caused the most trouble paid hundreds of dollars to gain access to the forums in new attempts to disrupt them.

And despite all of this, more users kept flooding in. Somewhere along the line, I can't quite remember when, either in 1999 or 2000, I was one. I was just out of high school, and so a little too old for this new iteration of teenage rebellion, more interested in literature than technology. But SA had its share of literature, a novel genre of writing in which disaffected users didn't so much pour out their hearts as probed the empty space where the organ ought to have been.

The definition of hacker had continued to shift, from artist seeking transcendence to freedom fighter battling corporate powers to something even more pessimistic, an idle generation using and abusing their power over virtual and real worlds to display their disinterest and contempt.

For example, in a 2003 thread in which goons swapped stories about how they hacked into AOL, one user, "aolice," told how, at the age of fourteen, he had earned supreme control over AOL's networks by first exploiting flaws in its security, then AOL employees as he befriended them via email.[15]

"When I turned 15 I finally realized that 'hacking' AOL was gay as hell and a waste of time," he wrote. "I decided to use my skills for profit rather than fucking around AOL." With the help of his parents, he set up an S-corporation, which used his knowledge of AOL chat rooms to lure users into banner clicks. By the time he was seventeen, aolice was making $17,000 a month, an arrangement that was mutually profitable, since he had to pay AOL $1,500 a month for 100 fictitious employee user accounts. The whole affair ended when AOL discovered his "business" and "employees" were illusory. They canceled his accounts, but insisted he still pay for them, in effect, scamming him. But the goon was not the only one being scammed. His virtual AOL company turned out to be a microcosm for AOL itself. After the dotcom collapse, the company became one of the largest examples of overvaluation in history, losing an unprecedented $206 billion of its $226 billion market share for overselling the value of advertising mouse clicks.[16]

Another famous tale on SA is "The Great Scam." The post relates how a young goon slowly became disaffected with human behavior as he is robbed, scammed, and bullied out of doing honest work mining space minerals in the virtual *EVE Online*, which he describes as a "beautiful" but "poorly designed game, which rewards the greedy and violent and punishes the hardworking and honest; and if you think about it, that's a good representation of capitalism."

Vowing to get revenge at all costs, he devises a scheme for scamming the richest guilds (societies of wealthy space merchants in the game) out of all of their virtual currency, a plan that rotates in and out of reality and the space world. To convince other players to invest in a spaceship he never intends on building, the goon "sockpuppets" various users on *EVE Online* message boards, conducting elaborate arguments with himself so that the threads are always bumped to the top of the page. When the marks finally bite, he is forced to sprint between his home phone line and a landline at his local library, pretending to be different satisfied investors in his project. The scheme works. He becomes one of the richest people in the game, and in doing so, betrays even those who were nothing but kind to him, going out of his way to wound the nicest people. The story ends when the goon dumps all of his currency (480,000,000 isk; approximately $40) on the first virtual stranger he meets in space, logs off, and never plays the game again.

Another tale, "The American Dream," relates how a goon calling himself "Moonshine" spent nine years moving up the ranks of a company while it paid for his degree in physics, until, in his late twenties, he's transferred to a department that doesn't exist, in charge of nothing. For months he spends the workday browsing SA, chain-smoking, and sipping Mountain Dew Code Red. How long, he wonders, can he get paid to do nothing? With the help of the forums, he starts treating his job like a meaningless game, trying to figure out how he can continue to live the American Dream.[17]

Fictional or real, these stories set the tone for SA: life is a joke. Life could be played the normal way, or as a situational absurdist comedy that tears at the curtain of fantasy. The question was, how ridiculous could you act to make that apparent to everyone else? This attitude would soon reinvent a previously obscure online character, the message board troll.

And the catalyst for all this would be a fourteen-year-old boy in upstate New York searching for porn, who would combine SA's culture and 2channel's format into a new site, 4chan.

PART II

4CHAN

Moot in Raspberry Heaven

Raspberry Heaven!
Hold me tightly in the fun dreams of Heaven
Raspberry Heaven, I'm coming back to you
When paradise's flowers have beautifully bloomed
You and me
Together we'll be
—"Raspberry Heaven," *Azumanga Daioh*

Around 2000, Richard "Lowtax" Kyanka, who hated anime, added an anime forum to Something Awful (SA), naming it Anime Death Tentacle Rape Whorehouse (ADTRW). By 2003, ADTRW existed a few planes down from more popular forums like the chaotic bin where the most obnoxious users met to insult each other, Fuck You and Die (FYAD). ADTRW attracted a slightly younger audience who lived in the shadow of older, cooler boys. As one SA user who later migrated to the chans wrote, SA "was also home to [a] wide collection of other losers, the third or fourth saddest of which was the ADTRW crew."[1]

One of these users was a fifteen-year-old kid who lived with his mother in Westchester, New York, named Christopher Poole. And at the time, he was deeply unhappy. "I was overweight bordering on obese," he wrote on his blog years later, "drank two liters of cola every day, spent a good 6–12 hours per day playing video games in a bedroom with blacked-out windows, and rarely went outdoors or socialized."[2] On his favorite message board, SA, Poole chose a name of bleak negation, "moot."

Moot also hung out in one of the many satellite chat rooms orbiting SA, an Internet Relay Chat (IRC) channel named Raspberry Heaven.

Raspberry Heaven was named after the sickly sweet ending-credits song to the anime series *Azumanga Daioh*, a comedy about teenage girls enduring the trials of puberty. However, the inhabitants of the channel were all teenage boys who directed their social life not outward toward the goings-on in the halls of their high schools, as *Azumanga Daioh* depicted, but rather inward and toward each other on the IRC channel, mediated by the fantasy of anime. "We quickly chased out the few women," a user named "Shii," who later became an influential early 4chan moderator, told me. "It became an all-male free-for-all for almost a decade." Another user, who went by the handle "Souldark" and also became an early moderator of 4chan, recalled that Raspberry Heaven was a realm defined by its constant mockery, adolescent ribbing that never ended.

In early 2003, the kids in Raspberry Heaven discovered 2channel (2ch .net) and became enamored of a copycat site called Futaba (2chan.net), which allowed users to post images. Raspberry Heaven users often skimmed 2chan for weird, odd, or gross pictures and then posted the links in the IRC or on SA. One of the teens who loved doing this was moot. And searching for a funny new email address, he registered 4chan .net on October 1, 2003, because, according to him, pant.su (Japanese for "pants") was taken.

After securing his email address, moot realized that he could replicate all of 2chan on 4chan and went about translating the board's PHP code into English and hosting it on his new domain, 4chan.net. When another user asked why he had chosen four rather than any other number, he reasoned, "its TWO TIMES THE CHAN MOTHERFUCK."[3]

In a moment that would have profound historical consequences, the fifteen-year-old translated the Japanese *Nanashii* ("Nameless") into "Anonymous," and "Anonymous" became the default username on 4chan. In this way, Anonymous was born.

2chan's alternate name, Futaba, meant "two leaves/flat sheaves," and the site's icon was two pixelated leaves. So moot named 4chan *Yotsuba* ("four leaves") and added two more leaves to his site's icon. Yotsuba also happened to be the name of the titular character from *Yotsuba&!*, a hyper-cute manga by Kiyohiko Azuma, the creator of Raspberry Heaven's namesake anime *Azumanga Daioh*. Yotsuba, who sported four green pigtails in the shape of leaves, became 4chan's unofficial mascot.

The manga character Yotsuba's four pigtails transformed into 4chan's "four leaves" icon.

Many goons quickly realized that 4chan was far more conducive to how they wanted to use the internet. SA's traditional bulletin board software was constructed around facilitating discussion, a structure that much of SA loathed. Users weren't debating topics to reach some sort of shared understanding or consensus. They were elaborating on jokes, sharing files, or generating something that was unique to the web—inverted discussions where the point was not communication, but the performance of sliced-up gibberish, in which disaffected teenagers all tried collectively to derail the conversation. Items like titled threads, usernames, elaborate upload interfaces, and an archive system organized chronologically were jettisoned on 4chan. All posts were regarded as garbage on SA, but 4chan actually treated them like garbage, automatically deleting its threads in a matter of days, if not hours. Users could create anonymous heaps of nonsense, funny images, file dumps, jokes, or porn, knowing that all of it would fade away as the site churned through new content.

While some of the appeal of SA was social interaction, many of its users employed it simply as a place to search for funny and interesting content. In this sense, 4chan was an evolutionary leap toward social media. Much of the appeal of social media would come not only from its use as an interactive social space, but also as a content aggregator. 4chan's design was not oriented around community or even discussion (there was no way to keep track of users and threads were easily lost), but it was addictive because the floating system pushed the most interesting content to the top of the site.

Other early content-sifting sites like Slashdot, MetaFilter, and Fark had all independently invented similar aggregating methods that employed some sort of voting system, but they were limited by content curation, approval by moderators, and other rules. 4chan, with its sloppy, unstructured approach, moved at a faster pace than all of them.

Then there was the content itself.

Another constraint that 4chan abandoned was common decency.

Libertine and experimental as it was, SA had a set of rules. And Lowtax had no compunction about drawing a clear moral line regarding what he would tolerate on his site. In fact, he delighted in purging users and content he found contemptible.

Moot would take a looser approach, or rather, the loosest. He set most of the rules next to the outer bounds of the rules that already existed, that is to say, the law. As he later phrased it, he was allowing 4chan's community "to define itself." But it was something only a shrugging teen boy would do, one who had not yet worked out his own value system and, as most adolescents do, was experimentally mirroring the culture around him, in this case, one of competitive transgression. As Lowtax described it to me, "[4chan] was like a race to see who could be the most crazy, fucked-up piece of shit possible. And they were all winning."[4]

Since SA's content was balanced on a razor's edge of hating on disgusting images and subcultures and reveling in them, SA ended up constantly tearing itself apart, banning, shunning, and condemning users at an increasingly frantic pace as it attracted the underbelly of the internet. For example, the ironically named Anime Death Tentacle Rape Whorehouse signaled to *genuine fans* of tentacle rape that such content was tolerated there, even if the original intention was to mock anime.

4chan's early userbase was born from one of these ADTRW purges, which SA called "the pedocaust." Or, as Lowtax told me, "I was tired of trying to figure out whether this sexualized drawing someone posted depicted an eleven-year-old girl or a 500-YEAR-OLD WITCH from princess whatever-the-fuck volume fifty-six."

4chan began as a place for moot and his friends to post Japanese anime images outside of SA, but immediately spiraled into what SA had been founded to mock: a collection of internet subcommunities where ostracized fetishists came to meet.

When moot began 4chan he added two sections: /a/ for "anime" and /b/ for "random bin." Almost overnight, 4chan filled up with all sorts of weird images that were part of the bizarre world of manga and anime. Scores of SA users flocked to 4chan to post pictures of watery-eyed anime girls not to prove to the world how ridiculous they were, but because they genuinely liked them. And these were followed by fetishists who desired to see the same watery-eyed girls chopped into bloody pieces as Japanese *guro*, or transformed into frolicking animals, and so forth and so on.

When a particular board became overwhelmed with disgusting pictures, moot often solved the problem not by banning users or setting up rules against content he found distasteful, but by creating a "containment board" where users could dump their files without intermixing them with the "innocent" images of anime girls in the /a/ and /c/ ("cute") boards. This resulted in an infamous /l/ board ("Lolikon," derived from *Lolita*, meaning sexualized drawings of young girls in the anime style), described by Poole as "fucking nuts." Incredibly, the board lasted a year until Poole, apparently discovering his own moral limits, deleted it. As he explained it in ADTRW, "It would work horrors on my personal life if friends/family found out I ran this site."[5]

Moot later described the beginning of 4chan as a funny project to amuse his friends, which almost instantly flooded with cartoon-obsessed weirdos from all corners of the internet. "I started 4chan when I was very bored, in need of porno, and wanted a cool email address . . . The immediate result was a cool 2chan clone that provided me with all such things, but a few unwanted side effects, the predominant one being ANIMU OTAKU KAWAII BAKA NEKOS-TAN-^_____^-PYO-NYOs" (anime, otaku, cute, idiot, cat with a diminutive Japanese term of endearment, a disaffected smiley face, the name of a cute, "superdeformed" girl anime character popular at the time). "Said people are complete wastes of human life and made running the site hell not only for me, but the original users [Raspberry Heaven]."[6]

In some ways, this characterization was ingenious. The vulgar anime fan communities from which 4chan derived its original userbase contained many otaku elements, and 4chan's own board topics encouraged the content. However, a fifteen-year-old boy does not expect a website he created on a lark to flood with hundreds of thousands of users all interested in living their entire lives (or at least pretending that they did) in a computerized stew of sparkling fantasy, magical creatures, outlandish pornography, and horrific gore.

Though 4chan would soon spawn communities of hackers and trolls who would come to define much of the present internet, the core of its culture remained in Japanese cartoons and fetish porn.

Where were these people coming from? Why did 4chan become the repository not only for an endless flow of fantasy worlds, but for fantasy debauched, chopped up into pieces or otherwise defiled, the desocialized center that accompanies the otaku lifestyle?

In a 1994 biopic, the indie cartoonist Robert Crumb described how his aunt allowed him to ride her boot like a horse when he was a toddler. The glee he felt imprinted on him a lifelong fetish for similar boots and mounting women like horses. As a child, Crumb's burgeoning sexual awareness cottoned on to all the comics and cartoons he absorbed. And his adult work became an avant-garde mix of anthropomorphic animals having sex with one another, art that was cited by Charles Reich as the forefront of the counterculture that had shaken loose the straitlaced mores of the 50s. But Crumb was also an advance guard for an entire generation of people who were deeply attracted to the cartoon characters of their youth.

The influx of screen-generated exultant fantasy worlds in the 80s and 90s mixed with the developing sexuality of young minds in a way that left the two permanently entwined. The phenomenon is probably not unrelated to how, in a frenzy of marketing, children's products were disturbingly mingled with marketers' tactics to sell through sexualization.

For example, one community of (then) closeted fetishists that flooded early 4chan was furries. These were people attracted to cartoonish depictions of animals, often rendered in a Disney style exemplified by the film *Robin Hood*.

Nowadays, furries are all over the internet, as well as real life. Big-box stores sell books with titles like *Draw Furries: How to Create Anthropomorphic and Fantasy Animals*.[7] Likewise, the 2018 Academy Award winner for best picture, *The Shape of Water*, centers on the furry theme of having sex with a human-animal hybrid fantasy creature. In 2005, however, furries were scorned, even on 4chan, where they were mocked and targeted for years.

Similarly, in 2007, the "brony" phenomenon emerged on 4chan. Bronys were a mixture of die-hard adult fans of the rebooted 1980s children's cartoon *My Little Pony* and fans who, in their exuberant affection, desired to have sex with the cartoon ponies, choosing otaku-style *waifus* from among them, and defiling their effigies in the form of toys and body pillows. (They would eventually be granted a board on 4chan, /mlp/.) The adult fascination was likely related to how the toy company "updated" the characters from the original designs, transplanting the hyper-glistening, receptive eyes and other female features of anime girls onto the once round, plump, and childlike cartoons.

Nightmare Alchemy

1981 design   traditional waifu   2003 redesign

The hyper-receptive eyes of teen anime girls were applied to a reboot of the American "My Little Pony" franchise, resulting in an unintended fan community of "bronys", otaku who often formed a romantic attachment to the cartoon ponies. The phenomenon began on 4chan circa 2011.

4chan used the strange content of Japanese anime to continue a race to the bottom that had been started decades earlier by media as they depicted ever-more-graphic violence and sexuality. This meant that by the 90s, media-saturated, desensitized teenagers like moot were sharing the vulgar images they found on places like SA, Raspberry Heaven, and 4chan not because they adored these things naturally, but because they were in the air(waves) all around them.

As with the original otaku phenomenon in Japan, this too had a lot to do with the complex game between pleasure and permission marketing was playing with people, in which sexual gratification was chopped up and sold in increments.

To combat this, counterculture attempted to decouple enjoyment from economic dictates and revel in boundless transcendence, sexual or otherwise. But, as we saw in previous chapters, counterculture's practices were soon picked up and used as yet another commodified gatekeeper for when to enjoy. And this in turn collapsed into the nihilism in which the early 4chan teens were born.

The conquest of not only sex but joy, intimacy, and pleasure through the commodification of romantic fantasy worlds didn't pass through the collective psyche of new generations without leaving a mark.

Herbert Marcuse argued that by the mid-twentieth century, people's understanding of the world had been fractured in two: a literal-minded deterministic view of reality (as dictated by the authority of experts and scientists), which closed off imaginative possibilities of better futures (personal or political); and an indulgent, outlandish fantasy life regarded as totally unreal. A contemporary example of this might be how nerds with the most narrowly focused, niche technical jobs—the computer programmers, scientists, engineers, and so forth—are the ones who indulge in the wildest romantic fantasy stories: worlds of elves, dwarfs, magicians, and superheroes. As the real world and our own personal circumstances feel increasingly predetermined and resistant to change, we are drawn into unreal realms where we can watch everything our reality lacks. In our twentieth- and twenty-first-century romantic fiction, super-effective heroes change not just their own lives but the entire world for the better. They are not simply more adventurous than us, but commune with transcendence itself in intergalactic Hollywood "infinity wars." To the nineteenth-century Romantics who invented this genre of storytelling (and the countercultures that followed), possibility, imagination, transcendence, heroic action, and creativity were internal qualities employed as tools to interpret the real world. In the modern era, these qualities were quarantined in external fiction. One person changing the world for the better seemed to be something that could only be found in a story, as could freewheeling adventure, and even the summit of human experience. It was there, in the unreal, that people were *really* living.

This system has been operating for over half a century. The externalities accumulating and coalescing as the oozing sludge on 4chan. The seemingly immutable "facts" of hard "reality" dictating you should live some way you don't want to live are packaged as escapist fantasy: sexual gratification as something you earned as a reward for work, powerlessness as hyper-effective heroes, and frustration as grotesque violence.

The illusory element is employed as an itch that inspires another scratch; the planned obsolescence that sells another product. Having isn't holding; looking isn't doing. The starlet is forever trapped behind the screen, the women behind the gloss of the magazines, the power fantasy in the bloody action movie. The goalpost is forever moving, and it's impossible to score.

What happens if, for fifty years, each scratch leads to more itch?

Where else would all this lead but to *more blood, more violence, more destruction, more sex, more debauchery,* and *more fantasy*? Until all of it becomes heaped on top of itself as millions of people flood onto the internet to fantasize together about transgressing the border of the screen and having sex with their fantasy creatures on the other side or obtaining a two-dimensional, watery-eyed princess as their bride and then chopping her to bits.

The internet *reversed the flow* of this process. The screen wasn't acting upon the viewer, it was allowing the viewer to generate content. And the first thing many people wanted to create was a nightmarish, home-grown amalgam of everything the screens had dangled in front of them. And the second thing people wanted to do was embark on quixotic efforts to pass through the looking glass and *actually somehow impossibly possess* the phantoms on the other side.

Japan was ahead of the curve on all this, outpacing American media in the race to the bottom. And so Western audiences sought out Japanese media as they found themselves in a similar position as the bean sprouts/otaku, outclassed by the solicitous content on their screen, and imagining themselves so powerless that dropping out seemed the only reasonable choice.

This is why, though first imported with the ironic air of SA, all of this media soon lost many of the trappings that framed it as silly. The mocking play became earnest. The sexual commodification of younger and younger girls, which was a feature of Japanese society, was appearing simply at a slower pace in the West.

The first American articles about otaku worshipping overpackaged young Japanese idol singers framed the phenomenon as a case of Japanese extremism that was considered far too distasteful to ever occur in the United States. But within a few years, the idol phenomenon arrived with performers like Britney Spears, Christina Aguilera, and Miley Cyrus.

Similarly, nerd stock characters in fantasy and science-fiction films, like the sexy female assassin, combined the objectification of female sexuality with the audience's demands for increasingly spectacular violence and gore. On the surface, the character seems to be expressing female empowerment: she is strong, active, and almost always takes revenge on perverts and those who wished to control or objectify their sexuality. However, if the ogling viewers resembled anyone, it was these villains. But rather than feel insulted by the slight, the audiences delighted in these moments.

This "empowered" aspect of the character was there to allow the audience to indulge in objectification and gore without feeling shame, without imagining they themselves were the perverts. But weirdly, throughout the 90s and aughts, this stock character kept getting younger.

In Japan in the 90s, the female assassin was often a young schoolgirl, as in the anime *Serial Experiments Lain* or the film *Battle Royale*. Eventually, this practice was imported to the United States. Literally. Quentin Tarantino cast the same actress from *Battle Royale* to play the young female assassin-schoolgirl in *Kill Bill*, who, in the scene before her own gory death, murderously rebuffs the advances of older men. It wasn't until the #metoo movement that we learned it was Tarantino himself, according to his star Uma Thurman, who held the schoolgirl's chain that choked her character.[8]

The female assassin stock character's age began to dip elsewhere into pubescent, then prepubescent, as in the nerd features *Kick-Ass* and *Sucker Punch*. In the former, a katana-wielding ten-year-old coats herself in gore.

Japanese culture offered internet audiences, now in control of their own screens, the same pornographic themes of American culture stripped of the polite disguises that allowed them to consume without shame. Japanese extremism was often the subject of mockery in the United States. Easterners, it was imagined, had a tradition of obsequious subservience to the hierarchy of Confucianism. Americans laughed at how Japanese people debased themselves on humiliating game shows in ways that seemed unthinkable to someone possessed of the inviolate dignity of the Western individual. In the 1987 film *RoboCop*, for example, audiences were meant to interpret a future game show in which a character was grubbing for money on the floor as a horrible dystopian vision of what TV might become. That is, until a few years later, when reality TV appeared in the West with programming that made *RoboCop*'s reality TV seem tame in comparison. The most notable program in this genre, *Fear Factor*, in which participants ate bugs and were drowned in tanks, was hosted by the comedian Joe Rogan, who would later become involved in the rise of the alt-right/lite movement (rebranded in 2018 as "The Intellectual Dark Web").

Yet 4chan's efforts to outrace transgression itself didn't condemn it to obscurity or even a shameful existence for long. Like all things fringe in the West, its path was toward the center. And as with any other subculture, mainstream society took a keen interest in it as it danced the weird looping dance of shame and satiety, condemnation and co-optation. Soon, 4chan was placed on the track to become the new mainstream culture.

Memes, Trolls, and Chan Girls

4chan's Depravity Goes Mainstream

Sunshine plays a major part in the daytime
—The Ghostface Killah

Only a few years after its founding, 4chan became one of the most popular sites on the web. And by 2008, it was being widely celebrated in the press. Articles bemused with its existence appeared in major publications like *Time*, *The Guardian*, and the *Wall Street Journal*.[1] Similar to 2channel, it was slowly being drawn into the entertainment complex. It wasn't so much that 4chan was being absorbed by mainstream culture as it was defining internet culture, which in turn was absorbing mainstream culture.

For all its pessimism and depravity, 4chan was also a wildly creative place. The fast-paced way it churned through content and voted only the best posts to live meant that it began generating art that had literally evolved to survive as sufficiently funny, interesting, or attention-grabbing. It was estimated that 40 percent of all posts on the site went unremarked upon and so existed only a few seconds before being swept away to the back pages of the boards and deleted. The most fascinating entries were "bumped" to the top of the site, saved, and reposted by other users.

A new culture composed of the sloughed-off psychic brainworms of catchphrases, old advertising slogans, and bits of media was bubbling out of 4chan. And it turned out that everyone needed a way to gain agency over the piles of psychic garbage entertainment marketing generated. People the world over soon learned the 4chan technique—the gag reflex of memes, in which the endless stream of invitations to indulge in something meaningless is vomited back up in a half-digested, colorful gush of irreverence.

To understand what the word "meme" means, it's helpful to learn its origins. Biologist Richard Dawkins coined the term in his 1979 book *The Selfish Gene* as part of an argument reframing how we think about evolution.

The central idea of *The Selfish Gene* shifted the focus of Darwin's competition for survival from the individual organism to the genes of that organism, the instructions that produce all its traits, from the shape of its eyes to its behavior. Evolution was often better understood, Dawkins argued, not as a struggle for the organism's survival, but for its genes to replicate themselves at the expense of other genes. For example, Dawkins suggested his paradigm more fully accounted for why animals often defend or feed their offspring or siblings to their own detriment.

Dawkins and his peers also realized that you could run such evolutionary competitions on early computers. In the 1980s, researchers created games that played themselves. Each computer-generated "organism" was programmed with a different survival strategy.[2] Then, all the different organisms would play not just one round, but thousands. They would compete over successive generations in one big simulation. One programmed strategy might direct an organism to cooperate with competitors, another might tell an organism to be selfish at all times, and yet another might recommend selfishness only some of the time. If the strategy scored high enough in a round, their "offspring" would compete in the next. Thousands of iterations of the same game were staged, simulating how different survival strategies played out not for the individual organism (who would only last one iteration of the game) but for the strategy itself over multiple generations. Losing strategies/genes "died off," while successful patterns of behavior begat "children" into the next round.

From this perspective, there's not much of a difference between a gene and an abstract idea. A gene is simply a way to store bits of information (eye color or an imperative to cooperate, etc.). Dawkins' next point was that we can imagine a set of genes that are simply ideas. They don't have a physical form, but they still replicate themselves over and over in an evolutionary struggle for our attention. These are memes.

As Dawkins puts it, "memes are tunes, ideas, catch-phrases, clothes fashions, ways of making pots or of building arches."[3] For example, in the 80s and 90s, we often heard the phrase "clean up in aisle two" in movies and TV shows. For whatever reason, that meme was replicated over and over at the expense of other ideas, thoughts, and expressions. Likewise, Darwin's theory of evolution could be considered a meme (or a huge set of memes), replicated over and over in the meme-verse (everyone's minds) because it is a useful tool for understanding the world. As a result, other memes proposed by his contemporaries (Charles Lyell's or Alfred Wallace's thoughts on evolution, for example) are replicated less, and some have pretty much died (i.e., no longer discussed). Darwin's superior memes killed them off.

In this sense, memes predated the internet. They are simply ideas— or more precisely, a way of thinking about ideas as replicators. But by the turn of the millennium, the internet had accelerated this process. Far more snippets of text and images were being replicated than ever before, and at much faster rates, with richer diversity. Therefore thinking of ideas as gene-like replicators became an increasingly apt way to understand them.

Many early message boards held memes, which back then were called in-jokes, but 4chan progenitors like 2channel and TOTSE, which encouraged frantic trash posting for the sake of entertainment over discussion, tended to have more. Technically, internet memes were invented on Something Awful (SA), where the first image macros (funny pictures captioned with white impact font) appeared, because there, too, people gathered not to exchange ideas but to compete to be funny. But around the same time 4chan was founded, Lowtax banned the practice, believing that simply copying someone else's joke and changing it slightly wasn't all that creative.

By contrast, 4chan defined itself as a pile of garbage posting with no rules (what later became known as "shitposting"), and so replicated the competitive evolutionary games Dawkins and his peers ran on the first PCs, where strategies "lived" or "died" based on how many times they were repeated. Except instead of virtual animals, the competitors were jokes in the form of recaptioned cartoons and images or snippets of text, which "survived" and were replicated if they were sufficiently funny.

By 2008, 4chan's memes had infiltrated mainstream culture, most notably LOLCats, the practice of slapping funny captions on cute pictures of cats, and "rickrolling," posting a link that seems important, but leads to the music video for the 80s pop single "Never Gonna Give You Up." In November of that year, the song's author, Rick Astley, popped out of a float in the Macy's Thanksgiving Day Parade to rickroll the audience. 4chan, SA, and a similar site dedicated to animated gifs called You're the Man Now Dog (YTMND) formed a "triforce" of meme creation that trickled out into the rest of the internet.

As for-profit social media began to replace open-source message boards, social media companies were particularly interested in co-opting memes. Sites like Facebook transitioned from voyeuristic quasi-dating sites to content aggregators with ranked 4chan-style feeds. When users logged on to Facebook, the point was no longer to check up on your friends, but to view the latest interesting content on the web, in particular, memes.

In 2008, 4chan seemed to be following the pattern history had established: counterculture becomes mainstream, from cartoon fetish site to Thanksgiving Day float. Now we could all enjoy 4chan's entertainment innovation—captioned pictures of cats—as a brief respite from our workaday routines. And indeed, 4chan's language and habits soon defined the rest of the web. Sites like icanhascheezburger.com and knowyourmeme.com became profitable internet institutions. Today, Twitter users compete with one another to elaborate on new memes while generating an endless flow of gibbering nonsense, as if it were 4chan in 2007. And users in Facebook and Instagram groups have replicated much of what 4chan once was using their real names.

As 4chan debuted in news articles, the corporate engine of co-optation began to rev up. "Although sometimes frivolous, every word-of-mouth marketer dreams of creating memorable memes that will catapult their product or client to fame," wrote the *Wall Street Journal* in 2008. "Over the last few years, 4chan.org has become one of the most talked-about sites when it comes to launching new memes."[4]

But 4chan was impossible to co-opt. Both memes and 4chan's ultra-transgressive culture were immune responses to commodification. When marketers mixed the backwater into the mainstream, this time, mercifully, something went wrong. The alchemy was off; they didn't so much spin straw into gold as breed weird new mutants, monsters it turned out, we've come to know as trolls.

Around the same time that the *Wall Street Journal* meditated on how best to monetize 4chan's creations, an article appeared in *New York*

Times Magazine about another confounding youth trend that was occurring on 4chan: trolling, the subtle art of acting obnoxious on message boards.[5]

Like memes, trolls had been knocking around the internet for years, but they only began to coalesce as a distinct phenomenon on SA and then 4chan. The term was derived from both the cranky creature sitting underneath the bridge disrupting the flow of traffic and a fishing practice in which chum is thrown into the water to attract fish.

Many of the internet's first trolls were inspired by the infamous "Eternal September" of 1993, when all AOL users were added to Usenet and the level of discourse dropped precipitously. As once-erudite Usenet boards disintegrated, trolls appeared as their defenders, baiting neophytes who were sounding off into defending silly beliefs or otherwise humiliating themselves.[6]

Other early trolls were situationists, disregarding the polite fiction that a message board was the equivalent of friends gathering in a room and delighting in one key difference—anonymity. By enabling people to meet virtually without actually having to meet physically, the internet enabled an unprecedented level of rude and aggressive behavior. For decades, this fact was counteracted by simple decorum, and because the early networks, composed of professionals, weren't quite as anonymous. The Well's one experiment with anonymous posting ended quickly because, according to the moderators, it was a disaster.[7] In its decades-long existence, The Well had banned only three users. By 2008, 4chan had banned 70,000.[8]

By the mid-2000s, the internet was transitioning from a society of professional adults to idle teens congregating in places like SA. These kids were less interested in defending discourse than in the situationist approach to trolling—playing the whole thing like a game. Nineties nihilism endured well into the 2000s, longer than most youth cultures. Like wine turned to vinegar, it could decay no further. Both culture and counterculture taught new generations to be so wary of being deceived and manipulated, it was best to hold nothing in your heart at all. Lacking convictions, the logic went, your desires could not be snagged or stolen. And no better example existed for this state of affairs than the unreal worlds of the screen. The art of cruelty, of tearing apart delicately wrought fantasy realms, thrived.

Previously, trolls had been isolated creatures, but as they shared their exploits on SA, they began to gang together. Threads about mischief-making in online games soon inspired collective "goon squads" in the vast new worlds of massively multiplayer online role-playing games (MMORPGs), where kids were already encouraged to create clans, tribes, and collectives. The genre of "griefing," at first a silly way of messing up your friends in cooperative games, became a pastime in which the goon squads attempted to "play" a game by disrupting other users' experiences as completely as possible. Popular destinations were the spaceship-themed *EVE Online*, where griefers massed in the Goonswarm Federation, and *Second Life*, where they called themselves the Patriotic Nigras.[9]

In the early aughts, *Second Life*, a for-profit digital fantasy MMORPG populated with elves and fairy princesses, proved a ripe target. But the temptations of *Second Life* were nothing compared to the much grander versions of *Second Life* that were coming out—social media. LiveJournal, Xenga, Myspace, Facebook, and YouTube didn't let you enter a typical fantasy world, but the effects were the same. Users duplicated their egos and imagined that their virtual interactions were somehow real. As social media invited millions of naive users onto the internet, it multiplied opportunities for mischief for trolls who exploited a widening gap between fantasy and reality.

The trolls claimed they were after lulz, a corruption of LOLs (laugh out louds). The term meant the laughs provided when a user was convinced to do something ridiculous in real life because of an event that took place on the internet, in effect, making the realm of the troll, the internet, real. While this tore at the fantasy of the virtual world, it also validated the strange duality of the troll himself, who, in his despairing nihilism, devoted his entire existence to online events.

Though most of 4chan's trolls were anonymous, we know a great deal about one of them. Andrew "weev" Auernheimer embodied each of 4chan's historical transformations: from meme creator, to troll, to hacktivist, then, finally, to neo-Nazi figurehead of the alt-right.

Since weev adored publicity and was one of the few people who self-identified as a troll, he became the subject of innumerable features between 2008 and 2011, including one in the *New York Times Magazine*. Short, with bulging, far-apart eyes; fleshy lips; cherub cheeks; and an up-turned, bulbous nose, weev bore an uncanny resemblance to a Greek satyr or, well, a troll. In interviews, he often claimed he invented popular 4chan trolling memes like "for the lulz" and "the internet is serious business."

Though weev liked to tout that he was born in "a trailer park in Arkansas," he spent most of his middle-class childhood on a hundred-acre farm in Virginia with his parents and sister. His mother was a real estate agent; his father, an industrial engineer for the poultry industry. His handle, "weev," was derived from weevils, a farm pest. As a child, he was something of a prodigy, or at least an autodidact. Sensing he didn't quite fit in at school, his parents enrolled him in George Mason University at fourteen. But there too he must have felt isolated, socially and academically. Like so many other 4chan denizens, he was technically adept but emotionally stunted. By sixteen, he had dropped out. He spent the next few years couch surfing across the United States with fellow computer programmers, hackers, and trolls he had met on the internet.[10]

Auernheimer and his circle of friends called themselves the Gay Nigger Association of America (GNAA) and recruited by advertising on content-aggregating sites like Slashdot. Initiates were required to watch the short film *Gayniggers from Outer Space* and answer questions about it. A queer-interest Dutch B movie in the hyper-transgressive tradition of John Waters, the film tells the story of a group of aliens, depicted as gay black men, who try to zap all the women off Earth and turn it into a "paradise." The message appealed to the society of nerdy white boys who wanted to cloak themselves in the coolness of 70s blaxploitation. (A machine in the film turns black men white.) The other trolling collectives on SA and 4chan would later adopt this practice, often referring to themselves, with a mixture of racism and envy, as "nigras."

Weev found 4chan in June 2004, when he was in his late teens. Unwittingly replicating the adolescent hacker otaku wars that sank the proto first channels on the Japanese Nifty Serve network, the GNAA programmed a similar auto-posting script to flood 4chan with pictures of goatse (guy opening his ass to show everyone), resulting in thousands of dollars of overage server costs that nearly shuttered the site for good. "What you miserable failed abortions seem not to realize is that the idiot actions of poorly executed cartoon drawings will never be your life," someone representing the GNAA, most likely weev, wrote on 4chan after the attack. "THE GNAA DECLARES FATALITY ON ANIME FAGGOTS."[11]

However, when 4chan finally went back up in August, weev and his trolling collective decided to settle there. Besides 4chan and SA, they also congregated on a wiki (an editable, encyclopedia-style site) that had once been dedicated to "LiveJournal drama," Encyclopedia Dramatica (ED). Previously, ED had documented histrionic feuds between the first generation of bloggers on the proto–social media site LiveJournal. But in the early 2000s, trolls began manufacturing the drama and needed a place to chronicle their "accomplishments."

But it was 4chan's culture that revolutionized trolling by treating collective harassment projects like memes. Between 2005 and 2008, 4chan became a hub world for trolling as the practice transitioned into a trolling-meme hybrid called a raid. First, a practical joke or target was floated on the boards. Most suggestions died immediately. But appealing ideas were bumped to the top of the site or otherwise replicated. Oftentimes these were invitations to invade another cyber world, be it a chat room, video game, message board, social media space, or rival chan-style site.

Users would meet to organize in various IRC channels that orbited 4chan. Oftentimes, to gather sufficient numbers, raids would spread from board to board in IRC networks and then back out again onto 4chan in loops and whirls. By 2005, there were dozens of copycat chan websites, constantly winking in and out of existence, often with even less oversight than 4chan. Many of these hosted invasion boards for the purpose of collective trolling.

But the most popular destination for trolling, and anything else in the burgeoning chanverse, was 4chan's random bin, /b/ (or, as Poole put it, "retard bin"), which carried 40 percent of 4chan's traffic. The name signaled an aspiration to be both silly and nihilistic, to make jokes, but also to tear constructive efforts apart whenever possible.

Ironically, "/b/tards," as they called themselves, had to gang together in complex networks to more effectively rip things to pieces. And like someone interpreting a Rorschach test, the userbase's attempts to be random soon revealed exactly who they were. Certain actions and language were met with approval or disapproval in the group. Before long these conventions evolved into a complex set of injunctions, memes, and code words. Absent usernames, behavior and language signaled insider status. If a user lurked for months or years on the board, they could learn to speak the dialect that told others they were part of the group. "In b4 summerfags," for example, means, "I'm writing this before young kids who have summers off come on 4chan and start replying to my comments with something stupid."

By 2006, /b/ had constructed a culture based on deconstruction and an identity based on anonymity. Users began referring to themselves and those who adhered to the void of their belief structure as "Anonymous," the author, as the joke went, of all posts. Users who wrote in a name were mocked as "namefags." And Anonymous soon codified their value system in "the rules of the internet," which were dedicated to tearing value systems apart: "Rule 8: There are no rules about posting . . . Rule 11: All your carefully picked arguments can easily be ignored."

The first rules were borrowed from *Fight Club*, a film about a male collective debased by modern corporate culture performing extreme acts of violence to regain their masculinity: "Rule 1: Do not Talk about 4chan. Rule 2: Do NOT talk about 4chan."

Anonymous was most cohesive when it was conducting a raid on another site, which varied from innocent to horrible. If nothing else was happening, anons would flood into a chat room where someone was streaming, often an adolescent girl, and try to convince them to place a shoe on their head. Anons often claimed they were from a rival site, newgrounds.com, enforcing Rule 1. In a few minutes, the chat log would reflect a repeated chanting demand: "Shoe on head. Shoe on head. Shoe on head . . ." When the streamer complied, a screenshot was posted in /b/ and a new target was acquired. But other projects lasted weeks, if not years.

An infamous early campaign targeted Mitchell Henderson, a middle-school-age boy from Michigan who had committed suicide. After his death, Henderson's Myspace page had been transferred to an ill-considered service called MyDeathSpace, which hosted the profiles of the dead. To the hordes of disaffected trolls on /b/, the idea of a Myspace death page was a tantalizing mixture of adolescent vulnerability and the unreal ego replication of the web they adored tearing to pieces. At first, trolls simply hacked the site and replaced Henderson's picture with a zombified image.

But soon, a rumor began circulating on the chans that Henderson had killed himself when "a bully stole his iPod." In this myth, Henderson and the sole picture that existed of him (depicting a sad-looking boy offering a fragile smile to the camera) became symbols of who the boys of 4chan had been a few years earlier. Now, safely ensconced behind their computers, the nerdy teens reveled in escaping Mitchell's fate. Tickled by the horror of a tale they had, in fact, made up, they began to act like a million cruel older brothers who would not let Henderson escape his humiliation, even in death.

For years, trolls called Henderson's parents pretending to be their dead son, pleading for an iPod. "Hi, it's me, Mitchell," they would begin. "I'm outside and I'm really cold. Please won't you let me back in?" Or, "I'm at the cemetery, where's my iPod?"[12] Other 4chan users made pilgrimages to Mitchell's grave, where they dropped iPods and snapped pics.

And as they scrutinized the mourners' posts on Mitchell's MyDeath-Space page, they cottoned on to a comment made by a young girl: "He was such an hero, to take it all away." Before long, the denizens of /b/ were encouraging each other to "become an hero." Suicide was already a topic frequently discussed on /b/. Whenever someone asked for advice, the two most common responses were "do it, faggot," and "kill yourself," to which the chorus of "became an hero?" was added.

Not long after, users on 4chan, YTMND, and SA coordinated an effort to flood a colorful virtual chat room for teenagers called Habbo Hotel with an avatar of an imposing black man in a suit and tie sporting an afro. On July 12, 2006, thousands of copies of the avatar (which /b/ referred to as "Nigras") cascaded into Habbo Hotel's network of Lego-style lounges to block access to the virtual pool. "Pool's closed due to AIDS," the men would declare whenever a child's avatar tried to get near. In anniversary "pool raids" conducted each year, anons would form enormous swastikas out of the avatars' afros they called "swastigets."

The original raid was inspired by vague rumors that Habbo Hotel was discriminating against avatars with darker skin. But a more likely scenario is that 4chan was long on trolls and short on targets. Raids lived or died by how many people rallied to the cause. Purported racism was an easy way to get mass consensus on whether a target deserved 4chan's wrath.

For the same reason, 4chan often targeted neo-Nazi radio host Hal Turner. Though Anonymous likely wouldn't have started molesting Turner if he hadn't livestreamed his shows, providing instant crank-call gratification. The same was true of Tom Green, the transgressive MTV comedian who hosted a livestreaming call-in show. When Green's show aired in the mid-90s, it was hard to imagine anything more vulgar. But in 2006, Anonymous attempted to outdo Green, flooding his phone lines with racial slurs and nonsense memes.

By 2007, trolling campaigns had reached a crazed fever pitch. This was partly because the raids were often wild successes. For example, the scorched-earth campaign against Turner only ended when Anonymous hacked him so thoroughly they discovered he was an FBI informant.

But the pace and scale of the raids was also increasing because 4chan's ranks were swelling. One way the community itself kept track was through "gets." Each post on 4chan was numbered, starting with one, so it was easy to see who, for example, had "gotten" the one-millionth post (which occurred in 2005). At the beginning of 2006, the ten million get had been achieved, and by March, the twenty-six million get. By more traditional metrics, 4chan was receiving somewhere between 900,000 and 3 million unique page views a month.[13]

This was partly because raids functioned as a recruiting mechanism. Despite Rules 1 and 2, rival sites' users often learned of the existence of 4chan through raids and soon joined. This meant that between 2006 and 2009, an increasing number of young women also began to use 4chan. The most frequently cited rules besides 1 and 34 ("Rule 34: If it exists, there is porn of it") were the two regarding the growing population of "femanons": the increasingly untrue Rules 30 ("There are no girls on the internet") and 31 ("tits or GTFO [get the fuck out]"). The latter meant that if a woman did appear on 4chan, she was obliged to post a picture of her bare breasts before she would be acknowledged.

Before long, a complex culture of "chan girls" emerged (here, referring not only to 4chan, but the diminutive term for girls in Japanese, "-*chan*"). Women would come to the site to garner male followers as ad hoc j-idols (Japanese idols), dressing up in costumes for their fans. The men, in turn, collected their pictures like they would Pokémon cards.

Many of these girls were chosen at random off the internet. Such was the case with the most popular of the chan girls, Catie "Boxxy" Wayne, a YouTube vlogger whom 4chan became obsessed with and who was soon dubbed "the Queen of /b/." Eventually, Boxxy parlayed her internet fame into a voice-acting career for Disney cartoons. Another chan girl, Allison "Creepy Chan" Harvard, who coated herself in blood in her pics, shared the details of her online following when she appeared on *America's Next Top Model*. But as much as 4chan was fun and games, it was also cruel horror.

One of the youngest chan girls, "Loli-Chan," was barely thirteen when she found 4chan. Like many kids at the time, she loved Gaia Online, an anime-themed children's message board that was played like a game. On Gaia, users could acquire not only status on the message board but currency (Gaia Gold and Gaia Cash), which they could spend on a host of virtual items (clothes, weapons, etc.) for their avatars. Thus caparisoned, they would then wander in an overhead virtual world like Habbo Hotel. Gaia was also the target of frequent 4chan raids. (By some metrics, 4chan was the most popular message board on the web in 2011, Gaia the second.)

In selfies she posted to 4chan in 2006, Loli-Chan appeared, as her nickname implied, like an anime girl-child come to life, with large brown eyes, a button nose, and short-cropped dark hair.

"I remember there was this one dress [on Gaia] I wanted for my avatar," Loli-Chan told me in 2018. "And I had put it in my signature that I wanted it. I saw other people do that, but an older person asked me if I would send them nudes and I learned from a young age that I could barter for commodities with sexuality."

When she found 4chan, she loved the freewheeling culture of silly jokes. Just as a friend at school had promised, it was "like Gaia only funnier." But when she posted pictures of herself dressed up as various memes, she was almost instantly elevated into a chan girl. And this drew her into a nightmarish society of fans, worshippers, "boyfriends," and pedophiles.

Now an artist whose work focuses on the depiction of women, she is still drawn to the chans' creative content, what she describes as "outsider-outsider art."

"The thing that made me angriest was [that] on my entry in know-yourmeme[.com]," Loli-Chan told me, "I saw someone left a comment: 'It was so easy to groom her.' I was a little kid. I blamed myself for a long time. I had to have a therapist tell me I'm not the only person this has happened to. That it wasn't my fault. Now I see women discussing it among themselves on these women-only message boards and I know it happens all the time."

And so by 2007, 4chan was a source of creativity at the center of a meme economy that dominated pop culture, but it was also a font of debauchery, trolling, and criminality into which kids fell—some thrilled to be there, others horrified.

"What I saw on 4chan on a daily basis was so fucked up it was only plausible to me because we were all just fucked up on 4chan," Loli-Chan explained. "It doesn't make sense now, looking back at it. There were memes that I saw when I was twelve or fifteen: 'crush-cat,' a woman crushing a cat with high heels, 'zippo cat,' a cat that was decapitated. An entire generation was desensitized . . . I think . . . what made 4chan go south is all the focusing on raids."

One day, some hacker might be leaking free Xbox coupons from a cracked coupon algorithm. The next day it might be a bomb threat, real or imagined. Another day, Anonymous might convince local news outlets that kids were collecting their feces in balloons and huffing the fumes to get high (code word: Jenkem). And it wasn't long after that anons began leaving their mothers' basements for their first real-life raids.

In 2007, anons dressed in wizard's robes made their way up and down lines of sleeping children in major cities as the tykes queued up in front of bookshops for the latest volume of Harry Potter. Fans awoke not to their dreamed-of purchase, but the spoiled ending: "Snape kills Dumbledore!" the anons bellowed over crackling portable loudspeakers as those in line screamed and stopped up their ears. Another sword-and-sorcery fantasy successfully shattered.

In the same year, an anon earned his first press coverage on a local Fox News affiliate in Los Angeles. The segment told the sad tale of "David," whose Myspace page was defiled by "domestic terrorists . . . hackers on steroids" named Anonymous. Meeting on their "secret website," the host declared, Anonymous quickly filled up hapless David's profile with gay porn, prompting his girlfriend to leave him. "We do not forgive. We do not forget," explained the blacked-out figure of a "former Anonymous member," his voice distorted. The declaration (Rule 5) was at best half-true. Anonymous rarely forgave, but they forgot almost every day as soon as something funnier popped up on the boards to fill the infinite void of their lives. When the report aired, Anonymous were so tickled, they adopted Fox's label for them as their new motto: "the internet hate machine."

Getting caught was a joke too. When someone was carted away, they were "brb fbi'd" ("be right back FBI [is at the door]"), or they had "gone for a ride in the 4chan party van," an allusion to a scene in *The Simpsons* in which Homer, being watched by the FBI, scrutinizes a suspicious truck out front labeled "Party Supplies."

But all of these isolated incidents fail to convey the constant stream of depravity and weirdness that flowed through early 4chan as though it were some river in hell; the daily chaos of teens, desperate weirdos, and just plain "normal" folks confessing the inner contents of their hearts, sexual experiences, humiliations, hang-ups, and deepest secrets. All of which were, well, insane; a mass excavation of the human unconscious on an unprecedented scale. At times it was pure trash. At others, it was art—the internal, in all its raw complexity, turned external, macabre and gross, subtle and sublime, interior monologues, previously the domain of fiction and private journals, flowing into pools of pornographic cartoons. This was, of course, the function of art, to reveal the nuances of imagination hidden under shame. But it was also art sans art, as 4chan negated everything, even itself. Art born from some insistent, frantic need mixed up with the Lost Boys nonsense of a generation of children who raised themselves online, sometimes Never Never Land, sometimes the carnival island in *Pinocchio* where wayward children, indulging in every excess, slowly metamorphosed into braying asses.

The result of all this was that by January 2008, something broke. The irreducible nihilism of 4chan, to use a favorite phrase from the opening credits of *The Fresh Prince of Bel-Air*, "flipped turned upside down," and a period of intense optimism followed, in which those who had retreated behind their screens suddenly found themselves imbued with a sense of agency and control over their own destiny, one that echoed around the world in radical political revolution. That is, until the party van actually came knocking.

And the tipping point, when it arrived, pivoted around Tom Cruise.

2008: Anonymous Accidentally Starts a Worldwide Revolution

"My name is Legion," he replied, "for we are many." And he begged Jesus again and again not to send them out of the area . . . "Send us among the pigs; allow us to go into them." He gave them permission, and the impure spirits came out and went into the pigs. The herd, about two thousand in number, rushed down the steep bank into the lake and were drowned.
—Mark 5:9–11

Late in 2007, double agents inside Scientology's organization leaked an internal promotional video of Tom Cruise giddily proselytizing the benefits of Scientology as the theme song from his latest blockbuster *Mission: Impossible* played in a mind-numbing loop over his meditations. In the video, Cruise came off as somehow both unhinged and vain, his language devolving at times into gibbering inanity as he waxed on in a self-congratulatory manner about the powers and responsibilities his high-level training granted him. "Being a Scientologist, when you drive past an accident," he mused, wide-eyed, "you know you have to do something about it, because you *know* you're the only one that can really help."

On January 15, 2008, the video was mailed to an anti-Scientology activist, who, in turn, sent it to NBC. However, fearing a lawsuit from the Church of Scientology, NBC didn't run it and the embarrassing clip ended up on YouTube. Though the Church sent a takedown notice to YouTube, it was too late.[1] As the story went viral, copies multiplied across the platform faster than they could be removed. Soon, the gossip website Gawker was hosting the video, refusing to take it down despite also receiving copyright violation notices from the Church.

Soon, an anon floated the idea on 4chan of a raid against Scientology in the name of one of the few values anon agreed upon: freedom of information on the internet. The image uploaded with the post displayed the snakey golden Scientology logo. "I think it's time for /b/ to do something big," the anon reasoned.

> People need to understand not fuck with /b/,
> and talk about nothing for ten minutes,
> and expect people to give money to an
> organization that makes absolutely no fucking
> sense.
> I'm talking about "hacking" or "taking down" the
> official Scientology website.
> It's time to use our resources to do something we believe is right.
> It's time to do something big again, /b/
> Talk amongst one another, find a better place to plan it, and then carry
> out what can and must be done.
> It's time, /b/

It didn't take long for Anonymous to become convinced. The mix of inane pop culture and the infamous bullying tactics of the Church made for a ripe opportunity. In fact, Scientology had been warring with information freedom advocates and hackers since the days of Usenet. 4chan's predecessor TOTSE adored following the action. But history hardly mattered to young Anonymous. At that point, raids were occurring at the drop of a hat. And without a good target, Anonymous often just targeted itself. For example, here is a description of a typical large raid that occurred two months before the Cruise video went viral from one of the wikis that kept track of Anonymous' exploits:

October 19–25 [2007]—The Caturday Nap-A number of users from Lulznet enter the 4chan IRC channel, demanding that it be moved from its current location on irc.rizon.net to irc.partyvan.org. Their request is not taken seriously and they are banned from the channel in short order. During the exchange, moot said "whatever, Im gonna go make soup." Angered, Lulznet begins a DDoS attack against 4chan. The attack is relatively successful, with all of the 4chan servers' timing out relatively quickly, in response moot simply plugs them out. Simultaneously, Encyclopedia Dramatica attacks Wikichan for the sake of it.[2]

To increase the amount of traffic flowing into a target, Anonymous often supplemented its numbers with distributed denial of service (DDoS) attacks in which enemy websites and IRC channels were deluged with meaningless requests for data until they crashed.

Compared to imagined slights on their own IRC channels, a vast, shadowy science-fiction-themed organization charging hundreds of thousands of dollars for "mental auditing" sessions (and restricting access to Tom Cruise YouTube lulz) was a far better rallying cry for a massive attack.

As usual, Anonymous retired to its IRC channels to sift through its bag of tricks: crank phone calls, pizza deliveries, and DDoS attacks, all of which began after a matter of hours. But soon things snowballed beyond their wildest expectations. The breakthrough moment occurred when a few anons uploaded a video to YouTube featuring the Anonymous character as he was depicted in the Fox News report, as a shadowy international cabal of powerful hackers.

In the clip, dark clouds drift double time over nowhere in particular, the only visible landmarks the tops of silver office buildings. Ominous synth music mingles with a techno war beat of drums. "Hello," a distorted, deep-set voice greets the viewer, emphasizing all the wrong syllables in the words:

We are Anonymous. Over the years, we have been watching you.

Your campaigns of misinformation; suppression of dissent; your litigious nature, all of these things have caught our eye. With the leakage of your latest propaganda video into mainstream circulation, the extent of your malign influence over those who trust you, who call you leader, has been made clear to us.

Anonymous has therefore decided that your organization should be destroyed.

For the good of your followers, for the good of mankind—for the laughs—we shall expel you from the Internet and systematically dismantle the Church of Scientology in its present form.

We are Anonymous. We are Legion. We do not forgive. We do not forget.

"We are Legion" was both Rule 4 and a reference to a passage in the gospel of Mark when Jesus, having trouble with a particular exorcism, asks the name of the demon inhabiting the victim, to which the demon replies, "My name is legion."

The video was an instant success. It was soon picked up by major internet news sites. The media seemed eager to believe the mad myth of Anonymous, which made sense because it was the invention of sensationalist media. Information began to flow in a weird whirlpool through 4chan, the pop-culture matrix, and then back out into the infotainment news complex. Recently, the whole news cycle had become infected with 4chan-style memes and *Buzzfeed* clickbait, blurring the lines between blogosphere rumors, YouTube videos, and actual events.

Delighted by the press attention and the Church of Scientology's angry response, more anons flooded into the IRC channels to take part in what was proving to be an epic raid on the scale of the Habbo Hotel, Tom Green, and Hal Turner raids. Anons took it upon themselves to order pizzas or make calls to Scientology buildings, while the more sophisticated hackers in the group coordinated DDoS attacks using a junk-packet spitter the original anon programmer had dubbed the "Low Orbit Ion Cannon."

But things were different this time. The number of people participating in the raids was of course larger. But also, Anonymous was no longer a loosely knit group of trolls demonstrating their impotence with nihilistic pranks. They had accidentally discovered agency. Now they were using their collective powers to enforce what they agreed was right and wrong. In their view, Scientology was an evil cult that deserved to be destroyed, and many imagined Anonymous had the capability to do it. No one knew the limits of Anonymous' strength. And many wanted to test it.

Major early decisions in the raid were made in an obscure IRC channel, which held the original video creators, including a young, left-leaning Boston activist named Gregg Housh. Debating what to do with all the new participants, Housh and the others eventually decided to put the crowd "in the streets." Protests were organized for a few weeks later and new messages were put out on behalf of Anonymous, promising that on the appointed day, thousands of Anonymous members would appear outside Scientology buildings around the world.[3]

The morning of the protest, February 10, 2008, was a brutally cold Saturday, at least where I attended, in New York's Times Square. I wanted to write an article on 4chan, which, at that point, no one had done. But I didn't have any sources. Anons I had reached out to adhered to Rules 1 and 2 and refused to speak with me. I had emailed Poole, but he never responded. I was hoping someone would show up for the protest, though I didn't really believe anyone would. At nine a.m., Times Square was totally deserted. Not even the tourists were out. All you could see was the trash billowing about on the streets. I had forced my roommate to come with me. He too looked around disappointed.

"We're being trolled," he complained. "No way these nerds are leaving their parents' basements . . ."

But as we turned the corner onto 46th Street, to our astonishment, several hundred people were screaming and shouting, cordoned off in front of the Scientology building. Anonymous. Every one. They all wore masks, mostly Guy Fawkes masks inspired by the Wachowski brothers' adaptation of *V for Vendetta*. This was, in comic book parlance, the mask's first appearance IRL.

I rarely checked the IRC channel, so I was surprised at how well coordinated it was. The cordons implied someone had notified the city some weeks prior. And the masks must have been ordered in advance too. There were other costumes as well. Several people were dressed as the avatar from the Habbo Hotel raids.

It was my first time acting as a reporter, and I had come prepared with a prop: a notebook a real reporter friend of mine had given me that read on the cover "Reporter's Notebook." So armed, I crossed the police line and interviewed the Scientologist standing between the columns of his temple. He was wearing a gleaming silver suit, the threads iridescent. He looked horrified and perplexed.

"These are terrorists," he insisted, of course having no idea who they were, which was message board users. "This is a terrorist organization. And we are a religion by the First Amendment." Then he handed me a packet, shockingly thick, full of glossy pamphlets about Scientology, like something you might get from a college admissions office.

Then I talked to the anons. Like at Otakon three years earlier, they were slightly younger than me and, somehow, impossibly paler. A few women and girls were in the mix, but not many. There were lots of punks with colored hair and teens in goth black.

I interviewed a pimply faced boy, his Guy Fawkes mask pulled up over long, curly orange locks.

"How was this protest organized?" I asked.

"It was organized on a site called newgrounds.com," he answered.

"Is the protest a joke or serious?"

"It's serious business," he replied.

"The internet is serious business" was a meme, a joke on 4chan. One that weev claimed he had invented. And so it went down the line: Anonymous protesters, all following Rule 1, trying to conceal 4chan from me, and obscure the source of the joke, just like a raid into a chat room, each hiding their motivations behind a mirrored chamber of repeated memes. Habbo Hotel by way of Lord Xenu, the space ruler who, according to Scientology's final revelatory secret, seeded Earth with souls one billion years ago by nefariously dumping them beside a volcano. Now anon chanted his name, which typically cost hundreds of thousands of dollars to learn. It was their only real political statement: all information was free now that we had the internet. Scientology acolytes the same age, handing out copies of *Dianetics*, stopped up their ears, their pamphlets scattering to the ground.

And thus proceeded the odd war between a group of internet teens and the ghost of a long-dead science-fiction author reincarnated as a celebrity-worshipping prophet. As promised, similar scenes were taking place outside of Scientology centers around the world: London, Los Angeles, San Francisco, and Perth. When the protest broke up around noon, a nerd dressed in a long black duster, like Neo from *The Matrix*, shouted, "Now back to our parents' basements!" and the whole crowd laughed.

Though Anonymous' war with Scientology would continue throughout the year, the February 2008 protests proved to be the high-water mark. The campaign made Anonymous more real than ever. However, the result was a schism between trolls and activists. Even before the protest, anons had expressed anger that the demonstrations would violate Rules 1 and 2, and threatened to expose the only community in which they had ever found acceptance. To the traditional nihilists, "protestfags" or "moralfags" had taken the joke too far and begun to believe their own lies.

A month after the protests, the troll collectives that frequented Encyclopedia Dramatica, which included the Gay Nigger Association of America, launched an attack on websites for epilepsy sufferers, filling the pages with flickering gifs intended to cause seizures in an effort to reclaim the name "Anonymous." "Circumstantial evidence suggests the attack was the work of members of Anonymous, an informal collective of griefers best known for their recent war on the Church of Scientology," an article in *Wired* read.[4] Hacktivists then insisted it was a *different* Anonymous, which in one sense, it was, and in another, it wasn't.

Eventually, Housh and the other activists migrated off 4chan to start their own sites. But now "Anonymous" had two meanings. To those using 4chan, it was still the collective of chan-board users. But it was also Anonymous, the shadowy cabal of hackers as reported in the press.

And both characters, it turned out, would soon leave the internet to wander the world at large.

2008–2011: From Hope to Despair to Change

There is more behind and inside V than any of us had suspected. Not who but what what is she.
—The comic book character V quoting the Thomas Pynchon novel *V*

As I walked to the protest, the first evidence of its existence I encountered was an older man scalping tickets on Broadway, the only other occupant of Times Square.

"Good to see you kids finally doing something!" he shouted at me.

His comment reflected something that's hard to remember ten years later. By and large, protesting was still considered a joke at the time, the domain of the past, not contemporary youth counterculture, which disdained everything, particularly action.

Weirdly, 4chan, in all its trolling despair, had drilled through the bedrock of nihilism and found a route to activism—just as the old 70s hackers had predicted—through the internet. And the template for the internet-organized protest would soon be copied, along with the Guy Fawkes masks, in Tahrir Square and Zuccotti Park. 4chan's 2008 transition from trolling to hacktivism was one part of a larger phenomenon that was taking place on 4chan in 2008, also known as the year of "hope" and "change," the transition from helpless despair to optimism.

The schism between activists and trolls belied a larger issue. 4chan was still experimentally groping for what it would become. Even before the Scientology protests, the combination of the collectives coordinating in IRC and 4chan's profound influence on culture worldwide made Anonymous feel powerful. And so the question on /b/ in 2008 was, "What are we?" But it was also, "What's next?" What new project would the user-base of the chans undertake that would change the world?

And to many, the answer seemed obvious. Themselves. Anonymous had chosen the radical V from *V for Vendetta* as their symbol because of the movie's revolutionary overtones. In both the 2005 film by the Wachowski siblings and the 1989 comic book upon which the film is based, V is an anarchist bomber fighting against a future fascist Britain that has beaten its populace into indifferent submission. But V was also selected because he resembled the typical anon, a scarred weirdo, unable to remove his mask, but witty and sophisticated. V lives in a basement (though not his parents') in an exaggerated nerd fantasy of old books, eclectic records, paintings, and pop culture, just as Anonymous used the chans to stockpile folders of MP3s, films, images, and books. Like the subject of the Wachowskis' previous film, the computer hacker Neo in *The Matrix*, V was a comic book super-hero, though he was more of a half-grown-up antihero. Instead of pursuing a normal romantic relationship with his love interest (played by Natalie Portman), V kidnaps her and converts her into a freedom-fighting radical.

Anonymous' icon, the man in a clean-cut black suit adorned with a Guy Fawkes mask, was not quite who Anonymous was, but who they desired to be. Someone like V—adroit, cultured, and capable.

V made a certain point obvious: If the collective could square itself against a big institution like Scientology, could they then face their central problem, that of their unhealthy personal habits and maturity? If they could "leave their mothers' basements" for the sake of intimidating Scien-tologists, couldn't they also leave for their own sakes? Could they become who they pretended to be—not just hacktivists, but a society of /b/rothers who lifted one another up out of otaku-ness and into manhood?

In this spirit, the Anonymous icon was soon plastered on a series of self-help guides written to help anons navigate real life. Mixed into all the usual instructions for mischief-making, hacking, and petty theft were how-to texts for education, grooming, and romance.

The most notable sought to teach anons things they had never learned in their isolation: the basics of hygiene, manners, etiquette, cleanliness, and self-education. At first these threads carried advice so basic it was endearing (e.g., "you must shower once a day"). And like everything on 4chan, the project grew in complexity as it was crowdsourced. For ex-ample, the second edition of the wiki began: "*The Return of the Well Cultured Anonymous* is an updated book, based on the original *Well*

The Evolution of Anonymous

1605
Guy Fawkes
attempts to
blow up
Parliament.

1960s-1970s
The folk tradition of
the Guy Fawkes mask
fades into British
comic books.

1989
The comic book
V for Vendetta
by Alan Moore,
David Lloyd, and
Tony Weare places
the mask on an
anti-fascist hero.

2005
A movie adaptation
by the Wachowski
siblings is released.

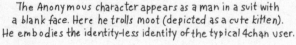

2004-2006
The Anonymous character appears as a man in a suit with
a blank face. Here he trolls moot (depicted as a cute kitten).
He embodies the identity-less identity of the typical 4chan user.

2006
4chan creates Epic Fail Guy ("EFG")
as a satire of the hyper-confident
V in V for Vendetta.
Unlike V, EFG always fails.

2008-present
V, EFG, and Anonymous merge to create "Anonymous",
the icon for an international society of hacker-activists.

Cultured Anonymous . . . It attempts to show others (primarily other Anonymous) how to be sophisticated, talented, and polite in today's modern world." The guide taught not only technical skills, but also how to appreciate music, literature, and art—sort of. ("Art is everywhere and shit. Understanding and appreciating it will set you apart from losers and make you feel better about your understanding of the world as a whole.") It also tackled the meta-questions that anons struggled with, the nihilism that seemed to pervade a nerdy life of inward-looking fantasy. Chapters offered instructions on how to self-improve not just in the real world, but in the more difficult terrain of your own mind. In a section titled "Why bother?" anons explained to other anons the trap of false pride that occurs in dwelling in virtual accomplishments like video games. "It's one thing to beat all your mates at *Mario Kart* even though they always seem to get blue shells on the last lap. That may feel good temporarily, but you'll know that most people IRL don't give a shit so you won't feel proud of it."

Nearly all of 4chan's original boards in 2003 were dedicated to some mix of anime and fetish pornography. But in 2008, boards were added to discuss fitness, fashion, and literature.

The creator of all these new sections was, of course, Christopher "moot" Poole. In the early years, moot had concealed his identity out of shame. Many users believed there was no Christopher "moot" Poole or that he was a fabrication of the FBI and 4chan an ensnaring honeypot. But by the summer of 2008, profiles in *Time* and the *Wall Street Journal* describing 4chan as a secret font for the hot new trend of memes brought 4chan's creator out of the shadows and into the limelight as a semi-celebrity/tech entrepreneur. When journalists came to interview him, they didn't encounter a jaded embodiment of /b/ who was sullen, isolated, and weird, but rather, an articulate, polite, skinny teenager with angular features and a mop of golden curls. At the time, he ran 4chan as a hobby as he attended college.

Poole's own experience tracked the transition from otaku to self-improvement. Shortly after founding the site, he had been arrested for throwing water balloons at cars from the roof of a building, a humiliation that convinced him to change his life by limiting his computer use, exercising, and channeling his screen time into productive projects. The success of 4chan provided him with friends and confidence. And now that it was growing into a worldwide phenomenon, he began to position the board as simply another helpful service in the style of trending social media giants.

As a typical post-90s teen, moot professed he hated politics and never endorsed Anonymous' transition into a hacktivist collective, favoring the site's role as a source for whimsical jokes. Every once in a while, he would prank /b/ by pretending to shut down the site or filling all the windows with raining dildos.

But the direction 4chan was moving can only be understood by setting it in the larger context of 2008 politics. As Naomi Klein detailed in her 1999 book on branding, *No Logo*, counterculture transitioned in the late 90s from identity politics to anti-corporate efforts, which appeared around the turn of the century as a sort of proto-Anonymous, in which masked hacktivists and graffiti artists subverted billboards and advertising technology in a practice they called "culture-jamming." By the end of the millennium, the unthinkable had occurred; these activists began organizing youth protests. In 1999, 40,000 demonstrators gathered in Seattle to protest the World Trade Organization, a symbol of global capitalist hegemony.

But the disasters of the Bush administration and the September 11, 2001, attacks derailed the left's focus on the growth of corporations and wealth inequality. Faced with "extraordinary renditions," new wars, the embrace of torture, and the decline of civil liberties (all themes of the film version of *V for Vendetta*), the left found itself on the defensive.

By 2008, many leftists considered Obama's ascendancy a way to put things back on track. Obama represented not only a clean break from the Bush administration, but the means by which the left could finally address the long-term problems of the neoliberal Corporate State, which had been described by Charles Reich in the 60s and solidified under the Clintons, his students, in the 90s. In a 2007 article in *The Atlantic* titled "Goodbye to All That," Andrew Sullivan imagined that the countercultural spats of the 60s were some baby boomer relic that could finally be set aside as irrelevant. And it was Obama who could do it. "Obama's candidacy . . . could take America—finally—past the debilitating, self-perpetuating family quarrel of the Baby Boom generation that has long engulfed all of us," he wrote. "So much has happened in America in the past seven years, let alone the past 40, that we can be forgiven for focusing on the present and the immediate future. But it is only when you take several large steps back into the long past that the full logic of an Obama presidency stares directly—and uncomfortably—at you."[1]

Similarly, a *New York Times* op-ed by John Broder titled "Shushing the Baby Boomers" read, "The time has come, Senator Barack Obama says, for the baby boomers to get over themselves."[2] And in a reissued edition of *No Logo* in 2009, Naomi Klein wrote, "Obama is a gifted politician with a deep intelligence and a greater inclination toward social justice than any leader of his party in recent memory. If he cannot change the system in order to keep his election promises, it's because the system itself is utterly broken."[3] Klein's take was the most pessimistic, but it turned out to be the most prescient. Obama, she observed, was a brand using "hope" and "change" as advertising slogans. And as such, a day might emerge when the customers realized they'd been cheated, sold not a product, but hype.

In 2008, /b/ supported the libertarian Ron Paul for president. In homage, anons modified their customary greeting of "sup /b/?" to "Ron Paul /b/?" But Obama was their second choice. The site was full of memes celebrating the candidate's youth, masculinity, and suave coolness— depicting him dunking on Hillary Clinton or smoking as Spike from *Cowboy Bebop*. And on Election Day, Poole changed /b/'s header from "RON PAUL 2008" to "O/b/ama."

However, by late 2010, it had become obvious that Obama had failed to restore America to a pre–War on Terror state. He was unable or unwilling to end the wars in the Middle East or even close Guantanamo. But he also disappointed those who hoped for a figure who represented a new "third way" and transcended the partisan baby boomer politics of the past, as all those op-eds had promised. He moved to the center while in office and hardly impacted, let alone dispelled, the big systemic problems on which he originally campaigned, such as the flow of corporate money into politics. By 2016, the presidential candidates who succeeded Obama, Hillary Clinton and Donald Trump, were both baby boomers relitigating how best to restore America to its 1950s ideal.

As Klein predicted, a counterswing began to build as all the Obama hype dissolved. In 1835, Alexis de Tocqueville had observed that the French Revolution did not occur in a period of hopelessness, but rather a period of rising prosperity where hope seemed on the horizon but expectations were not met. And indeed, it wasn't the Bush era that proved to be the catalyst for a new explosion of anti-corporate youth culture, but disappointed hopes for change that never occurred under Obama. And one of the centers of this new movement would be Anonymous.

The 2008 financial crisis that Obama inherited became an object lesson for the progressive left, spawning language to describe the disparity of power between corporations and people. Occupy Wall Street created slogans like "Banks got bailed out, we got sold out." And it spoke of how the U.S. government was serving the "1 percent" as opposed to the "99 percent." But Occupy Wall Street would not occur until 2011. And in 2009 and 2010, the expectation that Obama would address these issues, combined with a lack of language to even describe them, created a confused period of groping. Even among the left, the "end of history" notion—that there was no realistic alternative to globalized corporate capitalism—still endured. As Jean Baudrillard noted in 1990, to simply utter Marxist terms like "bourgeois" was to invite ridicule.

And so Anonymous, at that point a half-indifferent-troll/half-hopeful-activist amalgam, spent 2009 and much of 2010 flexing its collective muscle, figuring out what it was by performing cartwheeling pranks and cyberbullying. Two decades of 90s nihilism had many wanting to move on to something else. But the transition out of the philosophical vacuum was slow. The 2008 Scientology raid had hinted at new modes of empowered collective action. But no one knew quite what to do with the power.

In January 2009, Anonymous devoted itself to deluging a twelve-year-old YouTube star of the *No Cussing Club* with 7,500 profane messages, such as "i am going to find you And mutilate you with a scalple [*sic*]." In April, they spent thousands of man-hours hacking an online poll for *Time*'s 100 most influential people of the year in an attempt to make Poole *Time*'s Person of the Year (he made the list but didn't come in first).[4]

For much of 2010, Anonymous became obsessed with harassing a fourteen-year-old girl from Florida named Jessi Slaughter, an effort that snowballed when her father burst into the room during one of her livestreams screaming at Anonymous, "You dun goofed!" and threatening to "backtrace" them. When Slaughter appeared on *Good Morning America* to tell her tale, Anonymous launched "Operation /b/ipolar," posting nothing but positive messages for the day, hoping to convince TV viewers that 4chan was all about peace and love.

Meanwhile, anons were also donning their Anonymous *V for Vendetta* cowl to fight political battles, sort of. In 2010, angry that the Australian government was going to place restrictions on online pornography, Anonymous began performing distributed denial of service (DDoS) attacks on its websites in a campaign they called "Operation Titstorm." This in turn transitioned into "Operation Payback," when Anonymous heard several entertainment companies had subcontracted tech firms to launch cyberattacks against popular software and movie piracy sites like the Pirate Bay. In response, Anonymous launched an aggressive counterattack.

But as Anonymous spent the summer bullying Jessi Slaughter and defending porn and pirated software, the political landscape around hacking and activism was shifting radically. In April 2010, Julian Assange and WikiLeaks began releasing hundreds of thousands of government documents obtained from military contractor Bradley (now Chelsea) Manning. Among the various accounts of corporate and government malfeasance were videos showing American helicopters gunning down civilians in Iraq, including two Reuters journalists.[5]

Many anons considered Manning a hero, as he was soon jailed when a hacker to whom he had initially offered the leaks, Adrian Lamo, surrendered chat logs to the FBI. A sociologist specializing in Anonymous and hackers, Gabriella Coleman, described a bizarre scene in New York in July 2010 at the Hackers on Planet Earth (HOPE) conference, in which Eric "Emmanuel Goldstein" Corley and Mark "Phiber Optik" Abene, the cynical young hackers from the famous 1989 *Harper's/*The Well debate, sat on an impromptu panel with Lamo on the subject of snitches. It was rumored that Assange, a hacker known from the 90s scene, might appear via video conference, but he never arrived.

When Assange dumped 251,287 U.S. State Department files in November, it only heightened the feeling that vast institutional powers were committing crimes with impunity. Much of the world regarded the fiasco of the Iraq War as being the result of the larger military-industrial-complex quagmire, in which defense companies lobbied for perpetual warfare to sell services to the government. Between the false pretenses on which the war began (the infamous missing weapons of mass destruction), private contractors, private soldiers, oil opportunities, and bases replete with Burger Kings, the endless war seemed to embody the problem.

As "cablegate" progressed, a group of high-level former CIA, FBI, and government analysts, including the Pentagon Papers whistleblower, Daniel Ellsberg, issued a joint statement, writing that the old Russian propaganda paper *Pravda* was reporting on WikiLeaks better than Western media. "The corporate-and-government-dominated media are apprehensive over the challenge that WikiLeaks presents." They cited *Pravda*'s sentiment that "what WikiLeaks has done is make people understand why so many Americans are politically apathetic . . . After all, the evils committed by those in power can be suffocating, and the sense of powerlessness that erupts can be paralyzing, especially when . . . government evildoers almost always get away with their crimes."[6]

Soon Sweden had issued an arrest warrant for Assange on allegations of sexual assault, though he was then in the United Kingdom. And Pay-Pal and Mastercard confiscated the donations WikiLeaks had received through their services. Ironically, this prompted Assange to switch to Bitcoin, eventually making him millions after the currency's value went up over 1,000 percent in the next decade. However, it proved to be the final straw for Anonymous. Outraged, they organized DDoS attacks against PayPal and Mastercard that grew to the scale of the February 2008 Scientology protests. Once again anons flooded into the IRC networks and issued ultimatums to PayPal and Mastercard. And once again the press ran stories about the mysterious Anonymous and their shadowy threats.

One of the people in the IRC channels was me, watching as all the suffocation and powerlessness described by Ellsberg inverted itself. The feeling that overtook the boards was not an Obama brand of political "hope," but real, actual hope, a sense of collective agency.

In 1992, Baudrillard had written about how younger generations "no longer expect anything . . . [and] dig in behind their futuristic technologies, behind their stores of information and inside the beehive networks of communications . . . [to] perhaps never reawaken . . . [because] political events already lack sufficient energy of their own to move us." These sentiments directly inspired screen fantasies like the Wachowskis' *Matrix* and *V for Vendetta*. And now, the beehive was reawakening, buzzing with frenetic activity as it constructed a homegrown *V for Vendetta* in real life.

Once again, anons distributed the old DDoS Low Orbit Ion Cannon, this time aimed at PayPal and Mastercard. Many of the skilled hackers who hadn't been seen since the Scientology campaign reappeared to offer their services.

Though the effects weren't particularly spectacular. Most of the DDoS attacks bounced harmlessly off the corporate servers. PayPal's and Mastercard's websites went down for twelve hours, at most, and that was only because, as was later revealed by Parmy Olson in her book *We Are Anonymous*, the owner of a large botnet appeared in IRC to help. Botnets are created by infecting as many computers as possible with a virus that allows the hacker to control them. "Ryan" had 1.3 million computers that he had infected at his disposal and could work as he pleased.[7]

However, despite its middling results, "Operation Avenge Assange" finally succeeded in focusing Anonymous on the same countercultural enemies as the 90s hackers: the institutional powers of corporations and the state. Drawn to the reawakened activity, the most talented hackers and organizers coalesced into an ever-shifting network of elite IRC channels with names like #Anonops, #pureelite, #upperdeck, #InternetFeds, and #command.

Many of these people passed in and out of the channels and no one ever learned their identity. But the main players in the Anonymous campaigns to follow were a surprisingly small crew, and many of them were eventually caught.

Hector "Sabu" Monsegur was a twenty-five-year-old Puerto Rican living in a crowded apartment in a New York housing project on the Lower East Side. Christopher "Commander X" Doyon was a radical hippie who had been involved in activism and hacking since the mid-70s. Like Sabu, he had been attracted to the movement through hacking circles when he saw how the campaign was gaining steam. Jeremy "sup_g" Hammond was a twenty-six-year-old dumpster-diving freegan who had already spent years working as a hacktivist. At the time, Hammond was also a member of an obscure far-left activist group known as the black bloc or antifa. Mustafa "tflow" Al-Bassam was a fifteen-year-old computer savant living in the suburbs of London. And "Kayla" turned out to be a crew of teenage boys who got together to play online games and hack rivals during the chaotic chan wars of 2005–2009 by pretending to be a fourteen-year-old girl.[8] (On December 13, 2008, all the threads on /b/ were drowned out for the day by the auto-posted message "KAYLA > YOU" when Kayla apparently defaced 4chan for the sake of a rival site site called Raidchan.)[9] By 2011, only one Kayla remained (or at least only one was caught), a young British Iraq War veteran living in a suburb in Northern England named Ryan Mark Ackroyd. The owner of the botnet turned out to be Ryan Cleary, a teenage shut-in who lived with his parents in Essex, England. When the police finally arrested him, they dragged him out of a room with blacked-out windows. His mother, reportedly, would leave food for him outside his door.[10] Others, like "avunit," were never caught. (It's been speculated that if avunit still has access to the Bitcoin donations from 2011–2012, he or she, like Assange, would be a millionaire.)

And then there was the main subject of Olson's book, Jake "Topiary" Davis, a shy, walleyed teenager living in Scotland's remote Shetland Islands with his mother. Prior to #OperationPayback, Davis had spent his adolescence browsing /b/ and playing online games. In fact, he had made a name for himself on 4chan making crank calls. /b/tards would join him in chat rooms to watch him do things like phone up a big-box store in the United States, hack his way onto the loudspeaker, and announce that for a limited time all the items in the store were free.[11]

As he explained to the audience of a play based on Anonymous' exploits in London in 2014,

> I was literally playing Tetris in 2010 with my friend when he sent me this URL to a chat room. He said there's 12,000 people in this room taking down PayPal, Visa, and Mastercard in protest of funds being withdrawn from WikiLeaks. And I said, "Well that's completely ridiculous. There's no way a chat room could have that many people in it mobilizing in this ridiculous fashion." My experience with Anonymous activism before had been, sort of, these really disorganized trolls messing around for no apparent reason and it going absolutely nowhere . . . [B]ut [this time] it was sort of working, everyone was strangely organized and it was getting a lot of attention. Usually the attention span is sort of three or four days then everyone [returns to watching] videos of cats. But it continued for weeks. And I just ended up in the chat room instead of closing it.[12]

Though Davis knew next to nothing about hacking in 2010, he eventually made his way to the upper-level IRC channels, where he used the trolling skills he'd honed on /b/ to essentially play the Anonymous character to the press in a way that would draw attention to their exploits.

The month the campaign for WikiLeaks began, December 2010, also happened to be the month a twenty-six-year-old Tunisian street vendor named Mohamed Bouazizi set himself on fire to protest the abuses of his authoritarian government, an act that would usher in the Arab Spring. And on the heels of #OperationAvengeAssange, Anonymous launched #OpTunisia in early January, defacing the Tunisian government's websites with pro-democracy messages as the democratic uprising snowballed.

And then, as Anonymous began to foment revolution in the Middle East, events took an even stranger turn.

Anon Peeks into the Palantir

How long, I wonder, has he been constrained to come often to his glass for inspection and instruction . . . if any save a will of adamant now looks into it, it will bear his mind and sight swiftly thither.
—Gandalf the Wizard, regarding the Palantir, *The Two Towers*, J. R. R. Tolkien

CANTWELL: Do you think Palantir taught Cambridge Analytica, as press reports are saying, how to do these tactics?
ZUCKERBERG: Senator, I do not know.
CANTWELL: Do you think that Palantir has ever scraped data from Facebook?
ZUCKERBERG: Senator, I'm not aware of that.
—Transcript of Facebook CEO Mark Zuckerberg's testimony before the Senate's Commerce and Judiciary committees in the wake of the Cambridge Analytica scandal, April 10, 2018

By January 2011, Anonymous was all over the news for declaring cyberwar not only on Mastercard and PayPal, but on the government of Tunisia. And in early February 2011, a security analyst named Aaron Barr claimed to the *Financial Times* that he had infiltrated Anonymous and was soon going to unmask the leadership, including top lieutenants, to the FBI.

Barr's statements came at a time when the FBI had just turned its attention to Anonymous. Authorities had arrested several anons involved in the PayPal and Mastercard attacks in both the United States and the U.K. These included teenage boys in Ireland who had run the #AnonOps IRC server, which had coordinated the PayPal distributed denial of service (DDoS) attacks, and hapless college-age men in the United States.

Participating in a DDoS attack in the United States was, theoretically, a felony under the Computer Fraud and Abuse Act, a 1984 bill that was partly inspired by a teenage Matthew Broderick dialing into a nuclear war planner's computers in the 1983 film *War Games*. But the statute was vague. And in 2011, the law was still unsettled.[1] Advocates for the defendants in Ireland, prosecuted under a similarly broad anti-hacking statute, claimed the DDoS campaigns were the digital equivalent of a sit-in.

Moreover, the crime, if there was one, was difficult to prove. For example, Scientology and PayPal had provided the FBI with a list of the thousands of internet protocol (IP) addresses (unique numbers associated with each computer) that had deluged its servers with junk packets and messages like "WE'RE FROM EBAUMSWORLD." But an IP address, if it wasn't disguised by the user, pointed to an address in the physical world, not a particular person. Roommates, guests, or open Wi-Fi networks blurred the identify of who actually used the computer.

To avoid this problem, the FBI selected a handful of U.S. IP addresses out of the list and began paying visits to the associated physical addresses. Those who cluelessly told the FBI that they had used the Low Orbit Ion Cannon when the agents appeared at their doors were prosecuted with federal felonies.[2]

The FBI's strategy resulted in particularly unsophisticated parties being caught in the early stages of the investigation. Most of the participants in the PayPal DDoS were not so much hackers but, like the majority of the Anonymous collective, "script monkeys," only technically savvy enough to run code (in this case, the Low Orbit Ion Cannon). "Wait till they find out we're just a bunch of script monkeys" was a common sentiment expressed on IRC channels when yet another sensational article ran in the press depicting the masked Anonymous as potent hackers.[3]

So, when security analyst Aaron Barr stated at a conference in San Francisco that he had infiltrated Anonymous and knew who was at the top, he quickly attracted the attention of the FBI.

Barr had been lurking in one of the Anonymous IRC channels, but all the information he had gathered was wrong. This was because, it turned out, his method for discovering the identities of participants made little sense. It was largely rooted in arbitrarily friending people on Facebook who claimed they supported Anonymous. Barr thought that those he had friended were the same people in the IRC channels and began tracking when users logged on and off, attempting to associate IRC user-names with his new Facebook friends.

Barr even believed he was communicating with the leader of Anonymous, a man named Benjamin Spock de Vries, who was, in fact, Christopher "Commander X" Doyon, the older hippie hacker who had joined Anonymous, pumping him for information.[4]

Then, on the eve of Barr's meeting with the FBI, something strange happened. His devices began to blank out.

Hector "Sabu" Monsegur, Ryan "Kayla" Ackroyd, and Mustafa "tflow" Al-Bassam, among others, had remotely wiped Barr's iPad and deleted his company's server and its backups, but not before downloading some 68,000 of the company's emails. Gaining access to his website, they replaced its content with the message "Now the Anonymous hand is bitch-slapping you in the face."[5] They then invited Barr into an IRC chat room (#ophbgary), where the teenage prankster Jake "Topiary" Davis used the crank-calling skills he'd honed on /b/ to maximize the opportunity for lulz.[6] As Sabu, Kayla, and Gregg Housh, the cocreator of the Scientology video, looked on, Barr pleaded with the hackers not to release the emails.

The caper was so funny it made *The Colbert Report.* "To put that in hacker terms," comedian Stephen Colbert summed up, "Anonymous is a hornet's nest and Barr said, 'I'm gonna stick my penis in that thing.'"[7]

But there were reasons outside the obvious for why Barr begged Anonymous not to release the emails.

In their quest for lulz, Anonymous had inadvertently pried up the floorboards on what proved to be a labyrinthine and sometimes criminal effort of private defense contractors, the relevance of which only became fully known in 2018 during the Cambridge Analytica scandal.

Barr was relatively new to the security business. And his company, HBGary Federal, had been flailing. However, he had been thrown a possible lifeline. Washington, D.C.–based law firm Hunton & Williams had approached him with a job. Members of the U.S. Chamber of Commerce needed someone to investigate if a union had been "astroturfing" (manufacturing fake grassroots support online). Eager to get the contract, Barr teamed up with two other large but obscure security firms, Palantir and Berico Technologies, to form a coalition they called "Team Themis." Barr then put together a slideshow recommending a range of intimidation tactics and opposition research, much of it likely illegal, to create detailed dossiers on pro-union members of the U.S. Chamber of Commerce to embarrass them. Barr's proposal was an upsell; instead of purchasing just an investigation of astroturfing, anti-union members of the Chamber of Commerce could buy a subscription to a wide array of cyber-themed dirty tricks. The cost: $2 million a month.[8]

Hunton & Williams also asked Barr for another proposal on behalf of a major U.S. bank (rumored to be Bank of America) on how to destroy WikiLeaks. Here, too, Barr proposed illegal hacking, manufacturing of fraudulent documents, and intimidating the journalist Glenn Greenwald, who was then working with WikiLeaks. The slides for his pitches, all saved in his emails, read as, well, a little bananas. "Feed the fuel between feuding groups. Disinformation. Create messages around actions to sabotage or discredit the opposing organization. Submit fake documents and then call out the error," he wrote. "Media campaign to push the radical and reckless nature of Wikileaks activities. Sustained pressure."[9]

Before either of these proposals was bought, Barr experienced his unpleasant (and if it had not been for his boasts, totally unnecessary) run-in with Anonymous, who leaked all of this information online, along with the rest of the 68,000 emails. The story briefly became front-page news.

Why exactly had Barr embarked on his Anonymous side project? Despite owning a "security" company, Barr was not particularly technically adept at safeguarding information, as Anonymous proved. His emails painted a portrait of someone who considered himself an expert in cyber-stalking. Writing for *Wired*, Nate Anderson suggested the key to understanding the personality that emerged from the thousands of emails was Barr's attempt to get a contract several months earlier by showing a client how he had gathered information about the man's family on Facebook.[10] His big idea was to automate this process. He had hired a programmer named Mark Trynor to write a "fbook scraper" or "friend finder," which would gather information off Facebook to reveal things about users they hadn't explicitly shared (for example, where they lived).

But Trynor (who seemed far more knowledgeable about 4chan than Barr, since he often replied to Barr in 4chan memes) was skeptical. "I don't see the math working out," Trynor insisted over several email chains. "The more I look at this data the more it looks like :Step 1 : Gather all the data Step 2 : ??? Step 3 : Profit," citing a *South Park* episode that had become a meme on 4chan.

Nonetheless, Barr believed he could prove the efficacy of his ideas. He would unmask Anonymous with a presentation at a security conference in San Francisco. This would draw press attention to his company and get him a meeting with a coveted potential client, the FBI.

"Do you really think that . . . some hacker is going to have all his hacker buddies as friends on facebook?" Trynor objected.[11]

But Barr was adamant: "This group has some good points but is acting very recklessly I think. So if I can help to be a small balance, and get some press and customers in the process . . . yeah!"[12]

In the wake of the weird tale of Aaron Barr, two narratives emerged to explain what had happened, both equally difficult to believe: lone gunman and conspiracy.

As Anderson wrote, it was apparent Barr had gone a little nuts with his pitch to the U.S. Chamber of Commerce in his desperation to get the contract.

Palantir quickly distanced itself from the scandal by adopting the lone, crazed gunman narrative. Its CEO, Alex Karp, was a Marxist who had a PhD in neoclassical social theory from the Frankfurt School made famous by philosophers like Herbert Marcuse. He insisted Palantir was dedicated to progressive causes. Palantir blamed the illegal tactics on a single rogue employee, twenty-six-year-old engineer Matthew Steckman.

But Barr's emails contained a great deal of correspondence with upper-level management at Palantir. Palantir, Berico, and Barr had argued over their share of the $2 million a month. And an agreement that gave Palantir less than Berico and HBGary had to be signed off on by "Dr. Karp and the board." Other supervisors were cc'd and sometimes replied in the leaked emails.[13] Moreover, Palantir's scapegoat, Matthew Steckman, remained at the company for many years and was promoted after the scandal died down.

This fact implied the alternative to the lone-gunman theory: that Barr's proposals were business as usual, and the only part of the affair that had bothered the companies, law firms, and government officials was that Barr got caught.

In this telling, Anonymous had accidentally drilled a peephole into the weird security world where governments and corporations were using dirty tricks to grab power. At the very least, they were using the same illegal methods as the hackers they were jailing.[14] It was the 90s *Harper's*/The Well debate all over again. Existing power structures were using the internet more effectively than empowered individuals. And they were using it to curtail personal liberties.

The odd connections between Palantir, Facebook, and an antidemocratic ideology were only uncovered after Palantir became entangled in the 2018 Cambridge Analytica scandal.

In March 2018, a former employee of Cambridge Analytica named Christopher Wylie revealed that the company had used a quiz app to scrape data about millions of people off Facebook in 2014 without their permission to build "psychometric profiles" of voters in the United States and Britain. They then used those profiles to manipulate votes. On March 27, 2018, Wylie testified before the British Commons that Palantir had "helped build the models" using Facebook data. In fact, a Palantir employee had given Trump adviser Steve Bannon and billionaire computer programmer Robert Mercer the idea to scrape Facebook profiles.

When Palantir issued a statement, journalists with long memories noticed a pattern: Palantir offered the same excuse that it had in 2011 after the HBGary scandal—their involvement with Cambridge Analytica was the act of a rogue employee.[15]

Odder still, Cambridge Analytica was more or less Aaron Barr's vision of automated Facebook stalking realized.

And even stranger, one person was largely responsible for the advent of Facebook, PayPal, and Palantir: an eccentric, antidemocratic lawyer-turned-Silicon-Valley-investor named Peter Thiel.

Though Thiel was well known in the Bay Area, he only came to the public's attention in 2016 when he spoke at the Republican Convention as an early Trump supporter. Soon the media became obsessed with his bizarre supervillainish behavior. We learned that he had secretly funded Terry "Hulk Hogan" Bollea's case against Gawker out of spite after its Silicon Valley gossip blog Valleywag reported on rumors regarding his homosexuality. He invested in a "vampire" tech company researching how to prolong life by using the blood of the young. And, like Dr. Doom, Thiel had a sword-and-sorcery-inflected escape route if civilization were to collapse: a jet to New Zealand, where he had acquired land and citizenship, partly because that's where *Lord of the Rings* was filmed.

Moreover, in a 2009 essay published by *Cato Unbound*, Thiel laid out how the Enlightenment ideal of democratic voting was, in his mind, a failed experiment because people, especially women, rarely voted for what he called the "faith of his teenage years," extreme libertarianism.[16] For this reason, he believed democracy should be discarded because it would never bring about a libertarian society. Or as he put it, "I no longer believe that freedom and democracy are compatible." He then went a step further, explaining that tech companies like Facebook would be able to bring about the new libertarian capitalist societies that jettisoned democracy, a sentiment he rendered as, "We are in a deadly race between politics and technology."

His involvement with Facebook had begun in 2004 when it was a student-run website aspiring to become a profitable company. Its founder, Mark Zuckerberg, had dropped out of Harvard and moved his operation to Silicon Valley to look for funding. But venture capitalists were wary. Facebook was hardly different from Myspace or Friendster, and these were, as even the schoolkids using them assumed, stupid fads as transitory as Beanie Babies. But Facebook caught a lucky break. Thiel invested $100,000 and employed a team of attorneys to elevate the company into a major enterprise, even though, according to him, the nineteen-year-old Zuckerberg's pitch was "terrible."[17]

By 2008, Facebook had transformed the web from a network of open-source, information-sharing bulletin boards into a vast ego-replication project by building its platform around the most addicting feature of bulletin boards—social networking. Unlike most bulletin boards, Facebook was for-profit. It sold advertising. But most of its business model was based on collecting information about people and selling access to whoever would buy it.

Later, Thiel would attribute his decision to invest in Facebook to his study of the philosopher René Girard, who posited that human beings define themselves by observing and copying others. But another, far more down-to-earth explanation exists. A few months earlier, Thiel had received funding from the CIA's venture capital arm to start Palantir. Palantir would profit (immensely) from acquiring as much data as possible about people and selling it to large institutions, mostly the government and law enforcement. According to internal documents leaked by TechCrunch in 2015, "as of 2013, Palantir was used by at least 12 groups within the US Government including the CIA, DHS, NSA, FBI, the CDC, the Marine Corps, the Air Force, Special Operations Command, West Point, the Joint IED-defeat organization and Allies, the Recovery Accountability and Transparency Board and the National Center for Missing and Exploited Children."[18] Its most successful product was a piece of subscription software it sold to local law enforcement agencies that scraped data from all over the internet. But, as in the case with Barr's Team Themis, it sought out various business opportunities to sell the government, large financial institutions, and law firms data mining and other technological services.

"Palantir" was an allusion to Lord of the Rings, one of Thiel's favorite book series. In the fantasy novels, palantirs are magical crystal balls into which a wizard might peer to see anything in the world. But this knowledge came at a steep price; anyone else who owned a palantir could also see you. In the books, the dark sorcerer Sauron (the embodiment of all evil) secretly takes control of the entire network of palantirs, and uses them to dominate the minds of those who gaze into the glass. It seems likely that Thiel saw in Facebook another opportunity like Palantir—a way to collect, analyze, and sell large data sets.

A year and a half after Thiel's investment, Facebook introduced its "newsfeed" feature. Its users, mostly college students, howled in protest. Angry op-eds appeared in college newspapers objecting to the invasion of privacy. The newsfeed displayed everything your friends were doing in a constant stream (Alice poked Bob, Bob uploaded a photo, etc.). You could hide yourself from this stream, but at a price: you could no longer see it. Maybe the idea was inspired by Girardian nosiness—an assumed desire to see what others were doing. But it was hard not to notice that Facebook had become a palantir. To look you had to pay a price: you had to be looked at. Not just by other users, but by a third entity, the dark wizard Sauron, Facebook itself.

Previous generations imagined that one of the freedoms the United States provided was the ability to maintain a distinction between an interior private life and an outward professional one. Unlike the U.S.S.R., the United States safeguarded a constitutional "right to privacy" established by the Supreme Court.[19] Though it did not always live up to these ideals, the United States set itself up in fundamental opposition to sticking cameras in citizens' bedrooms like in *1984* or keeping elaborate dossiers on political opponents as the Stasi had done. But Facebook began to erode this conceptual split. One's external, professional world did not end at five o'clock; it lasted 24/7 on social media. The exterior and the interior were becoming one, the mask, the person.

Partly, this was what had given rise to Anonymous. As the web changed, few popular alternatives to social media emerged. And there was really only one that emphasized anonymity: the living fossil of 4chan. The chanverse's culture of trolling attacked social media–style ego replication. Partly, Anonymous dressed itself up like V because *V for Vendetta* was a meditation on this post-9/11 erosion of privacy. As Senator Maria Cantwell described to Mark Zuckerberg during his 2018 Senate hearing on Cambridge Analytica and Palantir, the Bush administration had championed "Total Information Awareness," which she described as former attorney general "John Ashcroft and others trying to do similar things to what I think is behind all of this—geopolitical forces trying to get data and information to influence a process."[20]

And absurdly, the mask-wearing superhero Anonymous first clashed with those who imagined themselves the dark wizards of the Palantir on the battlefield of Aaron Barr's loopy, shattered security company.

When Anonymous realized the enormity of what it had stolen from Barr, much of the early work of sifting through the emails fell to a freelance journalist named Barrett Brown. Brown lived in modest circumstances with his mother in Houston, where he was struggling with heroin addiction. His father had been a local real estate mogul, whose fortunes turned after he had been investigated by the FBI for fraud.[21]

Brown was present in the #ophbgary chat room when it was revealed to Barr that he had been hacked. And so, many of the second thoughts that occurred to the public about social media, Palantir, and the security establishment after the Cambridge Analytica scandal broke in 2018 occurred first to Brown in 2011.

Eager for sources on the story, the press soon cottoned on to Brown as an Anonymous spokesperson, though he identified himself as an investigative journalist. His handle in the #ophgary chat room was "BarrettBrown." And like the Occupy Wall Street movement to follow, Anonymous was so fundamentally opposed to hierarchies it somewhat impractically considered itself leaderless.

Nonetheless, Brown sat for interviews with major news outlets and tried to convey the vertiginous depths of what Anonymous had uncovered, cutting the odd figure of a Texas Cassandra.[22] He was skinny with light brown hair and large eyes that made him appear boyish at twenty-seven. Fast-talking and somewhat mumbly, but incredibly detail-oriented,

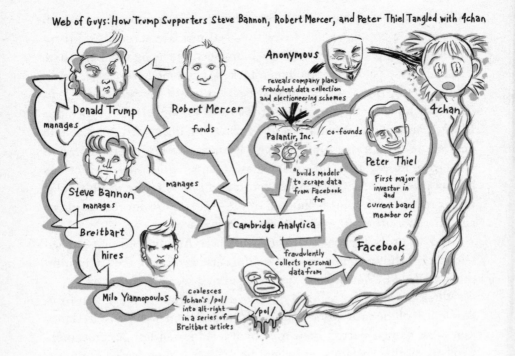

Web of Guys: How Trump Supporters Steve Bannon, Robert Mercer, and Peter Thiel Tangled with 4chan

he often said outrageous and conspiratorial things that turned out to be mostly true. It didn't help that, like the rest of Anonymous, he had the air of the prankster about him. Infamously, he held one news conference from his bathtub, swishing a glass of wine.

"What we got was just a single scoop," he told me over the phone in 2018. "What we've been talking about since 2011 has come back in this Russian troll operation [on Facebook during the 2016 election], except now it's much more widespread."[23]

Despite Brown's efforts, the scandal died down. As chronicled in Parmy Olson's *We Are Anonymous*, "Democratic congressman Hank Johnson called for an investigation into government, military, and NSA contacts with HBGary Federal and its partners Palantir and Berico Technologies." But nothing happened.

No one went to jail.

Except Brown and Anonymous.

Inspired by the success of the HBGary leaks, the hackers involved broke away and formed a splinter cell called Lulz Security (LulzSec) a few months later, consisting of Sabu, Topiary, Kayla, tflow, avunit, Ryan

Cleary, Jeremy "sup_g" Hammond, and two Irish hackers, Darren "Pwnsauce" Martyn and Donncha "Palladium" O'Cearbhaill. For the next year, LulzSec went on a high-profile hacking spree, targeting a mix of news and entertainment outlets like Fox and PBS; video game companies like Sony and Bethesda; and security agencies like the FBI, the CIA, and Britain's Serious Organized Crime Agency.

By September 2011, they had all been arrested (with the exception of avunit). After the FBI discovered the identity of Sabu in June, he flipped and began working as an informant. Those in the U.K. served lighter sentences and are now out of jail. But Hammond is still incarcerated in the United States.

In March 2012, Brown's home was also raided by the FBI.[24] The agency charged him with being part of the Anonymous criminal conspiracy. They even prosecuted his mother for concealing evidence. Unlike in the U.K. and most other legal systems, under U.S. criminal law, any conspirator can be convicted for the crimes of all conspirators. Brown took a plea deal and was ultimately fined $890,250 and spent over two years in prison. To many it seemed he had been "convicted of journalism."[25] And indeed, one of the few people reporting on Palantir was Brown, from prison. (Though Brown had already been released, in 2018 the government confiscated his advance from his publisher, Farrar, Straus & Giroux, for his book on the subject of the hacks.)

As I watched Anonymous spring up and dissolve nearly as quickly in 2011 and 2012, I was reminded of a science-fiction book I had read as a kid. In 1981, Vernor Vinge wrote the dystopian novella *True Names*. Back when the internet was mostly Usenet, Vinge imagined characters that today would be called hackers, though he named them "warlocks." In the physical world, they resided in landscapes of increasing urban sprawl. But in Vinge's internet, called the "Other World," they stole secrets from vast corporate and governmental institutions in the hopes of starting a revolution. Like in a massively multiplayer online role-playing game (MMORPG), the Other World is inflected with sword-and-sorcery themes. Warlocks, known only by nonsense handles like "Mr. Slippery" and "Erythrina," formed hacking covens that met in virtual castles. Like in ancient myth, the warlocks' weakness lay in their "true names," which, if learned by the FBI, would spell an end to them.

In the 90s, information theorist Oscar Gandy coined the phrase "panoptic sort" to describe the increasingly frequent collection of individuals' personal data by corporations and governments. The phrase was a reference to the "panopticon," a theoretical prison where guards could peer into all cells at once. The goal of the panoptic sort was twofold: gathering information for the security apparatus to maintain political control and gathering information to perfect marketing techniques, forming a seamless loop between inner desires and outer messaging. As the cofounder of Fox, Barry Diller, put it during the Cambridge Analytica scandal, "Since the beginning of media and advertising, the holy grail has been the precise targeting of the ads. Along comes the internet with almost perfect aim, and now the entire concept is being called antisocial. That's a most ironic but momentous thing."[26]

My 1999 copy of *True Names* came with an introduction by MIT computer scientist David Wexelblatt on the topic, in which he wondered if the entire internet would soon be devoted to Gandy's panoptic sort. The solution he suggested: abandon logins and create anonymous networks. And when reality played out like fiction in 2011, it was the internet's largest nameless network, Anonymous, cloaking itself in the video game language of wizards and superheroes, that first called attention to the vast panoptic sort by clashing with the self-styled dark sorcerer Peter Thiel and his company Palantir.

But unlike in *True Names*, the freewheeling hackers lost and the FBI won.

After the arrests of its principal members, Anonymous was never the same. The collective endured, playing a part in prosecuting the Steubenville rape case, throwing its support behind the Ferguson protests in 2014, and combating the alt-right. But 2012 proved to be its high-water mark. According to Brown, today Anonymous is "in shambles," though this was partly due to its loose-knit organizational structures. "It was a jellyfish," he told me. "It had no membranes, no walls; that had disadvantages and advantages."

And in the vacuum of hope and agency that remained, the alt-right sprang up in their place. The seeds had been there all along, but hardly anyone had noticed them.

When 4chan's trolling collective transitioned into hacktivist groups after 2008, Andrew "weev" Auernheimer, the former president of the Gay Nigger Association of America trolling collective, which had almost destroyed 4chan in 2004 before defining much of its culture in 2005 and 2006, followed suit. He created Goatse Security, which evoked the traditional 90s-style hacker security infiltration, though the cynicism of the old 90s hacker groups had devolved into a new nihilistic trolling ideology. If Goatse Security taught people about the growing powers of the Corporate State, it was only for the sake of lulz and the brief respite of more screen entertainment.

In 2010, weev and his new group, true to their promise that they would "expose gaping holes," revealed a security flaw that made hundreds of thousands of AT&T users' email addresses publicly available on the web. The end result was weev's arrest, prosecution, and conviction on federal felony charges for computer fraud.

In the trial that followed, often lumped into the other Anonymous prosecutions at the time, weev set himself up as a martyr of the old hacker cause of internet freedom. Indeed, the creation of LulzSec had been directly inspired by weev's Goatse Security. This message was amplified by McGill University sociologist Gabriella Coleman, who billed herself as an Anonymous expert. Partial to Anonymous' freedom-fighting causes, she spent a great deal of time, in the words of tech reporter Adrian Chen, on "the TED Talks stage, in documentaries and in countless newspapers to extol the unique power of Anonymous," stoking "Anonymous' mystical fire."[27]

Though some of her research was valuable, her efforts to scrub away Anonymous' more unsavory origins often appeared comical. In her 2014 book *Hacker, Hoaxer, Whistleblower, Spy: The Many Faces of Anonymous*, she described one popular IRC channel in which Anonymous was organizing, "#marblecake," as named "after one of their own found inspiration in the baked item he was eating." When, in fact, marblecake was a well-known meme on 4chan, meaning a mix of feces and semen, the ingredients Anonymous often felt it was inserting in its opponents. In the same book, Coleman declared weev "disgusting," but also garlanded him with elaborate mythological comparisons. His methods were not only "puckish," but similar to the Norse god Loki, the African trickster deity Anansi, and the Native American spirit Coyote.[28]

Far from silver-tongued, weev was rarely even cogent. In interviews, he sounded like a TV flipping channels. Reveling in the press scrums that followed his trial, he spoke one minute of America's "cultural decline," the next about the "shit-ton" of possibilities for drones, and then maybe about how laptop batteries could easily last one hundred years. When at last he came around to the subject of his legal troubles, he explained the

"Feds" were stupid. But journalists kept coming because he was always good for a sensationalist quote. Famously, weev called his judge "a mean bitch . . . I can see it in her eyes, she's a black Baptist Bush appointee and I don't think she's a fan of the GNAA."[29]

Weev loved being compared to gods by a scholar at a top university and quoted some of Coleman's passages on his own website. But he preferred to equate himself with the late Aaron Swartz.[30] Swartz was a child computer prodigy who cocreated Reddit, a website that was a mix of the old-style bulletin board system and the new social media. In many senses, it was 4chan 2.0. Swartz was also the understudy to some of the greatest computer scientists at MIT, many of whom had invented vital components of the internet. But in 2011, the FBI began aggressively prosecuting him for allegedly violating the Computer Fraud and Abuse Act. Like Brown and the rest of Anonymous, Swartz found himself facing the possibility of decades in prison and millions in fines. But Swartz's crime was barely political; rather, it was the absentminded result of a research experiment. He had attached a laptop to a server in a closet at MIT to collect articles from JSTOR, a database of academic papers. Swartz's act soon became wrapped up in a debate among academics regarding whether access to scientific journals ought to be free. But Swartz, according to those close to him, had simply been interested in collecting the information because he was always experimenting with large data sets. When the laptop was discovered, he was charged with breaking and entering and two counts of wire fraud for misusing the JSTOR data. Sadly, just before his case went to trial in 2013, he killed himself.

As with Swartz's case, weev's case was championed by the resurgent anti-corporate hacktivist counterculture and defended by the Electronic Frontier Foundation, an organization created by John Perry Barlow in the wake of the 1989 Harper's/The Well debate.

But weev made a poor martyr. In speeches, he often suggested mass genocide was the answer. And then, after his conviction, he declared himself a neo-Nazi, tattooing an enormous swastika on his chest. Though this act was reported as a conversion, he had been earnestly blogging about his neo-Nazi convictions since at least 2007. But no one had believed him, imagining that he was simply trolling.[31] In an early 2008 story about trolls, the New York Times' Mattathias Schwartz noted that weev suggested a large portion of the earth's population should be exterminated. But in the same interview, weev took Schwartz for a ride in an obviously rented Rolls-Royce Phantom, insisting to the reporter that he had made millions trolling.[32] (When I asked to speak with weev in 2018, he demanded a fee of $2,000 an hour.) Similarly, in 2011, weev hung around Occupy Wall Street holding up a sign that read "Zionist Pigs Rob Us All."[33] When reporters tracked down his mother, she explained her family was part Jewish. Ironically, just as the press was becoming enamored of weev, much of 4chan concluded that he was deeply mentally ill.

However, weev's influence over politics was just beginning. When he finally left prison in October 2014, he began collaborating with another young fascist, Andrew Anglin, to transform the Nazi site the *Daily Stormer* into the meme-soaked center of the emerging alt-right.

And beside it, an old site would emerge as the center of the new meme-ified far-right youth movement—4chan.[34]

PART III

THE PIVOT TO
THE RIGHT

From Gentlemen to Robots

I've come to represent an uncomfortably large single point of failure.
—moot's last post

While the drama of Anonymous was playing out on the world stage, 4chan itself endured, quietly separated from the hacktivists. By 2011, it was no longer a popular but obscure underground site, but one of the most visited message boards on the internet, receiving tens of millions of unique page views a month. Now, partially exposed to sunlight, it began to function a little more like an ordinary online community.

The vaulting of the hacktivists onto the world stage had created a hard split between older Anonymous (chan-board users) and Anonymous as the press knew them, as masked hacktivists. Chan-board users now called themselves "anonymous" (with a little "a"), and those who had gone off to become hacktivists "Anonymous" (with a big "A"). Despite the confusing similarity, the rest of the narrative will refer to the hacktivists as "Anonymous" and the chan-board users as "anonymous," though in some instances the distinction between the two might be a chasm of belief and in others a browser tab click.

After Anonymous had departed, the infamous random board /b/ began to deflate. Reddit was replacing or blending with 4chan's userbase. And 4chan itself became more Reddit-like, leaning into its traditional bulletin board structure. Fewer users came to lose themselves in an anarchic trolling collective, and more came to simply hang out in subsections dedicated to a particular topic, just as Christopher "moot" Poole had always wanted. To encourage this, he added many new niche boards to discuss comics, cooking, music, LGBT issues, science, toys, video games, and so forth.[1]

It might have seemed like the bizarre culture of 4chan was at last normalizing. But under the surface strange new forces were brewing.

The schism between anonymous and Anonymous, and the latter's defeat, resulted in 4chan ideologically retreating to its original position: 90s-style otaku nihilism. But belief, like nature, abhors a vacuum, and, once again, it could hardly remain that way for long.

Along with Anonymous, the intense period of optimism that had brought the political movement into being collapsed. The topic of self-improvement faded from most of the boards, and instead the userbase became obsessed with withdrawal and despair.

Nowhere was this more evident than on what had been 4chan's most optimistic project. During the height of 4chan's bright period in 2008, Poole had created a "new /b/," intended to be the throbbing heart of 4chan's creativity, absent all the darker and stupider elements that had afflicted the random bin. The new board was called "ROBOT 9000." "ROBOT" referred to a moderator program that automatically deleted spam, previously posted images, and copy-pasted text. "9000" was derived from a scene in *Dragon Ball Z*, when mighty warriors are astonished to discover that another warrior's power level is the highest they've ever heard of. "It's over 9000!" they exclaim. On 4chan, there was no higher number than "9000"; it meant the summit of achievement. Whatever worldwide phenomenon 4chan would invent next, it was expected to emerge from this new and better board.

In /r9k/, former self-identified /b/tards took to calling themselves "gentlemen." In their cartwheeling way, they converted their old jokes about how they were forever alone in their moms' basements, raging and frustrated, into jokes about how they would now become the height of sophistication.

Like so much else in this story, the transition can be told in the visual evolution of memes. On the /r9k/ board, the sad, scrabbly, forever alone /b/ user mutated into a sophisticated gentleman /r9k/ user. And in 2011, when Jake "Topiary" Davis chose the icon for LulzSec, he selected the classy "Lulz" guy from /r9k/.

But the board languished. By 2011, few people were using /r9k/ and Poole deleted it because it had "long since stopped being about original content."[2]

Full Circle: From Tears to Trolls to Gentlemen to Tears

2006-2007	2008-2009	2011	2012-present
4chan develops a set of popular memes to express their prevailing adolescent emotions: "forever alone", troll face, and "feels guy"	/r9k/ transforms the character into a "gentleman" to reflect the new 4chan	Topiary chooses the gentleman as the face of hacker group LulzSec	The character evolves into a "Wojack", a loser who lives in a world of constant rage and humiliation

However, /r9k/ *was* destined to become the new /b/. In the end, it did indeed become the place from which 4chan's novel inventions would issue to propagate around the globe. But these innovations would not charm or inspire but horrify the world and eventually drive even the phlegmatic Poole from his own site.

As often occurred in the neglected backwaters of the less popular boards, a group of oddball users had gathered in /r9k/. The board had slowly filled up with people who referred to themselves as "robots" because they identified as autistic or intensely withdrawn loners.

One of these robots was a boy from upstate New York named Fredrick Brennan. Brennan found 4chan in 2006 when he was twelve years old after /b/ had raided a *Sonic the Hedgehog* forum. When I first spoke to him via Skype in 2018, he was living in the Philippines, working as a programmer for 2channel.

"I felt like 4chan was this secret portal into what people were thinking," he told me. "I felt like everyone in the real world was lying, [that] they weren't telling me their true beliefs. I felt I was looking behind the mask. But in reality, I learned much later, that wasn't what most people were thinking at all. But as a kid I couldn't tell the difference."

Brennan described to me how /r9k/ began transitioning from /b/-style games "to try and thwart the robot moderator" to something very different.

We would write in the high Elizabethan style, hence the "gentlemen." Instead of saying "LOL," we would write, "this gave me such exquisite laughter." But over time . . . it started to evolve into stories, then personal stories. Then people started writing about their own lives. And we were all on 4chan so all our lives sucked! If our lives hadn't sucked, we would have been on Myspace or Facebook. The kind of person an image board attracts . . . it led /r9k/ into a lot of depressive stories. What's the common link between these stories? Well, we're all ugly. We're all alone.

The easiest way to get past the [original content] image filter was to just take your own picture. So people started posting photos they took. Their own face. Their own room. And what did they have in common? They were all sad.

When moot closed /r9k/, the then seventeen-year-old Brennan was devastated, as were the rest of the robots. "It was [an] affront to decency. My identity was so wrapped up in this site. It was psychologically damaging when he removed those two boards."

Instead of dissolving, the /r9k/ community expanded and hardened. Brennan used his programming skills to start alternative chans and IRC networks devoted to the new ultra-hikikomori, /r9k/ lifestyle. The largest and most dedicated of these sites was Wizardchan. The name derived from a joke among Japanese otaku that if you reached the age of thirty a virgin, you "became a wizard."

"We used to say that there's an oppression Olympics [in American culture], like, a competition among oppressed minorities to see who was the most oppressed. Well, instead of an oppression Olympics, it became a *depression* Olympics. So the most depressed people started to gang together and accuse anyone that had a single friend or went outside of just faking it."

In fact, Brennan, who went by the handle "HotWheels" online, had led an extraordinarily difficult life. Brennan suffers from osteogenesis imperfecta, also known as brittle bone disease, and is confined to a wheelchair. He is three feet tall with bright blond hair and a raspy voice. In an article he would later pen for Andrew "weev" Auernheimer and Andrew Anglin's fascist site the *Daily Stormer* during his darkest period, he called himself a "disabled supporter of eugenics," describing a life of both emotional and physical pain, in which he had broken hundreds of bones.[3] According to his account, his mother suffered from the same disease. And his father sired him to collect the benefit checks, knowing it was very likely his son would be disabled too. Perhaps it would have been better, his article argued, if he had never been born at all. Or, as he still maintains, if governments paid for genetic screening that could detect such conditions in utero.

Eventually, Brennan and the rest of the /r9k/ community convinced Poole to restore the board on 4chan as "Robot9001." And it not only endured, but ballooned into a place for super-otaku, who, in their extremity, put the otaku of early 4chan to shame.

American counterculture in the 1960s had objected to being evaluated by computerized tests and shuffled into a vast corporate-government hierarchy. A half century later, the hierarchy and the evaluatory techniques had not only endured but grown more refined. Each succeeding generation had encountered increasingly punishing, intense, and unnatural competition. Each year they had to work harder to earn a grip on the lowest rung, not only because the number of competitors was rising, but because what they earned for their labor was diminishing.

Combine this with the ever-expanding realms of fantasy, cyberspace, and screen diversions and it's no surprise that a youth culture defined by retreat from reality developed. It was these same dynamics that had created the first generation of hikikomori in Japan in the 1980s. Now, absent Anonymous, there was once again no recourse to break or change this system. And so the userbase doubled down on an otaku-style leap into the screen. /r9k/ soon developed an ideology that not only celebrated the otaku lifestyle but insisted that those born into it were doomed to remain that way forever.

Now that the wild transformations of /b/ were over, 4chan's culture had shifted back to where it began: idle young men celebrating retreat into cyberspace, video games, and anime.

As a society of ribald boys, 4chan had always been obsessed with masculine competition (and the subsequent humiliation when the contest was lost). The popular slang "epic win" and "fail" were 4chan inventions. But the robots of /r9k/ soon elaborated upon these, referring to themselves as "beta males," and those out in the world, enjoying romantic success, as "alpha males" or "Chad Thundercocks" (a buff jock who was healthy, social, and went outdoors), first as a joke, then earnestly.

This conception flattened the complexity of social interactions into a mechanistic game, like the computer simulations described in *The Selfish Gene*, or the video games the robots played to simulate feeling victorious. With little or no outside reference, robots imagined romantic interaction as a child might: as part of a schoolyard pecking order. According to their worldview, human beings were like wolves or walruses competing for dominance. Like so many other fantastical ideas in internet subcommunties, that skewed conception of the world was never dispelled, but rather strengthened into a shared article of faith.

For years, one 4chan image represented the beta's ideology more completely than any other: Pepe the Frog.

The Descent of Sad Frogs

2007
Pepe is excerpted from a webcomic
by Matt Furie and turned into a
meme on 4chan

2008-2013
Pepe's predominant emotion
evolves from glad to sad to mad

2014
Pepe becomes the face of the
Beta Uprising

In the original comic by Matt Furie, Pepe is a gross young dude living with roommates who gets high, plays video games, and eats junk food all day. The specific page from which he is co-opted features Pepe's roommates catching him peeing with his pants pulled down. When they try to tease him, rather than feel humiliated, Pepe owns it. "Feels good man," he replies, unashamed. And between 2007 and 2010, this panel, first on 4chan and then the rest of the internet, became associated with being a swamp-dwelling weirdo and owning your status as a loser.

But by 2011, something strange had occurred to Pepe as he evolved in 4chan's ooze. With every iteration of the Pepe-as-silly-loser meme, Pepe got unhappier. "Feels good man" turned into "Feels bad man," his smile flipping into a frown. And as the years ticked by—an astonishing amount of them spent at the computer—his 4chan-dwelling loserdom was no longer cause for lighthearted celebration. Pepe's sadness melted into despair, then rankling anger. By 2012, Pepe was crying and shaking with rage. And this rage was about to effect yet another transformation.

Borrowing a term from statisticians in the U.K., the Pepe-loving betas on /r9k/ soon began calling themselves "NEETs" (Not in Education, Employment, or Training), paring down complex social and psychological problems into a simple economic one. They viewed their own self-worth in terms of their economic status, or rather, their lack of it.

In /r9k/ they found commiseration, but they also found addictive withdrawal expressed in a strange, self-loathing duality. Popular posts featured tips on how to quit the board, stats on how long robots had managed to stay away, and many fond farewells. "Goodbye. My therapist says I need to let this place go," a typical post read, appended with replies like "good luck" and "maybe someday for me, too."

In /r9k/, all the protective layers of irony began to melt away and denial—let alone the infinite refraction of sarcasm—was no longer possible. The constant jokes about betas and their debased status revealed exactly who all the anonymous users were: people obsessed with status because their lack of status defined their lives. The jokes were an attempt to reduce it to the safe dimension of therapeutic play.

Betas developed elaborate memes about throwing tantrums in front of their mothers to get more "chicken tendies." If they behaved for their parents, they racked up "good-boy points." They compared their "cum jars" and "cum boxes" (often also filled with *My Little Pony* action figures), in which they accumulated the product of their loneliness. The humor functioned as a way for the young men of /r9k/ to express their hyper-sensitive, wounded misery with guarded sarcasm. But somewhere along the line (probably the cum boxes), the jokes stopped being funny.

With each iteration of memes, the sentiment became less lighthearted. Posters hardly bothered to cloak their anger and sadness in layers of irony anymore. Many simply confessed their abject resentment. Promises of murders, suicides, and mass shootings had always bounced around the boards, but often remained unverified or later proved to be hoaxes. Now these threads were becoming incrementally more real.

In November 2013, a young man posted in /b/, "Tonight I will be ending my own life. I've been spending the last hour making the preparations and I'm ready to go through with it. As an oldfag who's been on 4chan since 2004, I thought I would finally give back to the community in the best way possible: I am willing to an hero on cam for you all."

The anon then proceeded to open up a chat room in which to livestream his suicide. /b/ users gleefully piled in. And they weren't disappointed. Anon was slowly and methodically lighting his room on fire. As soon as the flames seemed large enough, he climbed under his bed to die. Some fifteen minutes passed before firefighters emerged to pull him out of the gloom. Incredibly, he survived unscathed. And when it was rumored in news reports his name was "Stephen," 4chan dubbed him "Toaster Steve."[4]

To some "oldfags," as veteran users were now called, witnessing an anon self-immolate was classic callous 4chan behavior. But something else was dying: 90s nihilism, from old age. What is the difference between being so miserable you would kill yourself on camera and being so miserable you'd want to watch someone else do it? Maybe at age fourteen, or nineteen, as a rude, angry adolescent, there was a big difference. But slowly, after a decade, the gap began to close.

"When I was administrator of Wizardchan," Brennan told me. "*Four* moderators committed suicide."

> In terms of /r9k/, that ideology is SO toxic. I used to be 100 percent on board with the whole thing. The top 80 percent will only breed, there's a whole ideology . . . Eventually the only way to come out of it: you either commit suicide or you realize all the flaws in that way of thinking. There are more image-board suicides than I can count. I can think of just four or five that I personally saw the note or the livestream. Imagine how many did it with *no note*. After a user disappeared on our IRC, we would wonder, did he kill himself?

A year after Toaster Steve, a Portland, Oregon, man named David Kalac strangled his girlfriend and posted graphic pictures of her naked corpse to 4chan. "Turns out its harder to strangle someone to death than it looks on the movies," he mused. Adding as he uploaded new pics, "She fought so Damn hard."

4chan shrugged off the live-posted murder and made jokes about it. But the jokes now functioned like the escapism and the junk food. It felt good for the moment, but later it felt worse. And soon, 4chan and /r9k/ became the center of a philosophical crisis. The wild party was over. All that remained was the grinding desperation of the late-night stragglers.

All these young people congregating in message boards had no value system, no context in society, and no reason to exist beyond the brief pleasures of consumerist gratification. Many suffered breakdowns, humiliated by their status as losers on the bottom of society, their only recourse cruelty and cynicism.

Though 4chan thought it had drilled to rock bottom in 2007, in 2012 it discovered a new, even more obdurate low that presented the same question: How long could 90s nihilism endure? How long could you believe in nothing? The answer, it turned out, was not indefinitely.

A watershed moment occurred in May 2014, when a slight, dark-featured, twenty-two-year-old man named Elliot Rodger went on a killing spree in Isla Vista, California. His stated purpose was to revenge himself on women for being a "miserable virgin" and end his life. He first stabbed his housemates. Then he traveled to a sorority house, where he shot three students. Afterward, he wandered into a deli, where he murdered another college student, before driving around shooting with abandon from his car window until the police caught up with him. After a brief gun battle, Rodger crashed his BMW and took his own life. When the dust settled, seven people had died, including Rodger, and fourteen had been wounded.

Rodger had prepared for his massacre by leaving two manifestos: a YouTube video filmed from his car titled "Elliot Rodger's Retribution" and a 141-page hybrid autobiography/confession titled "My Twisted World: The Story of Elliot Rodger." The lengthy manuscript, which began at his birth and ended at his decision to become a mass murderer, reads like an anti-bildungsroman, in which he used every opportunity to resist maturity and growth. Instead, Rodger boxed himself in as he grew increasingly detached from reality. "Cruel treatment from women is ten times worse than from men," he declared, describing a moment from childhood when a girl yelled at him for bumping into her. "It made me feel like an insignificant, unworthy little mouse." Humiliated, he drew inward, finding solace in video games, fantasy, and internet message boards.

Unable to understand social interactions, he dwelled instead on concrete statistics that he thought would make him appealing to the opposite sex: his wealth, his looks, his possessions, and so forth. In real life,

Rodger had close contact with the blockbuster fantasies most betas adored absorbing through the screen. Both his parents worked in the entertainment industry. He had attended the premiere of a Star Wars film because his mother knew George Lucas. His father had been a second-unit assistant director for *The Hunger Games*, a science-fiction tale about teens competing against one another in a murderous contest for supremacy. Rodger's favorite show, *Game of Thrones*, reworked old romantic children's fables about dragons and knights into a similar theme: life was a brutal and bloody competition for status and power. And it was this metaphor that Rodger extended into the world of competitive and conspicuous wealth and consumption among the youth of Southern California.

It didn't take long for 4chan to recognize a fellow screen-obsessed beta in Rodger. His killing spree was celebrated on /r9k/ and many other boards on 4chan in the only way it celebrated anything—in meme form. The antisocial users of 4chan had always reveled in crazed acts of violence. When the site went up in 2003, they were already memeing "Nevada-tan," the Japanese tween who stabbed her classmates with a box cutter while wearing a sweatshirt that read "Nevada," just like all the prepubescent girl killers in anime and movies. And in 2009, they spoke of "no one beating Cho's high score," a reference to Seung-Hui Cho's massacre at Virginia Tech, which was the largest massacre in the United States at the time. The number was surpassed in 2012 when Adam Lanza slaughtered twenty kindergarteners and six adults in Newtown, Connecticut. Like Rodger, Lanza was a withdrawn loner diagnosed with autism who had retreated into the fantasy world of video games under the financial guardianship of his parents.

Similarly, the Aurora, Colorado, killer, James Holmes, had been part of the 1 percent who succeeded in climbing the ladder of the academic hierarchy, literally. He had graduated in the top 1 percent of his college class and entered a highly selective PhD program in neuroscience. But the award only paid an annual stipend of $22,000. The next year, he found himself isolated, miserable, and slowly losing his mind. He settled on a massacre, stating his purpose as "the message is, there is no message," a philosophy that echoed the Joker's in the latest Batman movie, one of his favorite franchises. The role was played by Heath Ledger, who died of a drug overdose during filming. Ledger's already-dead Joker emphasized a nihilistic absurdism through meaningless acts of violence. For this reason, anonymous soon became obsessed with his character. When the film premiered, the boards exploded with troll-themed Ledger Joker memes.[5] The character also fascinated Holmes, who, in 2012, entered a movie theater dressed as the Joker, locked the doors, and began shooting just as the shooting in the movie began.

In 2014, Rodger seemed to echo Holmes' relationship with fantasy. He too was interested in the mad dream of creating a movie-style shooting within a movie shooting. Rodger's manifesto on YouTube betrays a canny cinematic eye. His face is positioned over a square of evening sunlight, what filmmakers call "the magic hour." In another clip, his reflection ripples into focus in the darkened window of his BMW as the sun fractures it. "Check it out," he tells the camera, "there's me." Though in fact he's barely there, cascading down the hall of mirrors of self-image. In the footage, it seems as though Rodger is not only stepping through the veil, but through the looking glass, into where he felt he belonged, on the other side of the screen, into the media narrative and immortality.

In *The Matrix*, the world of the screen attacks the legitimacy of the real world, condemning it as fake and suggesting its illegitimacy can be transcended through tremendous acts of violence, a deeply evocative message for a generation whose feelings were undermined by the hyper-real world of escapism. This produced a strange moment in 1999 when *The Matrix* seemed to mirror Columbine. And in 2014, Rodger evoked the same themes, seeking to enter the screen world by enacting the brutality celebrated there daily as a liberation fantasy.

Noticing the pattern, 4chan users joked about a "beta uprising." The Pepe-the-loser-Frog meme evolved again. This time, Pepe was masked and carrying a gun. He was ready for the revolution. And the betas adopted Rodger—half jokingly, half seriously—as their poster child, calling themselves the "the supreme gentlemen," a term Rodger had used to refer to himself in his manifesto. In 2015, a shooting at Umpqua Community College in Oregon was linked to the beta-uprising meme. Twenty-six-year-old Chris Harper-Mercer, also diagnosed with autism, killed ten people, including himself. "Here I am, 26, with no friends, no job, no girlfriend," he wrote in his manifesto, comparing himself to "Elliot Rodger, Vester Flanagan, the Columbine kids, Adam Lanza and Seung Cho," who "stand with gods."[6] It's very likely Harper-Mercer was responsible for a post on 4chan the day before the shooting with an image of Pepe: "Some of you guys are alright. Don't go to school tomorrow if you are in the northwest. happening thread will be posted tomorrow

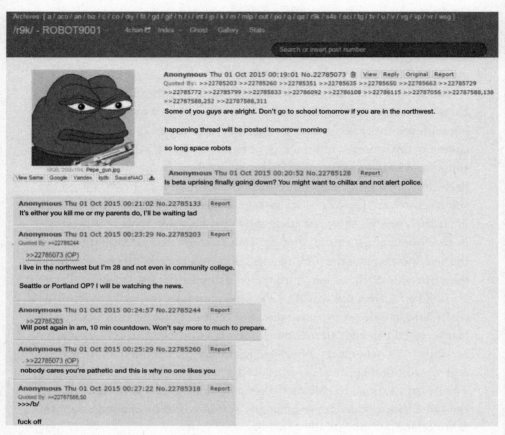

Chris Harper-Mercer's warning, it seemed at least, posted to 4chan prior to the massacre.

morning. so long space robots."[7] Though it's also possible the post predicting Harper-Mercer's massacre was simply a coincidence, since /r9k/ received threats of mass shootings daily. "Is the beta uprising really going down?" wrote the first thrilled robot-anon to reply. "[Y]ou might want to chillax and not alert police."

Though there's no evidence that Rodger visited 4chan, he frequented many of its offshoots, which employed its language and imagery. He often read a Reddit forum named after a 4chan meme, /r/ForeverAlone. He also visited pickup artist (PUA) sites, including PUAHate and several related YouTube channels. The PUA movement, popularized by a reality TV show and bestselling book, taught romantically unsuccessful men a cookbook-style method for picking up women. Like 4chan's culture, PUA told betas that they could ensnare women with a generous application of sociopathic manipulation.

Rodger's browsing history revealed to the public a ring of related websites for the growing population of beta/hikikomori called "the manosphere." The number of betas orbiting PUA sites and 4chan had expanded to fill a panoply of Reddit communities, in which men and boys could affirm their withdrawn existence as a lifestyle choice. The Men Going Their Own Way movement (MGTOW) began as a collection of subreddits, custom Reddit-style bulletin boards. And these were complemented by Reddit pages dedicated to the newly coined interest groups "incels" (involuntary celibates) and "vocels" (voluntary celibates).

In 2018, "incel" became a household term after twenty-five-year-old Alek Minassian was charged with ramming a rental van into pedestrians in Toronto, killing ten people and injuring fifteen. "[W]ishing to speak to Sgt 4chan," he purportedly wrote on Facebook immediately before the attack (though, by this point, anonymous had a long track record of falsely connecting the site to similar massacres). "The Incel Rebellion has already begun! . . . All hail the Supreme Gentleman Elliot Rodger!"

Women were often jokingly referred to as "succubi" on /r9k/, selfish monsters who would sap a man's attention and vital strength. This half-ironic, half-despairing meme soon evolved into an earnest philosophy on subreddits like MGTOW. On MGTOW, an idle reader could dig through fine-grained arguments on why "succubi" were more trouble than they were worth.

MGTOW logicians claimed to have run a cost-benefit analysis on the female gender and decided that, by the most important metric in life (the actuarial), they overburdened a man's balance sheet. In fact, the "researchers" concluded, the problem was getting worse. Feminism and what they perceived as a "gynocentric bias" against men was only upping the price tag.

Out of all the manosphere sites, MGTOW was perhaps the most tragicomic, since it was the most transparent. MGTOW logicians had obviously not worked out their "anti-gynocentric" philosophy from reason's eternal first principles, as they claimed. They'd just recast their disempowered retreat into internet forums as an empowered, principled choice. Just as Richard "Lowtax" Kyanka had described how, in the early days of Usenet, groups of "dollfuckers" had fallen into a bizarre, self-affirming groupthink. Young men, "alone together" on the internet, formed echo chambers of misogyny that offered them much-needed (though erroneous) explanations for why they had done so poorly in their romantic endeavors. Brennan, too, blamed the self-affirming community isolation of the internet for his descent into the incel belief system. "Image boards lead to these sorts of destructive ideologies. [On 4chan,] it was the incels, redpills, and National Socialism. But it was on all the boards, just different. 4chan's /lgbt/ board was full of people who were 100 percent convinced their lives would be totally miserable if they transitioned [because, though they wanted to, they believed they couldn't "pass"]. On the /fit/ board, they were miserable until they had perfect bodies. And though image boards are a great example of it, it's all the mainstream's platforms too. I know people who spend all their day on a Facebook group."

The betas' resentment of women soon pushed them to the right on feminism. And this also occurred with another issue—race. Elliot Rodger was half-Asian, but according to his manifesto, he longed to be "normally fully white." "How could an inferior, ugly black boy be able to get a white girl and not me?" he lamented. "I am beautiful, and I am half white myself. I am descended from British aristocracy. He is descended from slaves."

When Harper-Mercer copied Rodger's massacre, he echoed Rodger's themes, explaining that his racism emerged from humiliation. His understanding of black men seemed to be derived from online pornography, though he himself claimed to be "40 % black." "I don't hate blacks. Just the men," he wrote. "Elliot Rodger was right when he said his thoughts on the black male . . . Black men have corrupted the women of this planet. All they care about is sex and swag. All they care about is swinging their 'BBC thang' around in public."[8]

The same feeling of humiliation at having lost a perceived sexual contest with rigid metrics in which men "get" women (rather than enter into relationships with them) melded into racism on 4chan and the greater manosphere in the exact same way.

And soon, /r9k/'s sensibility blended with another board on 4chan that had become explicitly fascist—/pol/.

Within the year, many /r9k/ robots turned into Nazis.

From Robots to Nazis

Q: What conclusions would you draw from this data set?
A: Just from an Occam's razor approach, [the data] suggests that the men who want to read a site about little girl anime and gaming also want to read about right-wing political content. We should understand that there is a sub-section of the web population interested in both topics. . . .
Q: Are you saying that moe [little-girl-themed anime] media has conservative themes?
A: Not at all. Most of these series are made for pre-teen girls.
—Discussion from a 2012 *Neojaponisme* article on 2channel's new far-right bent

In January 2010, Poole created a news section for 4chan (/new/). But things did not go as expected. A year later, he was forced to delete the board because it had "become [S]tormfront."

Several years earlier, Anonymous had raided the infamous neo-Nazi site Stormfront. And, as had occurred with so many other sites targeted in raids, Stormfront users were not only clued into 4chan's existence, but soon became absorbed in image-board culture themselves.

However, when moot removed the board his neo-Nazi problem didn't disappear. The population simply took up residence in the international (/int/) and weapons (/k/) boards. In November 2011, Poole again attempted to address the issue by reversing his previous measures. He created a containment board to replace /new/: "politically incorrect" (/pol/). And in some sense this worked—Nazis flooded into /pol/. But the board didn't get crowded out in the marketplace of ideas. Rather, 4chan's new neo-Nazi section thrived.

It turned out a surprisingly large amount of 4chan's culture aligned with the sensibilities of /pol/. After all, a majority of the boards were filled with racist and homophobic slurs. Hyper-offensive trolls had defined 4chan's culture since the earliest days, when they had formed "swastigets" with "nigras" in Habbo Hotel. Moreover, the final split between anonymous and Anonymous meant that the trolling contingent remained in orbit around 4chan, while many who had possessed a moral compass had either left for activist sites or grown out of 4chan. Also, far-right fascism was not all that different from the extreme libertarianism that had defined much of 4chan's political beliefs from the start.

And another type of 4chan user was also drawn to /pol/: the growing population of withdrawn insiders. In a Q&A in 2013, moot described them as people who employed the "reverse of Occam's razor," cottoning on to the most improbable explanation for any question presented to them. It was difficult to say whether their poor reality testing was a result of spending all their time on the internet, or simply the only place where the desocialized could socialize.

Perhaps unsurprisingly, these credulous, cloistered people adored /pol/, which was awash in outlandish conspiracy theories and murky thinking, from "false flag" operations to centuries-old canards about Jewish banking cabals. Additionally, these ancient fascist conspiracy theories served as creation myths to explain something the conspiracists often wondered about—their own status as withdrawn losers who somehow couldn't get ahead in life.

Soon the betas on /r9k/ and the loopy, hateful denizens of /pol/ began to merge.

Many of the boards, but in particular /r9k/ and /pol/, became obsessed with "cuckold porn," a fetish in which men watch as their wives or girlfriends have sex with other, generally more strapping, men.

In William Shakespeare's *Othello*, the main character's cuckolding is a figment of his imagination, put there by the jealous Iago, who resents that an African man has ascended above him. And true to literary allusion, the fetish often features hyper-masculine African American men in the role of the surprise guest. Echoing Elliot Rodger's and Chris Harper-Mercer's manifestos, /r9k/'s obsession with masculine humiliation and /pol/'s right-wing racism merged into a single idea, a grade-school putdown they flung at each other constantly on the boards: "cuck," which by 2016 had found its way into mainstream conservative media as "cuckservative."

"Cuck" was a strange new territory for 4chan. The userbase had always been cruel and degenerate, but rarely that sincerely puerile. When moot livestreamed a Q&A in 2013, he was barraged with the same question from /pol/, who, unlike the rest of 4chan, despised him: "Are you a cuck?" "I went from being a 'faggot' for the better part of ten years to a 'cuck,'" moot concluded. "So I mean it was it is. I'm pretty amused by it."

But in fact, there was a difference in the terms. "Faggot," for all its offensiveness, was not laden with so much humiliated misery. When first employed on 4chan, faggot was a means of deflecting boyish ribbing by saying, "You can't offend me" and "I'm so secure you can insult my masculinity and I don't care." But it soon morphed into an expression of solidarity, a way of declaring, "I'm just a person who can be attacked like everyone else" and "like everyone else, I'm not straight. I have my own fetishes, quirks, aberrant proclivities, etc."

When someone came to the board and declared they were a "doctorfag," "oldfag," "policefag," or "fagfag," it was a way of humbling oneself, signaling to the anonymous community that the user was not putting on any airs by discussing their identity when they wanted to offer their expertise or discuss their background.

This notion of faggotry was connected to a lighthearted approach to gender norms, which would also disappear with the ascendancy of /pol/ and the betas. Though moot received a lot of hate mail, the majority of 4chan consistently showered him with an adolescent form of affection—they teased him. His nickname since 2005 was "Chris 'i wish to be a little girl' Poole." And to that end, anonymous shared pictures of him curtsying in a pink princess party dress, a tiara sparkling on his head, the photos snapped at parties in the halls of Otakon, where I first saw him sharing fan images of himself depicted as a sexy cat-girl. The feminization was not malicious; it dovetailed with rendering his name with hearts in the middle ("m<3<3t."), or as "mootles," "mootie-pie," "mootykins."

By contrast, /pol/ genuinely despised Poole. "Cuck" was not an expression of cartwheeling fun, but a product of sad bile, flung in sulky enmity hoping to wound by spitting out what the speaker loathed in themselves.

Thus, when /pol/ arrived on 4chan as a containment board for Nazis, it served as something more, a place where the orbiting clouds of racism and misogyny could condense. /pol/ not only endured on 4chan but thrived as a mixture of preexisting 4chan subgroups: to paraphrase a popular contemporary 4chan meme on the subject, paranoids, trolls, white nationalists, betas, libertarians, and directionless adults.

And indeed, by 2012 the phenomenon was growing not just on 4chan but around the world in countries that had copied the Western consumerist model. The Chinese equivalents of betas had taken to calling themselves "*diaosi*" (a play on the Chinese word "fan" that also meant "pubes"). The diaosi meme first emerged on the Chinese-speaking internet around 2012, just as the /r9k/ board was taking off. Early on, it mocked withdrawn Chinese loser nerds. But the term was soon co-opted by scores of young Chinese people groping to describe their sad state as losers at the bottom of China's new capitalist competition for status and wealth.

> They have no money, no background, no future. They love *DOTA* [*Defense of the Ancients*], they love the Li Yi BBS [bulletin board software], and they love their menial jobs. They are fated to kneel before the tall, rich and handsome. When the diaosi muster the courage to strike up a conversation with a "goddess," the only response they receive is a chuckle. They worship their god, Li Yi; they are diaosi.[1]

In Japan, the otaku movement had also expanded to become an enduring segment of the population. And as in the United States, otaku culture was based around image boards, in particular, 4chan's progenitor 2channel. By 2012, 2channel had evolved with otaku culture and become one of the foundations of the entertainment complex.

And also like 4chan, the Japanese otaku's politics began to shift to the far right. This baffled many people at the time, since the artists who created anime were generally on the far left.[2] In an article for the Japanese culture website *Neojaponisme*, the author concluded, "In general, 2ch[annel]'s brand of conservatism is mostly an identity politics based in populist resentment against other minorities—women, zainichi Koreans, Asians, gays, new religions, the poor, outcast populations—who are seen to be given an unfair attention from the government and society."

What about the betas' and otaku's new levels of despair pushed them toward fascism? And why did it occur around the world in 2012?

This question begs other questions: What is fascism? And how did it arise the first time around?

Though people often regard fascism as meaning something like "the state owns the means of production," this definition is nowhere close to the scholarly consensus on the subject.[3] While the exact meaning is hotly debated, there are several general markers upon which everyone agrees: Fascism is enamored of authoritarianism and a rigid code of "traditional" values that belongs to an ideal age in the past. It is often a response to a panoply of subjective value systems that accompany the modern industrial age of the late nineteenth and early twentieth century. It is opposed to Enlightenment values like democracy, freedom of the press, and human rights. Moreover, it also insists on a race-based style of thinking, which asserts nations should be composed of a single ethnic group.

A clear definition of fascism has remained obscure because both left and right attribute its rise to the other side of the political spectrum. The first appearance of fascism in the 1930s coincided with a resurgence of socialism, which caused some on the right, perhaps most famously the economist F. A. Hayek, to attribute fascism to the specter of socialism.

Today we can see this position disproved in real time, as fascism emerges in a smooth gradient from the far-right end of the political spectrum. In the United States, as well as in Europe, economically liberal capitalism has disenfranchised so many people that they have begun to search for alternatives to the status quo in socialism and fascism. All under the threat of being reduced, as Hayek puts it, to "serfdom."[4] From our contemporary viewpoint, it appears far more likely that radical political alternatives to Western liberalism have appeared because we have reached levels of economic inequality comparable to the 1920s and 30s. Or, as the philosopher Max Horkheimer put it, "Whoever is not prepared to talk about capitalism should also remain silent about fascism."[5]

Similarly, in *The Origins of Totalitarianism*, the philosopher Hannah Arendt argues that fascism, when it first appeared in the 1930s, was generated by the conflict between Enlightenment values and industrial capitalism, in particular a feeling of total powerlessness that industrial capitalism produced in Enlightenment societies.

At the end of the eighteenth century, industrial engines promised freedom from drudgery at a tremendous scale. In this new world, it no longer seemed necessary to divide society into a few wealthy and well-educated aristocrats and leave the rest to languish as resourceless laborers. As soon as it became apparent that machines could do much of the work that people did at the time, a new sort of politics formed. And it is from this politics that we derived our notions of technology as a radical emancipator. For Enlightenment thinkers, this promise of progress opened up the possibility of a government ruled by the people.

However, by the end of the nineteenth century, wealth disparity had reached a different extreme, somehow resembling the prior one but offering a glimpse of a better future. As one Communist manifesto from Chicago in the 1870s described it, the owners of industry were preventing this new society from coming into being one in which the age-old "selfish merciless struggle for existence" might be transformed into "a generous struggle for perfection in which equal advantages should be given to all, and human lives relieved from an unnatural and degrading competition for bread."[6] Or as Edward Bellamy put it in 1888, in the third-bestselling book of the time, *Looking Backward*, "nothing had . . . occured [in the nineteenth century] to modify the immemorial division of society into the four classes . . . the rich and the poor, the educated and the ignorant." Yet, he forecast, "elements . . . were already fermenting" that by the year 2000 would turn these divisions into mere relics of a brutal past.[7] There was a certain groping senselessness, he noted, that in the drive to better humanity, "The relation between the workingman and the employer, between labor and capital, appeared in some unaccountable manner to have become dislocated."

Like Bellamy, Karl Marx and Friedrich Engels predicted that eventually the workers of industrialized nations would notice the lopsided way wealth accrued to factory owners. Outnumbering the owners, the workers would band together to take control of the factories and redistribute the bounty of industrialization more evenly. But something far stranger occurred, that, in the words of Hannah Arendt, demonstrated the "absurd disparities between cause and effect which have become the hallmark of modern history."[8]

When we reached a zenith of inequality in the 1920s, industrialization hadn't neatly divided people into classes of workers and owners, each united by a set of shared interests. Instead, modern existence produced a vast new anti-class composed of isolated, *de-classed* individuals torn from the traditional social structures that predated industrialization. More joined this group when, in the throes of industrialization, market changes, and crises, they lost their jobs or perhaps their entire job sector and thus held no economic purpose and, by extension, no place in society.

This new anti-class was not necessarily the working class but composed of "the refuse of all classes." Arendt's description of this group, what she called "the masses," could easily be applied to the otaku today: "The truth is that the masses grew out of the fragments of a highly at-omized society whose competitive structure and concomitant loneliness of the individual had been held in check only through membership in a class . . . The chief characteristic of the mass man is not brutality and backwardness, but his isolation and lack of normal social relationships."[9]

These new de-classed masses did not necessarily resent the ownership class. Their mental landscape, like their own fragmented nature, was bro-ken into odd and sometimes loopy contours.

As society structured itself around its prodigious ability to produce factory-made products, human beings began to regard themselves as in-herently acquisitive beings whose very nature was bent toward nihilistic accumulation. As businessmen ascended to the top of society, more people imagined themselves as prospective robber barons and regarded their fel-low human beings as rivals. And by the early twentieth century, this self-image, what Arendt refers to as "Hobbesian" (in short, nasty and brutish), was growing more prevalent, particularly among the de-classed.

Similarly, entire nation-states began to see the world in terms of ac-quisition and power. The "commonwealth" was regarded as a tool by which the interests of big businesses that had roosted in government could search out raw resources and pry open new markets across the world.

People no longer felt like members of a cooperative association for betterment, as Enlightenment thinkers had envisioned the nation-state, but rather "degraded into a cog in a power-accumulating machine, free to console himself with sublime thoughts about the ultimate destiny of the machine, which itself is constructed in such a way that it can devour the globe simply by following its own inherent law."[10]

Soon, the view from the bottom and the very top looked very much the same. From both angles society did not appear to be an Enlightenment-style network of free individuals, but a wealth hierarchy, in which large interests at the top dictated the behavior of those at the bottom.

Thus, by the end of the nineteenth century, there was a bizarre align-ment between the masses and capital, of oppressed and oppressor. As today—when former Goldman Sachs banker Steve Bannon and a 4chan anime Nazi living in his mom's basement are in philosophic accord—the de-classed masses of the 20s and 30s viewed the world as a naked struggle for power and accumulation. And so, the goal of politics for the masses was not to establish a new Marxist-style horizontal order of equality, but to exert leverage and scrabble to the top of the dogpile.

Arendt described how, in the 1930s, groups of dispossessed people from the lower, middle, and upper classes all began to aspire to the cruel-minded values of a certain type of businessman who, like Trump today, was "flattered at being called a power-thirsty animal."[11]

It was this social Darwinist viewpoint that made the industrialist Dale Carnegie's 1936 self-help book *How to Win Friends and Influence People* a bestseller. His ideological outlook flattened relationships among people into a businesslike game of hierarchy and acquisition similar to contemporary bestsellers like *The 48 Laws of Power*. ("Law 2: Never put too much trust in friends, learn how to use enemies." "Law 7: Get others to do the work for you, but always take the credit.")

Just as friends were not made but "won," a man, according to the pickup artists' philosophy, does not enter into a relationship with a woman, but attempts to acquire as many women as he can to lift his status. In both schemas, people are approached not as fellow human beings, but as tools to be stockpiled, influenced, and manipulated.

This belief system soon engendered rankling enmity among all those who kept losing the perceived contest. People like Elliot Rodger suffered from its damning corollary: if one couldn't "achieve" status, wealth, and women, one was doomed to be worthless.

In Arendt's view, it was this sort of thinking combined with a declassed status that led to fascism. Fascism resulted when these previously apolitical masses dispossessed by capitalism began to rebel against it, *without discarding its cruel-minded competitive way of thinking.*

Unhappy with the status quo, the masses in the 1930s developed a new system of politics based on the idea that interactions between human beings are struggles for power and the winners of such competitions climb to the top of the power pyramid.

From this perspective, race-based thinking soon emerged because it was a last grasp at solidarity and belonging for otherwise atomized individuals who, in Arendt's words, found "no other unifying bond available between individuals who in their very process of power accumulation and expansion are losing all natural connections with their fellow-men."[12]

In this spot a cruel mirage appears. The fascist imagines that the only way to get ahead in life is to remove someone else—or a whole group of people—above you in the hierarchy.

To explain his place at the bottom of the pyramid, and to justify displacing those above him, a grand conspiracy is concocted: a group of devious people (immigrants, Jews, etc.) have *cheated* at the game and usurped a slot above your (race's) own. Therefore, their removal will help the new group in which you have found solidarity and belonging, your "race," to get ahead.

This sort of outlook emerges on the far right rather than on the far left because Hobbesian thinking rejects socialism as naive and utopian, since it's based on a view of human beings as inherently selfless and co-operative.

The masses also reject liberalism because it is pro status quo. After all, liberalism's central tenet is that the large forces at the top of the power pyramid—corporations and big government—work in tandem to maintain the Corporate State. This philosophy does not offer what the declassed want: fundamental changes that will radically alter the system so that they will no longer be on the bottom.

After World War II, both the Republican and Democratic parties in the United States have been uniformly "liberal," in the economic sense. They only disagree on the degree to which the state should regulate capitalism.

And now, in the twenty-first century, when inequality has reached levels only previously attained in the late 1920s, youth movements have once again emerged outside this narrow band of political thought. Fascism and socialism have become popular again.

Though modern alt-right fascists worship capitalism as a means to achieve power, like their idols Hitler and Putin, they want to create a grand upheaval that subordinates the power of capitalism to serve a particular race of people (themselves) and their values.

By 2012, groups of isolated, de-classed individuals began to appear on /pol/ and /r9k/. Cut off from humanity, they evaluated themselves by their use. They were not revolutionaries but NEETs (Not in Education, Employment, or Training). Weirdly, they defined their existence by their lack of employment, not, for example, by being the sons of mothers, good friends, artists, intellectuals, or members of a certain faith. And by this simplified metric, they considered themselves worthless, undeserving of meaningful company because they have not earned it.

Likewise, they imagined society and romantic interactions not as generous cooperative effort, but as a hierarchy of winners and losers, alphas and betas. Since the betas could not claim to be breadwinnners or playboys, they did not deserve the romantic and material rewards of either.

Stuck with this flattened worldview, they didn't rebel against capitalism as the left expected. Instead they aligned themselves with big capital. In their defeated and unquestioning cynicism, they saw the world as a video game—deterministic and drained of all meaning. Their (failed) purpose was simply to get ahead. They thought in simplistic terms of nihilistic accumulation. And therefore, only the language of the right-leaning bourgeois appealed to them.

The Jewish conspiracies revived on /pol/ were set in naive terms betas could understand and offered a convenient explanation for their debased status. If society was a hierarchy, there were only two ways to account for your status at the bottom: either you lost because of your own flaws *or* someone else cheated and took your place in the middle or at the top of the hierarchy. In this second scenario, conveniently, the onus is placed elsewhere (on Jews, outsiders, and so forth). And recall, the anti-Semitic conspiracies of the 1920s were all conspiracies of capitalists (as they are today), fables imagining Jews controlled the strings of finance, which then controlled the world. These ideas appealed to people who believed in the capitalist worldview but found themselves at the bottom of the power hierarchy. They served as explanatory myths for why they were brought so low despite the perceived perfection of capitalism.

Anonymous was a far-left effort to shatter the hierarchies of the liberal Corporate State, and it had been thoroughly crushed by the FBI. Those who remained on 4chan and the new boys and men who joined thought that they could simply retreat to their 90s-style nihilistic, otaku lifestyle. But soon, they found, just as Anonymous had, that it was no way to live. And with the left closed off, they began to grope for a new direction, this time on the right.

Liberalism appeared in England with the first factories. It was, as Engels put it, "the party of manufacturers," and its central issue in the early nineteenth century was free trade—convincing the other classes that what was good for factory owners would be good for everyone else.

Political philosophers such as Adam Smith and John Locke claimed that liberalism and free trade also meant freedom of the press, freedom of worship, freedom of lifestyle, and so forth. However, socialism made a competing claim for the mantle of Enlightenment, insisting that human rights did not stem from a freedom to do business. Rather, freedom of enterprise *interfered* with human rights. After all, a central goal of the Enlightenment had been freedom from drudgery through technology. Echoing Marx and Bellamy, Marcuse declared "technological processes of mechanization and standardization" would "release individual energy into a yet uncharted realm of freedom beyond necessity." But only "if the individual were no longer compelled to prove himself on the market, as a free economic subject."

To combat this idea, liberalism dangerously entwined the Enlightenment right to live as one pleased with the right of corporations to do business as they pleased. In the late 2010s, this fact did not go unnoticed by a new generation of fascists who resented the alliance between culturally liberated minorities and big business. Modern fascists sensed a relationship among their dissipated, consumerist otaku lifestyles; the liberal celebration of diverse lifestyles; capitalism's invitation to indulge in every self-gratifying pleasure; and the intractable power of the coastal elite.

Moreover, extreme conservatism addressed many of the de-classed otaku masses' complaints.

As socialist philosopher Slavoj Zizek points out in *Trouble in Paradise*, conservatism generates a "protective bubble" around the individual from capitalism. Though both traditional Republicans and Democrats are economic liberals, traditional conservatives are warier of the cultural problems capitalism generates. The constant invitations to enjoy a nihilistic lifestyle of empty materialism and acquisition can be rebuffed by holding fast to a set of religious values, which offer a fuller, more optimistic conception for the point of existence. And the inherently isolating way capitalism tears apart social bonds is similarly inured by clinging to traditional modes of behavior. People can retain a sense of enduring meaning by replicating ancient community structures: nuclear families, church groups, and so forth.

To isolated people adrift in nihilistic determinism (be it social Darwinism in the 1930s or game theory on 4chan today), the easy fix of tradition was a lifeline. It was, to the shipwrecked, at last firm ground.

Like a suit you buy off the rack, tradition offers a one-size-fits-all package deal of answers. How do I live my life? Live it like people lived

theirs in the past. What do I believe the purpose of existence is? You believe what people believed in the past.

It was this terra firma that Brennan found when he forsook the chans.
Now that he works as a freelance programmer in the Philippines, he at-
tends church, where he has discovered a supportive community. He recently got engaged and plans to start a family.

When I asked him how his conservative lifestyle evolved, he told me
that the personal problems that had drawn him into the chans had somehow stemmed from commodification and subjectivity. "Our society
today has become so commodified. Everything's a commodity and there's
all these products for every niche in this world. Even living decently is in
its own way a commodity. The Jordan Petersons [the pop conservative
thinker who sells responsible living to former betas] of the world [are] a
commodity on a commodity market. Even the anarchist in the black bloc
has to buy the thing he covers his face with, you know what I mean?
There used to be this national narrative. Now whatever that guid[ing]
light was has turned into darkness."

In the black hole of the chans, this core conservative belief in the lifeline of tradition combined with a number of bizarre ideas that idealized
the past. If power and privilege was a zero-sum game, betas figured, feminism and equal rights for minorities meant that white men had been
degraded in the hierarchy and had to fight for scraps of power, just like
any other identitarian faction. They imagined that white men had conceded power to other groups, and that this accounted for their current
debased status as betas. Hence the story in the /pol/ screenshot on the
next page about well-educated kids and economic security was predicated
on watching the police beat up a black man.

Thus /pol/ reveled in racist nostalgia for the 1950s, when white men
reigned supreme and the nation was ordered by agreed-upon traditions.
If they had been born in the mythic 1950s, they reasoned, they would
not be in their mothers' basements, broke and alone, but rather men supplied with good jobs, houses, wives, cars, and dignity.

They took this fantasy a step further when it came to women. Starting in 2014, a chart began bouncing around the chans that detailed how,
prior to the sexual revolution, men did not have to compete in the cutthroat Darwinian market for women. Instead, ancient tradition, in its
time-tested wisdom, had once simply supplied them with wives. This sys-

Anonymous (ID: QjxfOyJL) █ 01/25/17(Wed)09:45:48 No.108991904 ▶ >>108992100 >>108993039 >>108994093 >>108995505

>>108991663 (OP)

>be a man in the 1950's
>coming home from work from my high paying unionized job with pension and benefits
>drive my 8,000lb 8mpg 18' long car with huge fins on the back
>glance out the window and see a negro walking down the street
>stop at the corner bar and call the cops, watch as they beat him into a coma while sipping a Gimlet
>stop by the hardware store on the way home and buy several guns with no background check
>greeted by my submissive and dutiful wife with a kiss
>greeted by my obedient and well educated kids with a hug
>greeted by my Golden Retriever carrying my slippers
>sit own to a dinner of all-American grown products that is already on table
>after dinner the kids do their homework and the wife does the dishes
>pour myself a Canadian Club on the rocks and recline in my La-Z-Boy
>watch the nightly news and see America bombing Communist in some backward shithole
>smile as I remember all the Nips I killed on Guadalcanal
>plan our family vacation trip to the Poconos
>time for bed
>fuck my wife in the missionary position with no concern for her pleasure
>drift off to dream of the greatness of America

A typical /pol/ post from 2017.

tem appeared far preferable to what the modern world had seemingly allotted them—a computer terminal with a connection to pornography.

This new veneration of tradition extended to the ordering of the beta's internal feelings as well.

In January 2018, I stood outside a tony restaurant in downtown Washington, D.C., and watched as antifa heckled the alt-right conservatives who had gathered there. (To go inside, I would have had to pay the alt-right an admission price of $100, which I refused to do.) Antifa was mostly kids from a nearby college dressed in ragged black. Every so often, alt-right attendees, dolled up in literal off-the-rack suits, came out to smoke behind a metal gate and a line of police officers. They looked like particularly loose-faced frat boys, their features coated in a comfortable layer of fat. Though now and again weird aberrations would appear to break the pattern. Someone dressed like an anime villain, in a white top hat and coattails, hovered on their margins. Then the Nazi-worshipping former reality TV star Tila Tequila, the first person to have ever risen to fame via social media, came clopping out in six-inch heels (she was livestreaming with a selfie stick). Eventually, the alt-right began to heckle back.

"Maybe you forgot to take your antidepressants today?" they yelled at antifa. The implication being that their conversion to far-right conservatism rendered them, in contrast to their enemies, "based."

Developed by far-left black internet culture, this word was co-opted by the alt-right, who used it obsessively. At a time when young people on the left and right were quivering with uncertainty, mired in debt, and lacking jobs or places to live, "based" described a certain anti-state. It meant the opposite of how most young people felt all the time, walking a precarious tightrope to avoid mental and economic collapse.

In previous eras, human beings were defined by their place in a community. In the modern era, this was inverted. Each person was an isolated competitor ready to collapse under the cruel pressure of managing debts and assets. And most young people held far more debts than assets. "Based" was a response to this feeling, a sort of mythic mindset in which you had all your affairs in order, not only in the physical world, but the mental one. Your psyche, your assumptions, your ego, and your ideals were not paper-thin; you stood on solid, "based" ground.

This is what the alt-right attempted to project in their smug self-assurance, that in their loopy adherence to hundred-year-old conspiracy theories about Jewish financiers they no longer needed antidepressants. Ridiculously, they imagined they stood on the most solid ground of all in their rack suits with their rack-suit set of values.

They were waiting there that evening to hear two leaders in their movement speak, Milo Yiannopoulos and Mike Cernovich. Both men, it turned out, owed their fame to a strange moment in 2014 when, on 4chan's /r9k/ and /pol/, all the otaku-style resentment finally coalesced into the "alt-right" during a trolling and harassment campaign known as "gamergate."

And in the next chapter, we will see how in 2014 a sadder, sagging, bizarro version of Anonymous called "gamergaters" coalesced into a Trump-loving political movement.

Gamergate: 4chan's Depression Quest

Gamers have had enough of reality. They are abandoning it in droves . . .
These gamers aren't rejecting reality entirely. They have jobs, goals, work,
families, commitments, and real lives they care about. But as they devote
more and more of their free time to the game worlds, the real world increasingly feels like it's missing something.

—Jane McGonigal, *Reality Is Broken: Why Games Make Us Better and
How They Can Change the World*

"Gamers have had enough of reality," Jane McGonigal's bestselling 2011 book declared. The thesis was similar to Stewart Brand's 1972 *Rolling Stone* article about video games. Though it jettisoned all the talk about revolution, acid, and politics, *Reality Is Broken* asserted that games would "make us better" and "change the world" in a blander, vague sort of way. But the book had the embarrassing distinction of emerging just before "gamers" came to mean something very different, something so vile much of the industry attempted to retire the term.

"Gamers are over," games writer Leigh Alexander famously declared in 2014 during #gamergate. "'Game culture' as we know it is kind of embarrassing—it's not even culture. It's buying things, spackling over memes and in-jokes repeatedly, and it's getting mad on the internet. It's young men queuing . . . passionately for hours, at events around the world, to see the things that marketers want them to see. To find out whether they should buy things or not."[1]

Indeed, even in 2011 the hard sell wasn't that "reality is broken," it was McGonigal's polite caveat that gamers "have jobs, goals, work, families, commitments, and real lives they care about" even though they "devote more and more of their free time to the game worlds . . . [and]

the real world increasingly feels like it's missing something." If one really thought about it, this was an irreconcilable duality, one that finally reached a tipping point in 2014 when the world learned a vast swath of gamers had at some point in the past departed from the real world and begun making demands that appeared totally unhinged to non-gamers.

#gamergate was a self-described gamer revolt on 4chan that ended up briefly breaking the games industry and, a few years later, American politics indefinitely. To outsiders, it was a disturbing phenomenon that made little sense. And the hope was that, like so many other hyper-complex but foolish internet controversies, it would eventually melt back into the post-culture heap of internet sludge. However, just like Dennis Rodman visiting North Korea to practice reality TV diplomacy years before Donald Trump, gamergate prefigured a new kind of politics because it *was* cultural refuse.

The main event occurred in August 2014, when a jilted young man named Eron Gjoni decided to get revenge on an ex, game developer Zoe Quinn, by writing an angry blog post about her.

Gjoni's complaints were originally posted to Something Awful but were immediately deleted for violating rules against personal harassment. So Gjoni put them up on his own site, and they soon found their way to 4chan and the rest of the chanverse.

There was an age-old expression for what Gjoni was trying to do on the chans: "not your personal army." The label derived from anon's pat response to the scores of angry young men who beseeched the chanverse daily to take revenge on some acquaintance (usually a woman). Except, conveniently for Gjoni, Quinn was someone the chans already despised. And so his appeal for an anonymous-style hate mob in the tradition of those sicced upon teenage Jessi Slaughter and Mitchell Henderson was not only cleared, but moved to the front of the line.

The story of why the chans disliked Quinn had its roots two years earlier. In /b/'s vacuum, lighthearted boards were being sucked into the orbit of the new sagging center of 4chan, /pol/ and /r9k/. Soon, the denizens of 4chan's video game board "/v/" ("/v/irgins") found common ground with the fascist /pol/ "/pol/acks" and the sad beta /r9k/ robots in their deep resentment of feminism and liberal "social justice warriors" (SJWs).

To this new coalition, video games were the last line of retreat. Just as 4chan's userbase employed memes to reduce their complex problems into tiny cartoon characters with which they could enact a sort of thera-peutic play, these young men used video games to provide power fantasies in which they could simulate exactly how they rarely felt in real life—effective. These experiences weren't limited to sniper missions and sword play, but extended into wooing compliant virtual women, often depicted as shallow sex objects.

For decades, video games had been marketed to boys. However, as the industry grew to eclipse Hollywood, the customer base expanded to include the opposite gender. Threatened by the idea that games might become less boyish, /pol/, /v/, and /r9k/, as well as a number of copycat boards on other chans, began to obsess over the minority of women who had entered the games industry.

The most frequent subject of their grousing was feminist video game critic Anita Sarkeesian, who raised nearly $160,000 via Kickstarter in May 2012 to produce a series of YouTube videos on gender tropes in video games. The content was not particularly scandalous. One video dwelled on why Ms. Pac-Man was depicted with a pink bow, yet Pac-Man was considered male by default. Another, on why Mario rescued Princess Peach and not the other way around. However, critiques of Ms. Pac-Man and Princess Peach inspired boiling rage in the manosphere segments of 4chan, where anons seethed not only over Sarkeesian's ideas, but her financial success.

As one of the few female game developers, Quinn soon became an-other focal point of resentment. In February 2013, she released the semi-autobiographical, text-based adventure game *Depression Quest*. In design, the game resembled a Tumblr blog in which personal confessions spilled out onto the page. Like the sword-and-sorcery-themed text-based adventure games from the early days of computing, *Depression Quest* let users control the choices of the protagonist by selecting from a list of options. However, in Quinn's game, the main character is someone in a contemporary setting experiencing depression. As the story unfolds, the player can click through options that have their character going out to parties, interacting with friends, or staying home to despair. As the user proceeds, possibilities are crossed off the list. Instead of wandering in expansive new realms, the gamer finds their options dwindling, an effect meant to simulate real-life depression.

Depression Quest represented a sea change in video games. By 2013, technology had evolved to make it possible for individual auteurs to craft small games and distribute them at low cost through online stores. As with indie movies, the indie games movement freed creators from making formulaic content that would ensure that financial backers recouped their investment. *Depression Quest* was part of a new wave of avant-garde indie titles that broke out of the narrow confines of puerile subject matter and reconfigured old tropes to deal with a broader spectrum of subjects. For this reason, it attracted a lot of critical praise, though it was not quite fun to play in the traditional sense, much as *The Bell Jar* isn't exactly fun to read.

In their literal-minded way, game fans on the chans did not see the artistic merit of *Depression Quest*'s simplicity. They viewed its uncomplicated design as evidence that it was a bad game in comparison to what they were used to—elaborate AAA studio confections that immersed the player in a hyper-real fantasy world. Quinn was not demonstrating her skill in an overt way, in the manner boys compete in video games, one-upping each other in concrete achievements like points and kills. Thus, in their minds, the mystery of *Depression Quest*'s popularity could only be explained in one way: Quinn's gender.

The chans were organized much like Dante organized hell, in cascading layers of depravity. 4chan was only the upper crust. And in December 2013, resentment against Quinn and *Depression Quest* began to coalesce in one of the lowest orders: Fredrick "HotWheels" Brennan's Wizardchan, where one had to be a "wizard," a lifelong virgin, to post. (Brennan would eventually retire as administrator from Wizardchan because he had been, in their words, "seduced by a succubi" and "no longer qualified as [a] wizard.")[2]

The wizards were rankled by Quinn's gender and the fact that she claimed to have depression. What could a woman who "has physical and verbal contact with [the] opposite gender, has a job, [and] isn't autistic" know of depression, one poster reasoned.[3] How could her complaints compare to their lonesome suffering? (Or, as another wizard put it, "All females are sluts and have no right to be depressed. They can go out into the street, lie down with their hole open and have any man come and solve all their problems.")[4]

However, unlike so many other targets of the chans, Quinn had been on Something Awful for years and was very familiar with the chans.[5] When she began receiving harassing messages, she quickly traced the source back to a post on Wizardchan. And then, to the wizards' horror, she called them out on Twitter, lifting the rock on their obscure sanctum.

For the next six months, Quinn's name flowed in and out of the beta realms of the chanverse as a despised companion of Anita Sarkeesian.

So by 2014, when Gjoni decided he wanted revenge, he didn't need to do much to convince the chans to target her. Gjoni's whiny blog post would be the central document around which gamergate would revolve, though it's a bizarre read for anyone who lives their life out of doors: a rambling, 10,000-word document interspersed with memes, screenshots, and videos. Incredibly, many of the chat logs Gjoni presents as "proof" of Quinn's perfidy are conversations in which he threatens to malign her online.

However, the post was wildly popular in the chanverse because it was exactly what the sad man-boys wanted to hear. Women, many anons imagined, fed on attention and weaponized their sexual allure at the expense of men. Moreover, according to /r9k/ and /v/, they were using this technique to infiltrate video games, not only for their personal advantage but to promote a "SJW agenda" and steal away what they adored the most—their digital male fantasies.

Gjoni's post depicted Quinn as this character. The chanverse believed Quinn was leveraging her gender to promote her game, and for that purpose had used her relationship with a game reviewer to earn a favorable review for *Depression Quest*. (Gjoni later admitted that this was not true, and the implication was the result of a typo he had made.)[6]

Nonetheless, anonymous picked up the trolling tool kit of Anonymous and flooded into IRC to treat gamergate like the video game it wasn't. For a long time, they believed they would find evidence of a conspiracy in the games industry. Users attempted to score points by digging up obscure personal information about Quinn, hacking the accounts of those they believed associated with her, and sending hateful messages via phone, email, fax, and delivery services. Quinn's life soon exploded in an unprecedented level of harassment, even for the internet.

I happened to be working in indie games at the time. Many of those listed in Gjoni's post as targets were friends of friends. Gamergaters hacked the Skype account of the indie developer with whom I was collaborating, presumably digging through our conversations for concrete evidence of some SJW cabal. What they found instead was my boss patiently explaining to me how games were a carefully calibrated system of rewards—beat a level, get a cut scene.

The gamergate hackers often imagined their campaign would play out this way, just as a plot might neatly unfold in a point-and-click detective adventure. But in the real world there were shades of gray. It was disappointing. And as gamergaters rummaged through hacked accounts, they slowly lost interest. Though, as with previous chan obsessions, harassment of Quinn and other gamergate targets lasted for years.

In some sense, *Depression Quest* became the focal point of so much ire not because it was a bad game, but because *it was too good of a game*. It struck anon in his most vulnerable spot.

The thirty-year-old wizards who laid the groundwork for gamergate were adults with the habits of children. A life of playing fantasy video games had evolved into an existence that mirrored the life of the depressed character depicted in *Depression Quest* (referred to only as "you"). These men remained trapped in a small room, alone, their options in life slowly diminishing. What they imagined was their only recourse— a hasty retreat into a world of make-believe, where "old virgins" transformed into "wizards"—was, in fact, the font of all their problems.

Gamergaters claimed they campaigned because they didn't want video games like *Depression Quest* to replace their traditional games. And this was true. *Depression Quest* was a nightmare scenario for them. Instead of logging on to their escapist fantasy world, they found themselves thrust back into the hideous world they were attempting to flee—reality, or at least art that reflected reality so accurately it was horrifying to look upon.

As news of gamergate spread throughout the games industry, the effect was like lifting a floorboard and realizing the entire house was filled with mold. Misogyny had always been a problem for tech. But the nonsense "facts" of gamergate spread by the hate mob, the virulent harassment it inspired, and the sheer number of self-described gamers prying into a female game developer's sex life was a shock to many of the thoughtful and creative people who made games—and who, unlike so many of their customers, lived in the real world.

One of those professionals was Christopher "moot" Poole. For the past several years, the founder of 4chan had been working on a new online community called Canvas, focused around collaborative drawings, as often occurred on /b/ or the drawing sub-board /i/ ("*oekaki*," Japanese for "doodle"). But the start-up had recently collapsed.[7] In the months prior to gamergate, Poole had gone on vacation "to clear his head," traveling throughout Europe and Asia. When he returned to check in on 4chan he found his userbase causing a world of problems.

A few days prior to the Gjoni post, a self-identified "professional nudes trader" arrived on /b/ and dumped thousands of stolen pictures and videos, many of them sexual in nature, hacked from the iPhones of some of the most prominent female celebrities in Hollywood. The incident became known on 4chan as "The Fappening" ("fap" being the sound effect in manga when someone is masturbating) and was soon international news.

It didn't take long before the source of the photos was traced back to 4chan, where the leaks were being perpetually reposted. 4chan had never transformed into a multimillion-dollar corporation like so many other popular sites. But gradually, a few business-minded volunteers and moderators had fine-tuned an advertising system that allowed the site to remain in the black and save some money. Now Poole spent tens of thousands of dollars of 4chan's rainy-day funds on legal fees, as Hollywood stars threatened to sue 4chan out of existence. For the first time in years, it appeared 4chan might fall into the red again and sink for good.

Then gamergate occurred. Faced with dual crises in which his userbase was acting vilely toward women, Poole simply banned all discussion of gamergate sitewide, citing 4chan's rules against personal harassment; anonymous responded with outrage.

In many respects, Poole, now in his early twenties, had outgrown the adolescent sensibilities of the site. anonymous, by contrast, was drifting in the opposite direction, regressing to weird lows that defied common sense. Creative energy, sharp wit, and political movements had been replaced by moody complaints, irrational despair, and conspiracy theories.

The gap between Poole and anon had grown gradually, but gamergate precipitated an abrupt and dramatic break. Poole was pilloried on the site he was spending a fortune to keep afloat. The video game section had been one of the few boards that Poole read regularly. Now the most popular topic of conversation on /v/ was grousing about him, as he was lumped in with the hated Anita, Zoe, and the other public figures who had spoken out against gamergate. Just a few years prior, the entire site had worked tirelessly to make him *Time*'s Person of the Year. Now he was despised as a "SJW shill" and "sellout" who "betrayed us."

As during previous crackdowns, the gamergate ban inspired a

resentful exodus to copycat chans. At the height of the "chan wars" between 2006 and 2008, there had been hundreds of such places. But most had collapsed.

Eventually, the disaffected users settled on 8chan, a site created by none other than Fredrick "HotWheels" Brennan. To Brennan, 8chan had been a programming experiment. Unlike on 4chan, which had a fixed number of boards, 8chan, also known as "infinity chan," allowed users to create their own sub-boards on any topic they pleased, much like Reddit. The effect of combining this capability with customary chan depravity meant 8chan quickly became a rat's nest of weird, unmoderated mini-sites. And Brennan's policies for 8chan were somehow more permissive than 4chan's, even as it ballooned during gamergate from 100 posts per hour to 4,000.[8]

When 4chan rose to fame in 2008, moot had appeared at Ivy League universities and TED Talks to give lectures. Prior to gamergate, Brennan had made only one public appearance, in a short documentary in the Al-Jazeera America series "The Other America." In the piece, he was shown living in Brooklyn, dressed in *Super Mario Brothers* baby pajamas, and supporting himself as a programmer, but struggling with scant public services to help with his disabilities.[9] A *New York Times* story described how he had been mugged while traveling into Manhattan to buy a new wheelchair.

He was nineteen. And when he graduated high school, he was faced with a dilemma. "In the United States, you basically have two choices [for disabled people in my circumstances]," he told me. "You stop working completely or you pay [for] your own private nurse." Determined to be independent, Brennan began working as a "Mechanical Turk," Amazon's digital crowdsourcing service. The job typically pays pennies on the dollar for menial gigs and tasks people request. However, with his programming skills, Brennan managed to make $5,000 in his first year, eventually allowing him to move out of his mother's home in Atlantic City and into his own apartment in Brooklyn.

When the windfall of gamergate occurred, he viewed it shrewdly, as a means of personal escape.[10] "As far as gamergate goes, I don't even play video games . . . Do I regret giving them a place to congregate? I would say yes. There were some incidents that were really terrible, so petty. But this all goes to the question of do I regret creating image boards? I don't know if I regret it, because if I didn't what would have happened to me? If 8chan didn't happen, I probably would have never left the U.S."

Gamergate thrived on 8chan for a year before petering out—sort of. No evidence of SJW cabals or ethics violations in games journalism appeared because these were nonsense concepts. But the gamergate coalition endured. As had occurred during the Scientology protests of 2008, innumerable idle users of 4chan coalesced around a coherent axis of political issues. Gamergaters were anti-feminist, anti–identity politics, anti–social justice warrior, and in some cases, just plain anti-women. They believed that the narrative ought to be inverted: it was they, young white men, who were the marginalized outcasts, who had the true right to claim they were on a depression quest. Like their enemies on the identity-obsessed blogging site Tumblr, they too wanted to express their resentment as a mistreated subgroup. "Lgbt, women, people of color. These three categories, often in the spotlight of cultural debate . . . 'know' why they're oppressed," wrote one wizard in 2013 on Wizardchan. "They have people, communities, etc. [Y]ou [fellow wizards] have witnessed unbearable pain and have had no one to talk to."

In the short term, gamergate achieved an ironic result: it didn't ruin Quinn's and Sarkeesian's careers; rather, it underscored the importance of their work and made them wildly successful. In September, an article about gamergate appeared in the New Yorker. And Quinn and Sarkeesian went before the United Nations to talk about cyber-violence against women.

But in retrospect, gamergate opened up a new chapter for both 4chan and American politics.

By the end of the year, moot had quit his site, selling it to Hiroyuki Nishimura, the founder of 4chan's progenitor 2channel. Nishimura was free because he had lost control of 2channel as it, too, had pivoted to the right.

By 2012, 2channel had been more thoroughly incorporated into mainstream society than 4chan. And the government took notice. In 2013, a scandal erupted when it was revealed that 2channel sold a secret service allowing certain wealthy clients to delete unfavorable posts on the site. One of the secret customers was Japan's then ruling conservative political party, the Liberal Democratic Party. Many speculated that the government had been manipulating 2channel's content because a disturbing drift to the far right was occurring among otaku who spent a lot of time on the site.

2channel's server-hosting company was located in the Philippines, where laws were laxer than in Japan. The servers were owned by middle-aged, right-wing U.S. Navy veteran Jim Watkins. When 2channel began having financial trouble as a result of the controversy, Watkins used the opportunity to seize control of the site, citing its failure to pay its outstanding bills.

Right before Nishimura took over 4chan, Watkins managed to gain control of 8chan as well. As gamergaters migrated from 4chan to 8chan, Brennan was overwhelmed by server costs. He was approached by Watkins, who offered Brennan a job writing code for 2channel (later changed to 5channel) in the Philippines. In exchange, Brennan would sell him 8chan. Brennan agreed immediately because 8chan, like almost all image-based chans, was wildly unprofitable. However, in late 2018, Brennan also fell out with Watkins and left his employment, describing their relationship as "increasingly turbulent."

According to Brennan, it was Watkins' son, an 8chan user, who convinced Watkins to buy the site. "You know how a rich man will own a boat? Just for kicks? It's sort of like that. 8chan is alive because it's a toy. It loses money, but it's fun, I think, for him to have it."

After Poole departed, /pol/ became 4chan's new center of gravity. As much as Poole insisted he never put his hands on the wheel of 4chan's subject matter, in practice this was impossible. He did in fact determine much of the site's culture. When the first split with Anonymous occurred in 2008, it was partly moot's disinterest in politics that kept the site from tilting into political activism.

By contrast, Nishimura's style of running 4chan was shrugging and distant. His famously terse replies were even more abrupt in his limited English. His leadership might best be described as an echo chamber. When users asked elaborate questions about the direction of the site or the addition of certain boards, he would reply, "if u want." "Hiro," as 4chan called Nishimura, would make the site whatever its userbase wanted it to be.

So when the chans at last, in their depravity, turned like Frankenstein's monster on their own creator, they were left with a leadership vacuum. And as gamergate crystalized anons' resentment of feminism and social justice politics into a doctrine, a cottage industry of bloggers and vloggers popped up to fill the void.

Since gamergate was a campaign led by a group of people defined by their poor reality testing and their capacity to be deluded, these figures were often some combination of scam artist and clown, and as such were in a constant jostling state of replacing one another. Many managed to monetize gamergate by bloviating nonstop about the topic on YouTube and collecting ad revenue or by starting crowd-funding campaigns. Most faded from public eye as gamergate died down in 2015. But two bit players managed to successfully pivot from gamergate to a new cause: Donald Trump's presidential campaign.

Mike Cernovich was in his late thirties when gamergate began. He wasn't nerdy enough to play video games, let alone frequent 4chan. He was an unemployed lawyer living in Southern California and looked every bit the part, a disheveled jock who tended to squint and spoke with a lisp.

In a sense, Cernovich's life had been defined by women. When in law school, he had been accused of sexually assaulting an acquaintance. The case was eventually settled, but it prevented him from being admitted to the bar and practicing as a lawyer. He instead lived off his wife's income, who, unlike him, became a successful lawyer. After he divorced her, he lived off the settlement, which he claimed was seven figures. This allowed him to pursue his idle passion: blogging. And oddly, he chose a subject that, given his background, another man might be quick to put behind him: date rape.

His post–law school online journal was a hybrid of legal musings and self-help advice for men. Cernovich resented how he'd been treated by the law after the rape allegations were brought against him, and so he was drawn to the pickup artist (PUA) sector of the manosphere, copying its philosophy on his own blog. In his self-help book, he instructed men to embrace a "gorilla mindset" when interacting with women, to look for ways to exert their will upon women instead of asking for permission. He also counseled men to be "alphas." Betas, he argued, should work on impressing women through their animal-like displays of dominance.

Cernovich probably heard about gamergate through PUA boards. And it was through gamergate that he found a whole new segment of sad males: a surprisingly large population of chan-going men who desperately read any old bromide about what being a man meant.

On his law blog, he went to work tackling the "legal" issues of Quinn's request for a restraining order against Gjoni early on in gamergate, crack jurist reasoning that began by explaining that Quinn was an "alpha female." Gamergate dubbed Cernovich a "based lawyer," even though Cernovich did no legal work whatsoever for the cause outside of PUA-themed blogging and harassing people on Twitter.

The other blogger who rode gamergate to the top of the alt-right bubble was a wildly performative, openly gay British writer named Milo Yiannopoulos. After dropping out of Cambridge, Yiannopoulos had run a tech gossip site called *The Kernal*, which was known predominantly as a vehicle for his unique brand of catty personal attacks.[11] When *The Kernal* was bought by the *Daily Dot* in 2014, Yiannopoulos occupied his time writing for *Breitbart News* on whatever tech-related internet drama he could sniff out. However, tech-blogger gossip wasn't really a subject that held anyone's interest, even other tech bloggers', so when gamergate arrived, it was something of a gift.[12]

Soon Yiannopoulos was composing article after article filled with pro-gamergate invective on *Breitbart*. And through this, he was introduced to 4chan and 8chan. There he discovered his audience, an immense population of disenfranchised young men who were largely voiceless. Though he had next to nothing in common with them, who better to lead them, Yiannopoulos decided, than himself? It was Yiannopoulos who would tell them, as a wizard on Wizardchan wrote in 2013, "why they're oppressed" like other interest groups.

Like Cernovich, Yiannopoulos expressed no interest in video games outside of gamergate and had no connections to the industry (unlike those he attacked). A year later, however, he was explaining and defending "gamer culture" to *OUT* magazine.[13]

"I've never cared about having the hottest, or trendiest, friends," he declared to the reporter as he modeled in a designer blazer for the feature's accompanying photo shoot. "Most of the people I write for and who like me are not particularly fashionable. They may not be the hottest people in the world, they might not be the sexiest or the most socially fluid, but I like them. They're decent, real people, and they are being shat on by everyone else."

Six months after gamergate began, Yiannopoulos left trash talking other tech bloggers for the greener pastures of gamergate. He put his planned book, *The Pathological Narcissism of the Silicon Valley*, on hold and announced a new book on gamergate that he rapturously described as a white whale of tech-blogger gossip. "The biggest internet storm in a decade—a battle [that] has spawned an unprecedented four-and-a-half million tweets, death threats . . . [and] an unending wave of bitchy insults . . . [A] gigantic internet drama."[14]

However, a few months after his announcement, gamergate ran out of steam. Yiannopoulos and Cernovich found themselves rich in a new nerdy audience but short on controversy. And though gamergaters tried their best to search out imaginary ethics violations in games journalism, the topic was getting stale. The same angry resentment that had generated so much something from nothing remained, but it couldn't subsist solely on harassing women in the video game industry forever.

Luckily for all involved, a new controversy soon descended from up on high, inching down the golden escalator of Trump Tower.

Trump the Frog

> They will come in your palace and your bedroom and onto your bed, in the houses of your officials and on your people, and into your ovens and kneading troughs. The frogs will go up on you and your people and all your officials.
>
> —Exodus 8:1–4, as quoted on /pol/ during the 2016 U.S. election

When Trump announced his candidacy on June 16, 2015, from the lobby of his office, his speech condemning Mexicans as "rapists" was considered an offensive publicity stunt. However, it turned out that the politics of offensive publicity stunts aligned in an uncanny way with the vast group of netizens waiting for someone who spoke to their lived experience of racist jokes, screen performances, and garbage ads.

Trump's appeal was partly due to his strange talent for emitting both the bullying signals of an alpha male and an insecure, loser beta, who, no matter how vigorously he scrubbed, could not shed his status as an outsider whose desperation to be accepted among the elite prevented it from ever happening.

By 2015, the grousing denizens of /pol/, /r9k/, and other chans had turned sharp-elbowed, adolescent one-upmanship into an elaborate ideology framing the whole world as a schoolyard. Hypothetical interactions with women were deemed successful by displays of dominance and literal-minded manifestations of status: clothes, cars, looks, height, wealth, and race.

And this worldview was not confined to romantic interactions. When betas peeked out of their basements, all of life seemed to be a teenage pecking order that appeared to exist in accordance with the binary rhythms of a video game, an endless set of competitions to either win or lose. How else could you explain why you were in your mom's basement on your computer? Competition in school transitioned seamlessly into competition in an ever-tightening job market. Treating life like a computerized hierarchy drove the creation of the first generation of otaku and hikikomori in hyper-competitive Japan in the 1980s. And by 2015, it had created a vast new group of hikikomori fixated on competition because they seemed to be forever losing.

Trump's obsession with humiliation (his own and others'), his angry insistence on sorting the world into winners and losers, spoke to all of this. When Trump promised Americans that they would "win so much, you'll get sick of winning," who else was that message directed to but the losers?

This was the alignment that Hannah Arendt argued explained the dawn of fascism, when the "refuse of all classes" and the bourgeois businessmen who would be "flattered at being called power-thirsty animal[s]" agreed on how the world worked, viewing it from a distorted perspective visible from the very top and bottom. To both, the nuances of human interactions, relationships, and communities were abstracted into a cascade of zero-sum games.

And so, ironically, self-declaimed losers found their champions among the winners at the summit of the same hierarchy that they believed ground them underfoot. In similar loop-de-loops of logic, Trump claimed that because he himself had been a special interest donating to political campaigns, he was above special interests. Because he had avoided paying taxes for decades, he was a tax "expert." This reasoning won over not only the down-on-their-luck millionaires of the white working class and the one percenters who knew the rhetoric would ultimately benefit them, but also disenfranchised millennial and Gen X men under forty. Previously, they had not formed into a voting bloc because they considered themselves the failed margins of traditional liberal and conservative parties, struggling to move to the center and exist as either breadwinning family men or chic urban playboys, both of which required the economic success many of them lacked.

Trump skimmed the edges of these groups and formed a new coalition. As a "labyrinth with no center," as the filmmaker Errol Morris called him, he embodied their beliefs in how the world worked—as a series of flickering, promotional lies. What better described a basement with a terminal to an endless set of fantasy worlds than a "labyrinth with no center"? And who better embodied it than a late-night infomercial president?

In the first presidential debate, Hillary Clinton evoked her conservative father to appeal to the electorate. "My father was a small businessman," she said. "He worked really hard . . . And so what I believe is the more we can do for the middle class, the more we can invest in you."

No one noted how wildly outdated Clinton's picture of the average voter was because we were used to politicians holding up the same faded, sixty-five-year-old snapshot. Just as depictions of Christmas on Coke bottles are forever stuck in the 30s and 40s, so we expect politics to be eternally frozen in the 1950s. As a nation defined by its baby boomers, we viewed 1950s America as its idealized form.

But what does the American electorate look like if we put down the snapshot? Peel away how we perceive ourselves from what we actually are? How has that image of a 1950s businessman who owns his own home in the suburbs changed after decades of declining wages, middle-class status, and homeownership?

To younger generations who only had the myth of such jobs, America and perhaps existence itself appeared as a parade of empty promises and advertisements.

Trump made his fortune with casinos, correspondence courses, and pageants, swindling money out of aspiring-millionaire blue-collar workers by selling not even a bill of goods, but the hope of a bill of goods, the glitz and glamour of success to people who don't win, or in Trump's parlance, "don't win anymore." As if once, in the mythic past, they did win and soon would again. At its core, Trump's base were losers still interested in—against the odds dictated by their knowledge or experience—winning.

The older generation of Trump supporters the press often focuses on, the so-called forgotten white working class, are easier to explain since they fit into the 1950s-style electorate schema. Baby boomers were promised pensions and prosperity but received in return only promises. Here, the narrative is simple: workers were promised something and someone (the politicians? the economy? the system itself?) never delivered.

This telling of the story ignores the fact that, as Trump often points out, "it was a bad deal," a promotional lie. And so many of Trump's younger supporters on 4chan held a different sort of ideology. All they believed they could buy with their vote was the promotional campaign itself, the entertainment value of the fantasy world generated by the performance inside the screen. This, after all, was at the heart of the disappointment with Obama. As Naomi Klein had pointed out, Obama's "hope" and "change" had been a brand, an advertising slogan. And when Obama arrived but the promised hope and change never came, there was an inevitable emotional crash.

A generation born from 90s nihilism learned an old lesson anew: the ad was real, but the product wasn't. The screen was more substantial than reality. With the last connections to reality dispelled, twenty-first-century politics was purified into its essence. Young voters chose the candidate who would provide the best entertainment value. And who better to purchase a new ad campaign from than a former reality TV star?

Gamergate was a "consumer revolt" agitating for a fundamental right to be deceived by corporations in the ways that most pleased them. And Trump, too, as the prince of puffery, was an invocation of the same right—to choose the liar, the fantasy, the troll.

And as a bonus, he was what the beta losers wanted to be: a winner who presented access to the winner's world while somehow also being a loser like them. Boorish, brash, and ill-mannered, he was, to his fans' delight, an insult to everyone.

Like the offensive images trolls inserted into the media or on hacked websites, he spat in the faces of the self-satisfied, arrogant people at the top of society who had left them out. A loser crusader come to bring loserdom and lies to the homes of winners.

And soon, 4chan's emblem of owning your status as an offensive beta loser merged with Trump's campaign.

Trump became Pepe the Frog.

The Pepe meme had been floating around the internet for nearly a decade. But 2015 proved to be a banner year for the sad frog. His newfound popularity came from his ancient spawning ground, 4chan.org.

As /r9k/ robots posted and reposted Pepes to playfully mock their status as grotesque outsiders whose very visage was disturbing to "normies," they ushered in a renaissance of frogs that soon appealed to all the netizens who every year had a little more in common with withdrawn, internet-soaked hikikomori.

When Pepe memes exploded into the thousands in 2015, this in and of itself became a meme as users pretended to stockpile "rare" images of

Pepe as they might collect gems or stamps. Robots placed USB drives full of Pepes up for sale on eBay. Subreddits orbited around memes' "future markets," the joke being that the meme generation had neither the wealth of the past nor all the grandiose promises of the future, but was simply worthless scraps of rehashed media in a world obsessed with meaningless accumulation. Or, as one of the most popular memes of 2015 put it, "Born too late to explore the world . . . Born too early to explore the galaxy . . . Born just in time to explore dank memes."[1]

At first the game was make-believe. However, the advent of cryptocurrencies soon allowed the internet to fulfill its ultimate dream—to render an online joke a reality. The 4chan meme "doge," a cute, clueless Shiba Inu, already enjoyed his own virtual security—Dogecoin. And eventually, alt-coin PepeCash would power art auctions of rare Pepes using blockchain. And this, in turn, would fuel the viral success of a man claiming to have made a fortune trading Pepe crypto, "PepeCashMillionaire," as he came to be known on Twitter and Instagram.

Though the rare-Pepe meme extended well into 2017, its initial success meant that Pepe, like so many memes before him, had escaped 4chan and was now coming into vogue as a pop-culture symbol. Nicki Minaj posted a female Pepe with her butt in the air on Instagram. Katy Perry tweeted a crying Pepe while complaining about her jet lag.

As they had since the mid-aughts, 4chan resented "normies stealing our memes." Robots attempted to pull Pepe out of the chute of the entertainment complex by inventing "peepeepoopoo Pepe," depicting a gelatinous Pepe leaking bodily fluids. But to no avail. In 2015, the scatological was far too tame to prevent corporate media co-optation.

"What's your reaction going to be when Pepe eventually gets on a TV commercial or show?" went a typical /r9k/ lament.

The irony was that things like PepeCash were so popular because they mocked Pepe's inevitable transubstantiation into a commodity. Pepe, a symbol of the worthless everywhere, had been born of counterculture's helpless disgust with the cycle. The left-leaning artist Matt Furie had come up with the idea for Pepe while working in a junk shop, sorting through the garbage of old knickknacks and action figures. In one page from Furie's original *Boy's Club* comic, Pepe stares vacantly at the TV. "What are you watching?" his roommates ask him. "Commercials," he replies, the joke being that Pepe vibes out on the dregs and enjoys the packaging as much as what's inside. But here it was happening nonetheless. It seemed Pepe, un-usurpable garbage commodity, would soon simply be Pepe garbage commodity.

That is, until 4chan, ever the pop-culture meme alchemists, at last discovered the secret ingredient that would render the frog poisonous— Donald Trump.

Soon after Trump announced his candidacy in the summer of 2015, /pol/ and /r9k/ produced a few Donald Trump Pepes, depicting him as "smug Pepe," the loser candidate who would represent their issues, and then smug Pepe locking immigrants out of the United States (depicted as wojaks).

And incredibly, on October 13, 2015, Trump himself retweeted /pol/'s depiction of him as Pepe along with /pol/'s tag line, "You can't stump the Trump." Calling it to the attention of *Breitbart News* and the *Drudge Report*, he linked the image to a raucous meme-ified YouTube video that remixed his performance at the recent Republican debate with dance music, Illuminati jokes, and audio clips from a documentary about a centipede with killer pinchers.[2]

Trump's October 13, 2015, tweet.

The Trump-Pepe association that so delighted Trump didn't stick at the time. However, a few months later, Trump would fuse with Pepe for all eternity in a matter of hours.

The conversion of Pepe from loser frog to hate symbol happened on January 7, 2016, at around seven in the evening. It began when cable news pundit and "Never Trump" establishment conservative Cheri Jacobus noticed the strange connection between Pepe and the trolls harassing her on Twitter gamergate-style.

Jacobus didn't understand anything about 4chan, /pol/, or even gamergate, but she saw that Pepe appeared frequently in the nasty comments from young Trump supporters that appended her tweets.

"The green frog symbol is what white supremacists use in their propaganda. U don't want to go there," she tweeted at a colleague.[3]

The statement was both valid and ridiculous. Pepe had not yet been successfully co-opted by /pol/. On January 7, 2016, what proved to be Pepe's last innocent day on earth, he was just a silly cartoon frog.

At first, the response to Jacobus' statement was mockery. Many were delighted at the notion of nonsense internet culture being elevated to political discourse. Pepe had always been a symbol of contempt expressing how the world was a milieu of byte-size media garbage. Where else did he belong but in digital garbage—in this case, the naive Twitter speculations of a second-tier media pundit?

However, others insisted there *was* an association, citing articles about white supremacists rejoicing at the hordes of Twitter accounts with Pepe avatars. Somewhere on the internet, the link was being made. But no one, at least on Twitter, could say where; though this secret chamber happened to be the Pepe meme's hatchery, the original source of his meme-ification, 4chan.org.

Within an hour of Jacobus' Pepe tweet, someone had posted it to /pol/. And to /pol/ocks, the next step seemed obvious. They wanted to make the connection real, and so they began flooding Jacobus with the most offensive, racist, and pro-Trump Pepe memes they could scrape from the bottom of the chans: Trump-loving Pepes gripping assault rifles; Pepes with swastikas on their foreheads, Manson-style; smug Pepes in yarmulkes watching the twin towers fall.

Jacobus rewarded the trolls who sent the most shocking images by retweeting them to prove her point, cementing the connection /pol/ wanted to make: that Pepe was indeed a white supremacist symbol. And as a bonus, each tweet flung the filthiest Pepes /pol/ could devise into Jacobus' followers' social media feeds, the "cuckservative" Republican establishment.

The threads on /pol/ and then /r9k/ filled with a frenetic creative energy that only occurred in the rare instance when something was actually happening on the boards.

A YouTube video compilation made by a 4chan fan depicted the most gleeful replies:

pepe will be reclaimed from normies in your lifetime

>/r9k/ tries shitty memes to take pepe from normies
>all it really takes is pepe for Trump

TOP FUCKING KEK

we've got him back, lads
'Pee pee poo poo' didn't do it
But Trump got him back for us

Absolutely BASED

Is there anything this man can't do?

one part wants to run with and see how far we can take it.
the other part thinks it might be bad for Trump

we need more people to send her racist peepees. we need an anti woman one now. that will probably double trigger her.

>being this shoe on head retarded to think a caricature of a frog is racist

4chan stealing back its meme?
I thought I would never see the day

>Pepe now too hot for normies to handle

"trump's white supremacists adopted the meme"-jacobus

>/pol/ literally trolling and writing national political history
>mfw [my face when] i'm part of it all

someone link this thread over at /r9k/
inform them we are saving pepe & that they should contribute
HURRY FAGGOTS
THERE IS NO TIME TO WASTE[4]

The drama ended when Mike Cernovich stepped onto the stage, the gorilla-minded missing link between the chanverse and the credulous internet conspiracists of *InfoWars*, who lapped up any invention the trolls could concoct.

Echoing gamergate, Cernovich asserted that Jacobus was harassing herself in a "false flag" operation.

When the dust settled, the chanverse had succeeded in associating Pepe with both white supremacy and Donald Trump—a connection that would soon be championed and promoted not only by Trump, but his longtime confidant and political adviser.

It was not all kismet and /pol/ that joined the betas to Trump and Trump to Pepe. Below the meta-connections of mass culture, there was in fact an earthly human link between Trump's campaign and the gamergaters. When Trump first retweeted an image of himself depicted as Pepe, he mentioned *Breitbart News*. And this was because the transition from gamergate to Pepe-splattered Trump campaign would have likely never occurred if not for Milo Yiannopoulos' boss at *Breitbart*, Steve Bannon.

Steve Bannon: Nerd out of Time

Agrippa crosses to Brutus and grabs his crotch.

AGRIPPA: Hey motherfucker, you. What you think you? As the great dick of this . . . assembly

BRUTUS: Did you call me a . . .

AGRIPPA: A dick.

BRUTUS: You motherfucker . . .

Agrippa grabs Brutus' crotch a second time.

—Opening scene from Steve Bannon's unsold 1990s screenplay for a hip-hop musical, *The Thing I Am*

Steve Bannon took a peculiar career path to politics. A conservative Catholic baby boomer from suburban Virginia, he had begun his adult life in the Navy, before transitioning into a career as an investment banker at Goldman Sachs. From there, he moved to Hollywood, where he traded in film rights and aspired to be a writer and filmmaker. Although his fictional screenplays were nightmarishly bad, he experienced some limited success producing proto-historical far-right documentaries after experiencing a 9/11-changed-everything radical conversion.

During this period, he often worked with David Bossie, who aspired to make films in the style of leftist activist Michael Moore, only for the right. One of these experiments, *Hillary: The Movie*, became the center of the 2010 *Citizens United v. Federal Election Commission* Supreme Court case. When Bossie's partisan film was challenged by the Federal Election Commission as a campaign contribution, the Supreme Court issued a surprisingly broad ruling: corporations counted as people and therefore had free speech rights. The judgment gutted campaign finance law and opened a floodgate of unregulated corporate money that poured into politics, much of which would flow to Bannon in 2016.

And it was in the realm of conservative filmmaking that Bannon met Andrew Breitbart, who ran a far-right clickbait website of news chunklets in the style of *Buzzfeed* called *Breitbart News*. Impressed, Bannon began working for *Breitbart* before taking over the business after the founder's sudden death from a heart attack in 2012.

Like Trump, Bannon had the cheesy whiff of memes about him, where, on the fringes of money grubbing capitalism, serious businessmen were steeped in the same silly excesses of pop-culture scraps drizzled on consumers. Bannon had sponsored Biosphere 2 (not the Pauly Shore movie, but the actual project) and made a fortune when he acquired subsidiary rights to reruns of *Seinfeld*, more by accident than design.

An aesthetic of excess united Trump and Bannon. For the doubly eager outsider Trump, it was fine suits worn badly with too-long ties. For Bannon, instead of wearing a jacket he simply layered several polo shirts on top of each other for a casual jock-going-off-his-rocker look. Both of them sported overdone duck-tailed 80s hair. All of this created an outlandish impression of someone representing a not quite right, doubled-up, mocking copy of someone else.

Bannon's personal motto was based on a meme: "Honey Badger Doesn't Give a Shit," a line from a viral YouTube video in which a comedian overdubs a nature documentary about an aggressive honey badger rampaging his way through nature's thorny problems in a series of vicious frontal attacks.[1]

In his 2017 book *Devil's Bargain*, Joshua Green describes Bannon as he first encountered him in 2011, as "a recognizable Washington character type: the political grifter seeking to profit from the latest trend." Though Trump later claimed "Steve Bannon has nothing to do with me or my Presidency" after a falling-out in January 2018, Green details how Bannon began advising Trump on a potential presidential run as far back as 2012 and soon became a key figure who shaped his strategy.[2]

When Bannon encountered Yiannopoulos in the backwaters of hyperconservative punditry in 2013, he recognized him as a fellow Honey Badger, smitten by the histrionic title of Yiannopoulos' never-to-be-written book *The Pathological Narcissism of the Silicon Valley*.[3]

Bannon hired Yiannopoulos just before the young blogger discovered his vast new audience of "shat-upon" gamers. Neither Bannon nor

Yiannopoulos likely had ever heard of 4chan or 8chan at that point. But Bannon was very familiar with gamers.

From 2007 to 2012, he had been the CEO of a multimillion-dollar video game gold-farming scheme.[4] "Gold farming" was a term for hiring third-world laborers to do the same repetitive tasks in massively multiplayer online role-playing games (MMORPGs) to acquire in-game currency. Eventually, the virtual gold, minerals, armor, real estate, or whatever it may be can be sold for real American dollars to gamers who don't want to work to earn in-game items. The self-proclaimed anti-globalist Bannon ran the scheme by subcontracting Chinese labor. According to *Wired* writer Julian Dibbel, who visited one of the Chinese business partners who employed miners for Bannon's company in 2009, the digital laborers "slept upstairs on plywood bunks, day-shift workers sat in the hot, dimly lit workshop." They earned about four dollars a day with eighty-four-hour workweeks.[5]

In a sense, Bannon's scheme was a continuation of the nihilistic virtual adventures of the griefers and goons from Something Awful in the 90s as they cruelly hacked their way to profit in *EVE Online* or on AOL. Except that Bannon's scheme was performed in deadly earnest. And it was a failure. Bannon had taken over the company from its founder, Brock Pierce, a former child actor from *D2: The Mighty Ducks* and *First Kid*. Bannon had been brought on board to raise $60 million in Goldman Sachs seed money. But when the operation began to falter, the wary investors replaced Pierce with Bannon. However, unlike Pierce, Bannon knew next to nothing about gaming and drove the operation straight into the ground.

Gamers, as a rule, despise gold farming. Green describes how Bannon's business made him aware of not only gamers but their tenacity when they sued his company. But by 2014, when Yiannopoulos linked up with the same population via gamergate, Bannon thought he could use gamers as he had used his Chinese gold farmers. "I realized Milo could connect with these kids right away," he explained. "You can activate that army. They come in through gamergate or whatever and then get turned onto politics and Trump."[6]

But Bannon also shared a profound spiritual affinity with gamers, one stronger, in fact, than Yiannopoulos' superficial connection.

It was this core aspect of Bannon's character that had led him to gold farming in *World of Warcraft* in the first place. And it is best understood by noting that Bannon and /pol/, prior to their first meeting, shared (and still share) a favorite philosopher, Julius Evola.

In 2016, the *New York Times* ran a short piece on Bannon's puzzling fascination with an obscure midcentury Italian writer named Julius Evola and a related philosopher in the so-called Traditionalist School, René Guénon.[7] Bannon often mentioned Evola fondly, which was strange considering the philosopher had collaborated with the Nazis until the regime got sick of him. After the war, Evola escaped prosecution by explaining that he was not a fascist, but rather a "super-fascist," his saving grace being that he was critical of the fascists for not going far enough to extinguish modernism, women's rights, and democracy.[8]

Little has been written about Bannon's affinity for Evola partly because the writer's work is difficult to process, not so much reasoned-out philosophy as mystical gobbledygook. Consider this typical passage from one of Evola's more popular books, often on /pol/'s "required reading list," *Men Among the Ruins*:

> The State is under the masculine aegis, while "society" and, by extension, the people, or demos, are under the feminine aegis. Once again, this is a primordial truth. The maternal domination, from which the political-virile principle subtracts itself, was also understood as the domination of Mother Earth and the Mothers of life and fertility, under whose power and tutelage existence was believed to unfold in its physical, biological, and collective-material aspects. The common mythological background is that of the duality of the luminous and heavenly deities, who are the gods of the political and heroic world on the one hand, and of the feminine and maternal deities of naturalistic existence, who were loved by the plebeian strata of society on the other hand.

Where is it found that "demos" is "under the feminine aegis" and is a "primordial truth"? Certainly nowhere in the Greek texts from which Evola plucked "demos" and "aegis." In fact, the word "demos" is masculine in Ancient Greek, as were, of course, Greek democracies. To make sense of what he is talking about we should first note that Evola categorizes nearly everything as something like an aegis. If it is not an ancient shield, it is a spear, or a harsh warrior's trial, or a clan. Indeed, Evola was a type occasionally encountered in scholarship, the latency-period boy trapped in the skin of a man, rooting through history to move around tin soldiers, be they Roman legions, conquering satraps, or Japanese samurai. The core of his philosophy was that the foundational pillar of civilization, man's primordial warrior spirit, was being debased by modern effeminate culture.

Evola worked as a sort of comparative mythologist, though not a scientific-minded one. Rather, he was a mystic. He imagined myths held ancient "primordial truths," practical guides for living in a wise and traditional manner, but also sublime, unutterable, and transcendent wisdom, singular and obscure, "world myths" that could be sussed out not by dissecting the past, but by venerating it. He did not so much present arguments as appeals to what he felt were eternal ideals hiding under "world myths."

And what did all of these gut feelings he interpreted as universal verities have to do with "luminous," virile man-gods freeing themselves from the "domination" of divine "Mothers"?

In a metaphor Evola himself might appreciate, it is easy to cut through this Gordian knot by simply noting that the sage produced these endless unscholarly passages on men "subtract[ing]" themselves from women while living most of his life as a bachelor with his mother.

Indeed, this is the same skeleton key that unlocks why hordes of gamergaters suddenly fought a nonsense war against people they deemed to be feminist *warriors* of social justice. Or why gamers, trapped Evola-like "in their mother's basements," are obsessed with RPG-inflected concepts of masculinity.

Beneath Bannon's career as a producer was a deeper ambition to become a screenwriter in the style of Evola, telling fables about bellicose men establishing civilizations, an interest that eventually led him to fantasy-themed video games. His production company, Glittering Steel, which funded *Brietbart*, Yiannopoulos' tour, and Cambridge Analytica, was sword-themed, as were most of his proposed movies. His most prominent success in Hollywood was a film adaptation of Shakespeare's bloodiest play, the sword-and-sandals drama *Titus Andronicus*. However, Bannon's screenplays were often too bizarre, hyper-masculine, and apocalyptic even for Hollywood. As a companion from his mostly failed screenwriting days recalled, "He was constantly telling stories about great warriors of the past, like Attila the Hun, people who had slain empires."[9]

After the 2016 election, journalists continually reminded their readers that when Bannon said "winter is coming" to express his political

philosophy, he did not mean *Game of Thrones*, the sword-and-sorcery
TV show that flattened out the spiritually obsessed Middle Ages into a
deterministic, gore-smeared video game. After all, Bannon's screenplays
read like a cheesier version of *Game of Thrones*. "One is VOLUMNIA,
dragon-lady mother of Marcius," began one of Bannon's character de-
scriptions in his mid-90s attempt to combine ancient Roman history and
the L.A. riots into a hip-hop musical. "A proud lioness, statuesque,
regal—'Madame X' of South Central. 'Abandon hope all ye who fuck
with her!'"[10]

But the alignment was slightly more than coincidence. Evolian warrior philosophy connected Bannon's historical theories to the near-
duplicate philosophy expressed on popular fantasy TV shows. Bannon's
"winter is coming" statement derived from a line in one of his documentaries, *Generation Zero*, an adaptation of a modern book called *The
Fourth Turning*, which uses number-crunching to shoehorn the nuances
of human behavior into a facile set of game theory–like rules full of "archetypes" and cyclical mystical ages called "turnings."[11]

In *The Origins of Totalitarianism*, Hannah Arendt carefully traces the
font of such ideas and their relationship to race-based thinking through
the Comte de Gobineau and Oswald Spengler. These efforts are characterized by an effort to enshrine a generally accepted opinion among the
nobility "into a full-fledged historical doctrine, claiming to have detected
the secret law of the fall of civilizations and to have exalted history to
the dignity of a natural science."[12] Evola was not significant enough to
mention in her survey, but he falls under the same category.

In the 1930s, Evola and Spengler relied on early nineteenth-century
romantic fiction for their interpretations of history as a series of exciting bloody battles punctuated by magic and sex. These ideas found their
way into the Nazis' obsession with mysticism, Richard Wagner, and Teu-
tonic Knights, ushering in a new but somehow also ancient cyclical age
called the Third Reich. By the twenty-first century, the same apocryphal
but entertaining swashbuckling vision of the past that the Romantics had
invented had worked its way through the late Romantic heroic adventure novels of Edgar Rice Burroughs and Rafael Sabatini to superhero
comic books of the 1930s, fantasy novels of the 1970s, and finally to
the HBO soap operas and Xbox games of the 2000s.

There was hardly any difference between the video game–style plot
of *Game of Thrones* and what Bannon meant: Human conflict is assumed

to be as natural and inevitable as the seasons. The West (Westeros) will be besieged by foreigners (despite an enormous wall built to keep them out), and civilization will crumble in an all-consuming war because every leader cannot help but pursue selfish interests.[13] These thoughts were barely an inch away from the blinkered ideology of the gamers who viewed all of life as a succession of competitions. Bannon's philosophy, like that of his meme-soaked companions on 4chan, was composed of scraps of Romantic fiction.

In other words, though both Evola and Bannon imagined themselves men of the warrior past, they might be better understood as figures born *before* their time, historical outliers from the vast populations of early twenty-first-century gamers.

In Evola's work we find the content of all the games that self-described gamers sought to defend in gamergate, in which men (when they were dressed as supereffective barbarians, chieftains, warlocks, and pirates) were men and women (when they were monsters to be tamed, or prizes to be collected) were women.

Evola's texts read like a potpourri of the heroes, mysticism, and adventure that are mashed into comic books, unsold Bannon screenplays, and PlayStation 4 games in which gods from Asia battle trolls from Norway for ancient scrolls devised by Christian demons guarded by Greek centaurs.

It's easy to see why Evola appealed to gamergaters. Gamers spend their lives absorbing fantasy stories of unfettered masculine heroes wandering the earth wild and free. And it seems only natural that they eventually regard their romanticized escapism as what all that Hollywood art works so hard to convince its audience it is—a lost ideal that must have been very real in a vanished past.

Gamers and fantasy consumers then reasoned that in this fictional past, they would not have been entrapped by video games in their moms' basements. They would have been wandering actual moors as ax-wielding Scottish chieftains, not digital ones. And like the fable-soaked Evola, they blamed modernism for their debased condition.

How is this puerile veneration of a vanished warrior lifestyle possibly connected to fascism? It was a reaction to the same modern consumerist nihilism that unmoored the gamergaters from any context in their lives.

We often regard fascism, like racism and fundamentalism, as a perennial evil that must be trimmed back each time it grows. But as Hannah Arendt points out, fascism emerged seemingly ex nihilo in the 1930s as a brand-new idea that devoured the globe in less than a decade. Both fascism and Evola's obsession with tradition were knee-jerk reactions to the extreme changes that had occurred in the first part of the twentieth century, as modernity unraveled ancient modes of existence almost overnight.

For example, Japan in the early 1930s was undergoing such a crisis as guidelines for society dissolved in the pleasures of Western consumerism and new modes of living. As the historian Ian Toll put it:

> There was a craze for all things Western, especially among the city's huge population of university students. Young men (and even more scandalously, women) wore Western clothing and Western hairstyles, smoked Western cigarettes and drank Western cocktails. They whiled away the hours in cafés and nightclubs. They listened to jazz and learned how to dance. They watched the films of Charlie Chaplin and Buster Keaton. They steeped themselves in Western literature and philosophy. They argued the merits of alien creeds like feminism and Marxism.[14]

It was during this period that Japan invented the hyper-depraved comic book genre of *guro*, sexualized stories about women being chopped into bits. And it is no coincidence that guro was one of the first boards added to 4chan in 2003. As in Japan in the 1930s or 4chan in 2012, fascism arises in places where modern consumerist hedonism has pushed people so far out to sea that they swim desperately to the terra firma of traditional values (mixed in with a great deal of apocryphal past-themed fiction).

4chan often functioned as an object lesson in the limits of liberalism's invitation to invent one's own moral compass. Could one really say everyone ought to live any odd way they pleased when the boards filled up, each day, with lifestyles that were so grotesque they, at the very least, nudged up against the bounds of infinite tolerance?

I recall times when my own tolerance was challenged as I browsed the boards. For example, in a now-infamous thread from 2010, a man began posting pictures of creepy dolls that filled his house. They were human size, svelte, and female, and all had different animal faces with snouts that were a cross between Miss Piggy and an old-fashioned teddy bear. Some were dressed in skimpy underwear, others in cheerleading outfits. The images were so weird that even 4chan, den of freaks, freaked out.

As the anon kept posting, it became clear that he did not possess simply a room full of the dolls, but a house populated with thousands of them. They slept in bunk beds, sat at tables, and lined every wall. Moreover, the man had a family. His wife and young children lived among the dolls in this house. Many of the photos were of normal family activities. Here his wife and children were eating, there they were watching TV on the couch, except in each scene of domestic tranquility were limp knots of human-size rag people strewn about like seaweed.

Eventually an anon asked what everyone else was thinking, "Do you have sex with the dolls?" To which he responded, "Well I never 'fuck' them. I made them and as such I am their god and can instill my will upon them. I have a wife and children who also enjoy our times in the 'fantasy room' but it is nothing bad or wrong."[15]

It was moments like these that threatened to break the old liberal countercultural perception that letting people live as they pleased was always the right answer. Viewing things like that, one had to at least consider the possibility that not all moralities were equal. And that there was perhaps an objectively right and wrong way to live, and that, well, it should be enforced.

Oddly enough, Bannon and his protégé Yiannopoulos became a sort of yin and yang, representing both sides of this extreme, but also demonstrating where the two opposites met.

Yiannopoulos was the professed classic 4chan nihilist of Western extremism, a champion of untraditional sexual adventures, fame-seeking, and decadence. He encouraged his fans to indulge in consumerism, play video games, abandon real women, and masturbate to pornography. On tour, Yiannopoulos built shrines to Mariah Carey, bought $30,000 jackets, and demanded endless buckets of de-skinned KFC chicken.[16]

Bannon was just an inch further along this scale, because a half-step after Yiannopoulos' hyper-modernist nihilism came repentance—a fundamentalist veneration of strict and unequivocal stoic tradition derived from the ancients (or what the ancients were imagined to be like by unscholarly, fantasy-obsessed men like Evola).

The contradiction of Yiannopoulos or 4chan embracing a fundamentalist libertinism is better understood by placing them on the edge of a graph of liberal permissiveness where the model finally breaks down—occupying the very limits of the spectrum in the "creepy-doll guy zone" (aka, the 4chan zone). Yiannopoulos and 4chan abuse their modern liberal liberties so frequently by living a life dedicated to weird pornography, consumerist gratifications, etcetera that the device finally breaks from constant use.

These are old themes that arose with liberalism in the nineteenth century. And indeed, Yiannopoulos often alludes to the nineteenth-century figures who explored them before they were labeled "accelerationist" by twenty-first-century libertarian tech bros. (In the accelerationist schema, popular among nerds who got it from science fiction, modern problems are exacerbated to cause a collapse that will allow society to be rebuilt from scratch. "Just like in *Star Trek*," as one longtime 4chan user put it to me.) This Bannon/Yiannopoulos duality was perhaps best expressed by the nineteenth-century French writer Joris-Karl Huysmans, whose novel *À Rebours* ("Against Nature") defined the decadence genre that meditated on the death of Western civilization. Huysmans was so repelled by the emptiness of modern Western life, he eventually abandoned writing for an existence devoted to fundamentalist Catholicism.

This same theme was mirrored in the far-right French novelist Michel Houellebecq's 2014 novel *Submission*, in which a Huysmans scholar at the Sorbonne lives a hollow life of diversion, sex, and modern pleasures (ordering sushi, sleeping with his students, etc.) in a near-future Paris. However, he finds it all to be a sad dead end. The professor's plans echo those of Huysmans' protagonist in *À Rebours*. When a fundamentalist Islamic party is voted into power (having won narrowly over Marine Le Pen's fascist National Front), the scholar schedules a half-fulfilled trip out of his life before abandoning the project. In this, the character follows the protagonist of *À Rebours*, who launches a similar failed attempt to flee his decadent existence in Paris. Both characters arrive at what they feel is the final cul-de-sac of the dissolute West. The main character in *Submission* converts to fundamentalist Islam as Huysmans converted to fundamentalist Catholicism. Echoing Huysmans' apostasy against the life of a liberated writer, Houellebecq implies that the future of Western culture is a dead-end loop back into the Middle Ages. And in a larger sense, the protagonist is a metaphor for France itself, as both reach a point of helpless despair in a narrative that has them surrendering to a foreign value system.

This metaphorical device is often used in alt-right rhetoric, in which a personal crisis of liberal dissolution is extended to apply to the West as a whole, which is seen as "committing suicide" by letting in immigrants. As Yiannopoulos spoke on those exact same anti-immigrant talking points, he was also performing the associated personal libertinism that is the traditional conservative's nightmare scenario. And this duality eventually was his undoing.

Though Yiannopoulos imagined he was cutting-edge by diving into the void with buckets of diet chicken and praise for sex machines, he was in fact a little behind the curve. After Trump's ascension to the presidency, the conservative establishment managed to knock Yiannopoulos off his media pedestal by digging up his statements countenancing manboy love. But the "fans" Yiannopoulos had hastily claimed ownership of post-gamergate used the opportunity to abandon him for a different reason.

Yiannopoulos' celebration of retreat was bad life advice. Gamers soon preferred the Bannon/Evola philosophy: the rigid structure of hyperconservative values. In 2017, Yiannopoulos would be replaced by a new youth figure, a Harvard-educated clinical psychologist named Jordan Peterson whose philosophy regarding traditional values and male domination founding civilization echoed Evola's.

Peterson's first book, *Maps of Meaning*, expressed the same unscholarly, simplistic thesis as Evola. According to Peterson, all myths were moral and could be used to guide "how a human being should act." Furthermore, order, as expressed in myth, is masculine, represented by the "Wise King" and the "Tyrant," and chaos is feminine.[17]

To make this absurd generalization, Peterson ignores not only hundreds of years of far more nuanced scholarship on the topic of myths and morality, but primary sources. A constellation of counterexamples exists that would take an eternity to list. Suffice it to say, schoolkids might recall that in the second book of *The Republic*, Plato explicitly states that Greek myths make for incredibly poor moral instruction and proposes that all myths be rewritten. Or that one of the most famous goddesses of all, Athena, is a female deity who represents law and order.

After Peterson inherited Yiannopoulos' audience of betas, he published the bestselling *12 Rules for Life* in 2018. The self-help book is based on a popular post Peterson made on Quora, a Reddit-style site infamous for being a place where literal-minded computer programmers go for basic life advice. And indeed, the book offers just that, explicit instructions for how to exist, accompanied by a /pol/-style, loopy, cruel-minded philosophy.

For example, to justify rule number one—"Stand Up Straight with Your Shoulders Back"—Peterson makes an argument for social Darwinism, suggesting that human beings are equivalent to animals. Just as songbirds, chickens, and lobsters organize themselves into "pecking orders," so too, he asserts, do human beings. "If you're a number one, the highest level of status, you're an overwhelming success," he writes. "If you're male, you have preferential access to the best places to live and the highest-quality food. People compete to do you favors. You have limitless opportunity for romantic and sexual contact. You are a successful lobster, and the most desirable females line up and vie for your attention."[18]

He further asserts that from "a Darwinian perspective" all of civilization is a "pecking order" in which a disproportionate amount of wealth will always accrue to a privileged 1 percent. In fact, Darwin often argued against the facile analogy Peterson was making, which was derived from the common-minded prejudice that accompanies the mindset of big business, not science. Darwin asserted that human beings were distinguished by their capacity for compassion. Their natures, like those of many primates, were bent toward caring for others in a community, particularly the weak and sick.[19]

But before Yiannopoulos was replaced by Peterson, he would go on a weird roller-coaster ride of ultra-fame and disgrace. The adventure began in early 2016, when he started work on an article that attempted to survey all of the Trump-supporting internet coalitions calling themselves the alt-right.

#War on the Sea Owl

These guys, these rootless white males, had monster power.
—Steve Bannon

In 2016, the term "alt-right" referred to someone on the far right who possessed contempt for the traditional conservatives of the Republican Party. This included anti-globalist fundamentalists like Bannon, opposed to how the Republicans colluded with corporations for globalized free trade. Others were radical accelerationist tech bros in the style of Peter Thiel, who wanted to demolish our present society by pushing extreme laissez-faire capitalism to its limits.

But tapping into this new vein of young internet conservatives was problematic. The alt-right also included a great number of fascists. Some alt-right groups were explicitly fascist, while others were coy, from crypto-fascist deniers to free-market libertarians who claimed to be coolly examining the "scientific" issue of race-based hierarchy. Many mainstream Republicans wouldn't go near them. But for Bannon and Yiannopoulos, a grassroots pro-Trump youth movement couldn't be ignored. They tried their best to separate out the fascist elements as marginal, but this proved to be a difficult task.

The alt-right consisted of three large subgroups with a lot of overlap. First, there were Yiannopoulos' fans, the hordes of right-wing young men on 4chan, 8chan, and the rest of the manosphere—a mix of hard-core fascists, racists, libertarians, men's right activists, and betas.

Then there were the older Nazi groups that had endured in the margins of American society and the street-brawling neo-Nazi groups on sites like the *Daily Stormer*.

Finally, there was a subgroup of oddball suit-wearing white supremacists who imagined themselves intellectuals. This organization was the most cohesive. It had a name, the New Century Foundation; a magazine, *American Renaissance*; and was led by Yale-educated academic Jared Taylor, who argued that whites were scientifically superior to blacks. His de facto protégé Richard Spencer had largely invented the term "alt-right" in 2010 when he registered the URL alternativeright.com.

Spencer was a crank who predated the phenomenon of the alt-right, not so much a visionary as a lucky weirdo who had his boat pushed up by the rising tide. Arguably, the only force that had marginalized Spencer was his own unhinged ideas. He was a silver-spoon Republican who tipped so far to the right he ended up an explicit white nationalist, debating the pseudoscience of race-based theories with other *American Renaissance* writers. Before dropping out to begin a career in white nationalism, Spencer had pursued a PhD in philosophy at Duke University, where he was friends with other vocal campus conservatives, among them Trump administration official Stephen Miller (though Miller denies the association).[1] Spencer arrived at his cutting-edge insight that the antebellum South had the right idea about race relations from a familiar old perch. He is the heir to a large Southern cotton farm fortune.[2]

In the uncanny way that the original dimwitted Nazis on the margins of society pretended to be erudite gentlemen rather than armchair cranks, so too did members of Taylor's New Century Foundation aspire to be intellectuals. They held "seminars" in ballrooms, where white nationalists gathered as if dressed for a wedding. YouTube videos capturing these occasions are somewhat comical to watch, as Spencer ascends a podium beneath a convention center chandelier, welcomes an open-minded audience interested in hearing new ideas, then promptly begins expounding on how all his enemies are ugly hairy monkeys, especially the women.

At the end of March, Yiannopoulos completed his survey of these groups with the help of a ghostwriter, Allum Bohkari. The result was an oft-cited long-form piece in *Breitbart* titled "An Establishment Conservative Guide's to the Alt-Right," illustrated with several Trump-as-Pepe memes culled from the chans and the subreddit /r/TheDonald. The article was edited by Bannon, who was delighted it mentioned Evola.[3]

To distance the alt-right from fascists, Yiannopoulos and Bohkari divided it into four categories: "intellectuals"; "natural conservatives"; the "meme team"; and the "1488ers," the alt-right neo-Nazis (1488 being a common coded reference to white supremacy and "Heil Hitler"). Leaked emails later revealed that the authors hoped to legitimize the burgeoning movement by splitting the alt-right into subgroups and dismissing the neo-Nazis as the least important.[4]

In reality, each of the article's four spurious categories contained a significant portion of white supremacists. The "intellectuals" the piece cited were Richard Spencer and *American Renaissance*. "Natural conservatives" was an illusory classification for which the piece presented no concrete examples. The meme team consisted of 4chan and 8chan. And the authors neglected to mention how threads that expressed pro-Nazi sentiment appeared on these sites daily, if not hourly.

When Yiannopoulos' emails leaked to *Buzzfeed* in 2017, they revealed how he had used the piece to strengthen his ties with the same fascist groups he affected a distaste for in his writing. Yiannopoulos let the neo-Nazi Andrew "weev" Auernheimer review and comment on multiple drafts of the article. And a few days after the article ran, he was singing "America the Beautiful" in a karaoke bar with Richard Spencer and fellow white nationalists as they threw up Heil Hitler salutes. (In response to the leaks, Yiannopoulos denied being a fascist and claimed that Spencer had "tricked" him.)

However, when Yiannopoulos' article premiered in March 2016, it was a success for the young blogger, cited by major press outlets as a possible description of what was still a confusingly amorphous movement.

As a reward, he was finally clued into the mysterious donor behind the scenes. When Bannon went to Cannes in May 2016 to premiere his latest film, a documentary based on Peter Schweizer's *Clinton Cash*, he brought Yiannopoulos with him to meet Robert Mercer. Mercer sponsored not only *Breitbart* but Bannon's films.[5]

In the 1970s, Mercer programmed machine-learning artificial intelligences to process vast sets of data and so predict what was supposed to be the central mystery of capitalism, the movement of markets. And, well, they did—and still do. The hedge fund for which Mercer worked, Renaissance Technologies, has earned an average yield of *70 percent each year*, making Mercer one of the richest men on the planet. This has allowed the eccentric Mercer, who prefers the company of computers to human beings and, by some accounts, whistles more than he speaks, to live a life suspended in latency-period unreality that echoes Bannon's and 4chan's obsession with swordplay and ancient warriors. But if Bannon and 4chan were perpetually frozen in adolescence, Mercer preferred his regression dialed back a few years younger. Prior to his entrée into politics, the only press he garnered was for the elaborate model train sets he commissioned to run through his sprawling estates. Later on, it was discovered that once a year he traveled to a small town in Arizona to use his gun permit and play at being a deputy sheriff.[6] He often threw lavish costume balls, though he rarely spoke a word at them, opting instead to play the piano for hours. Squiring him in 2014 was a costumed Steve Bannon, who soon convinced Mercer to back Trump by funding Bannon's film projects, *Breitbart News*, Cambridge Analytica, and Milo Yiannopoulos.

Mercer shared Trump's (and /pol/'s) interest in conspiracy theories and pseudoscience. Acquaintances of Mercer's recalled offhand remarks about how radiation was good for people and that Hillary Clinton was a murderer. And in a nod to classic billionaire bonkers, Mercer also funded a vast urine-hoarding project. One of the only candidates he promoted for public office before Trump was a fringe scientist in Arizona who has collected thousands of samples of human waste to search for the secret to eternal life.[7]

It was the power of computers that gave Mercer his billions, but it was the *Citizens United* ruling that allowed his billions to flow into politics. Disappointed at how his money was squandered after Mitt Romney's defeat to Barack Obama in 2012, Mercer sought to build his own set of funding networks for the 2016 presidential election that would promote his extreme libertarianism. To this purpose, he first preferred the platform of Tea Partyer Ted Cruz over Donald Trump. But Bannon soon convinced him otherwise, channeling millions of Mercer's funds through his production company, Glittering Steel, to *Breitbart*, Yiannopoulos, pro-Trump projects, and the alt-right.

One of their most successful projects in this realm was Cambridge Analytica, a data analytics company founded in 2013 with Bannon as CEO and Mercer and his daughter Rebekah as principal investors. In 2014, Cambridge Analytica used a quiz app to fraudulently siphon personal information from 87 million Facebook users to build elaborate personality profiles with the aim of manipulating voters in both the U.K.

during the Brexit vote and the United States during the 2016 election. As described in chapter 8, the data breach was revealed in 2018 by a whistle-blowing former employee named Christopher Wylie. Soon after, the BBC aired a video alleging that Cambridge Analytica's CEO Alexander Nix had offered undercover reporters posing as Sri Lankan officials an array of blackmail, fraud, and other illegal electioneering services on behalf of the company, including an offer to ply a political opponent with "beautiful Ukrainian girls."[8]

When Wylie testified before members of the British Parliament, he detailed how Peter Thiel's data collection company Palantir had been working with Cambridge Analytica. Anonymous had hacked the security contractor Aaron Barr in 2011 and accidentally caught Barr and Palantir trying to sell similar illegal electioneering techniques to the U.S. Chamber of Commerce and attempting to build a Facebook "scraper." According to Wylie, it was Palantir (owned by Facebook investor and board member Thiel) who first suggested siphoning profiles from Facebook using a quiz app. Palantir "helped build the models," Wylie testified, and "senior Palantir employees" came to work on the data on many different occasions.[9] When the connection came to light, Palantir used the same excuse they'd used in 2011: Palantir's work with Cambridge Analytica was the act of a single rogue employee. Though the extent to which Thiel and Mercer are acquainted is unclear, in December 2016, Thiel appeared at one of Mercer's costume parties dressed as Hulk Hogan. (The theme was heroes and villains. Kellyanne Conway came dressed as Supergirl and Trump as himself.)[10]

In late May 2016, Bannon escorted Yiannopoulos aboard Mercer's wood-paneled, pirate-themed yacht anchored in the Mediterranean, the *Sea Owl* (so named because Mercer considered himself a night owl).[11]

There, in chambers covered in hand-chiseled reliefs of myths and fairy tales, a plan was hatched to secure yet another line from the billionaire's virtually limitless funds. The new strategy was similar to Cambridge Analytica—an unconventional, secret internet project that would help Trump win the presidency. The sum was rumored to be a million dollars. The idea: send Yiannopoulos to what Bannon called "#war." Bannon would hire a "top-level team" to activate the blogger's new audience, the swarms of alt-right and right-leaning youth on the chans.

However, the #war, soon to be renamed by Yiannopoulos "The Dangerous Faggot Tour," faced a conceptual hurdle. Yiannopoulos reigned over the insubstantial world of internet disputes. How would his brand of harassing people online function if it went outdoors? Whom would he harass?

Yiannopoulos was not a particularly dynamic speaker. In fact, most of his speeches were a series of disconnected personal insults in the style of someone perched on a couch dishing out celebrity gossip. The blogger thrived on conflict. And so the left-right gamergate dynamic would have to be made manifest in the physical world.

And to understand how, our narrative takes another strange turn. 4chan had a rival.

In another corner of the internet, an equally popular, predominantly female image board had developed an entirely different set of values, culture, and politics.

Though the two communities had many common interests, they were mirror images of one another. And absurdly, these two online rivals came to define distinct poles of modern politics on the right and left in 2016, with Donald Trump reflecting the alt-right that centered around 4chan's /pol/ board and Hillary Clinton representing the online identity politics of 4chan's brighter, more optimistic twin sister—tumblr.com.

Tumblr and the Mosaic of Identity

Anime was a mistake.
—Hayao Miyazaki, creator of some of the most beloved anime of all time /
popular meme on Tumblr

Much of Tumblr's relevance has now been drained away, a significant portion of it flowing into the image-sharing mobile app Instagram, owned by Facebook. However, between 2008 and 2014, tumblr.com defined a great deal of the internet's culture that wasn't already in 4chan's orbit, declining only when it was purchased by Yahoo! in 2013 for $1.1 billion and run straight into the ground.[1]

The site was founded in 2007 by yet another New York–born tech entrepreneur just barely out of his teens, David Karp. Karp's creation melded a social media–style image-posting community with a LiveJournal blog format in which the user could write about themselves in a public diary. Tumblr users also had access to a constantly updating feed that displayed all the posts of the blogs they were following in chronological order. If a user saw a post they liked, the software invited them to reblog it. At the press of a button, the post would reappear on the user's own blog and in the feeds of all their followers.

In effect, Tumblr transformed blog posts from personal log entries into little snippets that could be replicated over and over. The result was a rapidly developing ecology of memes. If a post was sufficiently interesting, it would begin to be reblogged. Likewise, boring ideas went unreplicated and soon disappeared into obscurity.

In this sense, Tumblr became the 4chan 2.0 that so many entrepreneurs, including Poole himself, had struggled to create—a vibrant meme factory absent the disgusting content. When I joined around 2008, I was astonished to find Tumblr was just as witty, clever, and creative as 4chan, but positive and celebratory. At the time, it was a thriving center for visual arts, animation, and comics creators. Several early artists on Tumblr went on to create popular kids' animations, like *Adventure Time* and *Steven Universe*, which in turn became popular on Tumblr. The content was similar to 4chan's: anime, manga, comic books, fantasy, science fiction, photography, fine art, fetish pornography, and personal confessions. On Tumblr, however, these items weren't posted to mock yourself and others mercilessly. In the positive atmosphere, aesthetic interests were granted reverential respect in a circle of mutual support.

Anything could be posted on Tumblr, but the software encouraged small snippets of media. Images were the most popular medium. And this practice solved a problem that had afflicted Tumblr's predecessor, the proto–social media site LiveJournal. Adolescents interested in establishing a network of friends/followers no longer needed to compose long, classically structured paragraphs of prose. Instead, the system invited users to express their interests and ultimately their identity not through the complexity of words, but through jpegs. Like on 4chan, these pictures were most often pieces of pop culture. The transition from text to images appealed to a media-saturated generation. Perhaps more significantly, this approach freed bloggers from the burden of creating their own content. The personal diary was transformed into a mosaic of images reblogged from friends' blogs. In a uniquely adolescent way, users expressed their online identity through their friends' identities, which were in turn pieces of other friends' identities, ad infinitum. Teens, anxious to figure themselves out, posted how they felt and what defined them. And this quest for definition blended seamlessly with the celebration of fantasy. Sliced-up bits of culture from films, anime, and TV would often be appended with Tumblr's most popular hashtag, "#me."

As a self-deleting image board, 4chan inspired a value system built around deconstruction and fatalism. Personal confessions and arguments poured into a garbage furnace on page ten (the last page before deletion, later changed to page fifteen). Selfhood was annihilated by anonymity. By contrast, Tumblr's software invited the user to construct a complex identity out of the tiny fragments of images and text a user replicated from their friends and idols. The culture that grew out of Tumblr was not an everything-is-garbage nihilism, but a certain preciousness around cobbling together a mosaic of identity.

Posts endured for years, bouncing around the site to be polished, well, like gems in a tumbler. Often this replication made the images and memes funnier or more interesting. But this also meant that many posts were argued over and annotated with each reblog. Even stranger, the annotations rarely ran on forever, as one might expect. Eventually, the various sides in the dialogue reached a consensus and what was then reblogged was like a rabbinical commentary, a settled piece of cultural law.

For example, for several years starting in 2014, some hundred thousand Tumblr users debated whether it was appropriate for Asian women to be depicted with dyed purple hair in film and TV, an issue that eventually migrated up to Twitter, then *Buzzfeed*. (The ultimate verdict: it was.)[2] But the process covered all the big questions: concepts of self, belonging, meaning, and politics.

4chan responded to the glut of traumatic media flowing through the screen by outpacing it and getting even grosser. Tumblr employed the opposite strategy. To replace the now long-vanished concepts of polite decorum in media, Tumblr invented "trigger warnings," a helpful label added to disturbing content. 4chan responded to screen media aggressively dangling idealized versions of people in front of you by becoming a space where users shared versions of those ideal bodies debauched, defiled, and cut to pieces. In response to the same problem, Tumblr users invented "body positivity," attempting to eradicate the very concept of the ideal body by insisting that all bodies were equally beautiful.

Adults reading this book may remember trying to "figure it out" as a teen, sifting through competing ideologies of television shows, parents, bands, and friends. Defining yourself meant coming up with a moral system: what to believe, what was right, what was wrong. Then, once that was settled, a new question arose: How do you go about fighting for it? Tumblr allowed all of this to take place on a scale of not tens or hundreds but millions of teens. Tumblr's project was no less ambitious than all this: all of its users would develop a code of laws. Collectively they would agree, disagree, edit, refine, and append until a consensus was reached on what was cool and what wasn't cool, what you should do and what you shouldn't, and what's right and what's wrong.

Such a philosophy naturally focused on issues relevant to adolescents.

Young people struggling to find a group that accepted them created groups that championed "radical acceptance"—their creed, everyone should be accepted for being different, unless of course you didn't believe this, in which case you were out of the group.

In a beautiful recursion loop (or, less charitably, a short circuit), teens used this core belief in the right to define oneself (and the software's invitation to do so) as their system of defining themselves. Those who believed that they were free to define their identity any way they pleased became a member of that clique. Indeed, subscribing to this belief determined their identity. Those who took issue with portions of the canon (for example, the rejects of 4chan) were shunned and condemned. Depending on how you looked at it, teens had either solved their problem with their problem or dug their escape route back into their prison.

The end result was a philosophy that emphasized an ultra-respect for personal identity and others' viewpoints. In other words, Tumblr's moral code became the exact inversion of the values of the adolescent boys of 4chan, who eschewed identity and insisted that nothing was sacred.

Outside of the moral code, the content was very much the same. Like on 4chan, Tumblr users employed the site to find unique groups that shared their particular interests, including sexual ones. Kink and pop culture blended together on Tumblr in fan groups that depicted pornography mingled with viewers' favorite fantasy books, television shows, cartoons, and celebrities. Along with the usual amalgams we have already encountered on 4chan like furries, bronys, and yaoi ("boy love," sometimes classified in Japan as "girls manga" because it was marketed to young women who preferred to read about romance occurring exclusively among young men), there was a great deal of "slash" fan fiction depicting romantic encounters between two male companions in films, TV, or books.[3] For example, after the premiere of *The Hobbit*, Tumblr filled with imagined romantic encounters between Bilbo Baggins and Thorin Oakenshield, king of the dwarves.

In this vast melting pot of sexuality, identity, and kink, Tumblr soon incorporated a borderless fluid theory of gender identity into its growing moral system. For this new generation in the soup of internet fetishes and subgenres, being "in the closet" wasn't limited to homosexuality. Similar to the LGBT+ Alliance (whose acronym had extended to so many letters it was shortened to just "+"), it was inclusive of all possible permutations.

To Tumblr users it was evident society accepted only a narrow range of sexuality, and that these people enjoyed the privilege of being considered "normal." And in this atmosphere, the politics that the userbase developed focused on rights and recognition for a panoply of marginalized groups and mingled with feminist theories addressing women's longstanding unequal treatment in society.

Similar to 4chan users, Tumblr users regarded the world as a power hierarchy, though they termed it a hierarchy of privilege, employing a term generally used to describe what a parent might permit a child to do. On top of this privilege hierarchy were heterosexual, cisgender white males. Tumblr's moral goal was to lift other people not possessed of these privileges—women, minorities, transgender people, and so forth—to that level. Users were encouraged to "check their privilege" (which might include additional traits such as one's health and economic status) to make way for otherwise marginalized or oppressed subgroups. This idea in turn melded with the values of intersectional feminism: the notion that all lines of injustice "intersect" and that women cannot lift themselves up to a better condition in society if they leave marginalized subgroups like African Americans and Latinos behind, and vice versa.

Like 4chan, Tumblr also hosted a large community of trans people. And erasing the borders between sexuality combined with eliminating the division between male and female. Once the gender division was dissolved, people would be able to move freely along the "spectrum" of gender and sexuality, not fenced off from certain privileges and ways of being, as women in particular have been for most of human history.

Though, as these ideas developed in "fandoms" (groups devoted to particular media franchises, which often denoted one's identity or sexual interest), murky philosophical questions and schisms arose. As Tumblr users declared their sexuality or gender and asked for recognition from the community, other users declared that their preferred identity was their "fursona" or that they were "otherkin" (meaning they defined themselves not as a man or woman, but off the human spectrum as a cartoon wolf, dwarf, elf, dragon, faerie, etc.). And these subgroups argued that it would be immoral to deny their declared identity.

Recognition of those who identified as queer or trans soon became entangled with a contingent of Tumblr users who wanted similar recognition as fantasy creatures. And fierce debates raged in the community as to whether this equivalence was valid. A consensus soon emerged: it was not. But this did not end the struggle. For example, as late as 2015, controversy sprang up over a new subgroup, "Hamilkin," composed of people who "identif[ied] with cast members of the 2015 Broadway musical *Hamilton*."[4]

Where did this weird mingling of trans theory and entertainment products come from? And why couldn't the movement, try as it might, jettison it?

Though the creepy-doll guy on 4chan professed to be simply following his natural sexual inclinations to build life-size mock-ups of cartoon characters and live intimately among them, obviously somewhere along the line his desires and the other side of the screen got mixed up. This isn't surprising, since the past half century could be defined by the screen's efforts to mingle real-world desires and those in fiction.

As online communities organized themselves into places where sexual fantasies and fetishes could be indulged, they also encouraged deep dives into fantasy lives that never came up for air.

The result was a group of internet users who felt trapped behind impenetrable glass. A frustrating gap formed between who they wanted to be and who they were, a desired fantasy and a cruel deterministic reality. And the two would never meet. Ironically, unlimited personal exploration and choice became a fishbowl prison, where isolated subcommunities looked out on a world they believed they could never access.

For incels, the forbidden realm they would never enter was the sexual one. For betas, it was being a successful man. For hard-core otaku, it was the better life on the other side of the screen. And indeed, around 2015, the /lgbt/ board on 4chan filled up with men who desired to transition into women but believed they would never be perceived as female. And so they remained, sadly longing to be something they thought they could never become. In a popular video on YouTube, trans vlogger "ContraPoints," who used to frequent the /lgbt/ board (called jokingly by its residents "/tttt/"), described how it devolved from a place where "the twenty-five gay men who actually liked Milo Yiannopoulos" met to something that resembled the sad incel boards one click over.[5]

Tumblr's online community championed the idea of gender fluidity for moral and political reasons. Trans people were still struggling to gain acceptance not just in society at large, but in the LGBT community, from which they had also long been excluded. But to leave the explanation for Tumblr's cultural movement there ignores its uncomfortable proximity to social media, marketing, and fantasy entertainment.

Modern capitalism convinces consumers to buy a never-ending stream of products to cobble together their always incomplete identity. The bachelor pad defines the playboy, as does his cologne or brand of alcohol. Similarly, social media built around advertising was a mirrored chamber designed to enthrall people with the constant activity of self-definition. Just as the playboy must continue to buy to inch closer to the ideal version of himself sold by magazines, so too must we maintain a perpetual stream of personal uploads to social media if we are to chase after, but never quite attain, a certain ideal screen version of ourselves.

As the conceptual theory of LGBT rights flowed onto social media, it became subverted by commodity marketing. Just as the hippie's ideal of boundless transcendence was co-opted, so too was the subversive idea that all human beings have the unlimited right to choose who they are, what they do, and how they define themselves. This dovetailed almost exactly with the disposition industry wanted people to take toward the commodities they manufactured: buy to live, buy to be, buy to indulge, but also buy to define. By the twenty-first century this system wasn't employed simply for physical commodities, but for the products of entertainment fiction. Fantasies in movies and TV reflected who you were, as did the images you chose to represent yourself and your lifestyle online.

When first developed by feminists in the mid-twentieth century, these theories of personal liberation were designed to smash the confining, socially constructed gender roles like "housewife," "mother," and "breadwinner." But by the twenty-first century, capitalism had managed to bend these escape implements into a new prison, one of constant self-obsession. Ironically, limitlessly self-defining became a new role that society constructed as much as any other.

One might have expected Tumblr's feminist theories to appeal to the loser betas of the chans, who defined themselves by their inability to live up to oppressive cultural ideals of manhood. More than anyone, betas would have benefited from no longer regarding themselves as failed "breadwinners" or "playboys." And a minority perhaps did.

However, the hard-line manner in which belief was settled upon on Tumblr, then vigorously defended, soon brought it into conflict with 4chan's trolls. Particularly when it came to the subject of gender theory. The trolls regarded Tumblr users as their favorite sort of target, people who believed a fantasy constructed on the internet. And anonymous adored tearing apart any rigid belief structure.

By 2014, the Tumblr-based obsession with identity and trans theory began trickling down to the pop-culture entertainment complex. After reality TV star Caitlyn Jenner's transition from male to female, *Vogue* would declare 2015 the "Year of Trans Visibility."[6] However, the betas on 4chan began to move in the exact opposite direction.

In the same way the dissipated pornography-celebrating philosophy of Yiannopoulos could be pushed a step further into the stoic, hyper-traditional value system of Evola, so too did 4chan begin to deeply resent fluid concepts of gender, associating their absolute freedom to choose and liberal freedom of consumerist escapist diversions with the hyper-subjective nihilism that had trapped them into their present circumstances. Soon threads began to appear in which transitioning was depicted not as a path toward liberating self-determination, but as yet another way to escape life by layering fantasy on top of reality. The chans' trolls mockingly joined together what Tumblr's debates had worked so hard to separate: internet subcommunities of people who sexualized screen fiction and trans communities. The fact that trans visibility was being championed by the corporate entertainment complex only strengthened the association.

Furthering 4chan's resentment was the fact that in Tumblr's hierarchy of privilege it was white cisgender (as opposed to transgender) males who were the most privileged. Therefore, Tumblr's logic went, their share of cultural power needed to be diluted and redistributed. 4chan was a community of largely cis white males who did not feel privileged at all. Victimized by capitalism like everyone else, they imagined themselves competing against other groups who also felt they were on the bottom, because, well, capitalism had placed an unprecedented number of people on the bottom. And so Tumblr's dissolution of the concept of male identity read as an attack against their own identitarian subgroup, yet another attempt to erode their already shrinking share of power.

As Tumblr pushed leftist politics to a place that seemed, to 4chan, exceedingly polite, 4chan's disenfranchised anger boiled over. Self-condemned to a life of wallowing misery, the site's betas were hardly interested in a politics centered around deference and respect. To the betas of 4chan, Tumblr's belief that "gender is a construct" was not a liberating message of salvation. As men, they were still at the bottom, constantly losing. The advice "it's in your power to define manhood anyway you choose" was not helpful.

Having been raised on the internet, they weren't looking for a way to dissolve their identity in the acid of conceptual theory. Drifting in nihilism, they were groping for a concrete value system that defined their place in society and offered them guidance on how they could be accepted and regarded as men.

As self-described beta losers, some did long to escape the prison of their masculinity. Even prior to the /lgbt/ board, many used the chans as a place to discuss transitioning or gender theory. I frequently saw threads on /b/ authored by those claiming to be depressed, nerdy beta men slowly transitioning into women to begin life anew. Transwomen on 4chan were referred to as "traps" by its sex-starved population of man-boys. Though statistics are scarce, other authors writing on anonymous have attempted to account for the noticeably large trans communities on the site by noting that there seems to be a connection between identifying as trans and frequent computer use.[7] But for all the users exploring identity-bending on the site, there was a great deal more who wanted to understand how to more closely conform to some baseline definition of personhood, to join society and become men as society defined them.

The philosophical lineage of the freedom to choose that Tumblr adopted can be traced from Jean-Paul Sartre to Simone de Beauvoir to Judith Butler. The technical term for it is existentialism or, as Sartre phrased it, "existence precedes essence." Simply put, this means that human beings are free to self-define: to make any choice at any point in their life, unconstrained by their past, their upbringing, or their inherent nature. Consciousness grants us absolute freedom. And to conceal this terrifying truth, we invent the illusion that our decisions are limited—that we must do something or make a certain choice—when in reality at each point in our lives the only constant is that we are "doomed to choose."

De Beauvoir's conception of gender extended this absolute freedom to choose into the realm of sex. And Butler, in her 1990 book *Gender Trouble*, asserted that de Beauvoir did not go far enough. Categories like "sex" and "gender" ought to be abolished, she maintained, as unreal mental constructs.

As discussed in chapter 4, cultural critics like Herbert Marcuse and Charles Reich noted how the modern world closed off the possibilities contained in the insight that existence precedes essence, that human beings have a far-ranging capacity to choose and self-define. Instead, what was "practical" was dictated from above by "experts," who told people how to think and what was realistic. In order to participate in the hierarchy, one had to become an expert, agreeing to only offer one's interpretation of a narrowly defined subject, never the system as a whole.

And as a result, wild worlds of fantasy sprang up, full of elves and dwarves, wholly split off from what was real. Imagination and the infinite array of possibility became unnaturally walled off in people's minds from their experience of the real world. These gaps became encoded in communities like the incels and betas who felt they could never transcend reality to get to their fantasy.

And now, cracks were appearing in this wall.

As they came into conflict, Tumblr and 4chan began to employ escapist fantasy from TV, films, and video games to champion radical new political and personal philosophies.

Absurdly, the chosen battlefield was the online realm of children's fantasy entertainment products. Yiannopoulos and 4chan harassed the stars of the new *Ghostbusters* film on Twitter, and Cernovich would do the same for *Star Wars*. All of this was in the mold of 4chan's 2015 "troll Tumblr" campaign that targeted *Steven Universe* by making Tumblr-style fan art in which all the diverse characters were made white, blond, and skinny.

Judith Butler's "gender as a construct" became a rigid moral philosophy, or rather, the online interpretation of it did, as Tumblr's userbase's philosophy crystallized into a concrete moral code. It's not often that one is condemned as immoral if one disagrees with "existence precedes essence" (as occurred frequently online and off with gender is a construct). Rather, it is more often employed as a tool to achieve perspective, a lens by which we might gain insight. But strangely enough, for Tumblr it was problematic to consider gender is a construct as a construct itself—that is to say, to treat the idea the same way it treats sex and gender, as a set of concepts equally true and untrue.

And this rigidity created a widening fissure between the two fantasy-soaked communities, amplified by social media's capacity for a "pile on," in which once a stance on a moral issue has been decided, users rush to echo the original conclusion and condemn those who disagree.

Indeed, the sociological problems of the betas are better understood by setting down the gender-is-a-construct tool and applying another.

In the novel *The Left Hand of Darkness*, Ursula K. Le Guin describes men through the eyes of a genderless character who has never seen one: "There is a frailty about him. He is all unprotected, exposed, vulnerable . . . To match his frailty and strength, he has a spirit easy to despair and quick to defiance . . . He is ready, eager, to stake life on the cruel quick test of the precipice." This passage pinpoints the betas' problems.

For betas, it is not always helpful to regard flaws as culturally constructed roles. Instead, they should be viewed as feelings churning at the root of their beings—and their sex—mingled with their most basic desires for recognition, winning, and defiance. They longed for a framework that was the exact opposite of Tumblr assertion that "sex" and "gender" were mere cultural performances.

The identification of traits like Le Guin described is not always used to exclude or trap people into rigid definitions of masculinity (i.e., you are not a man unless you feel defiance). They can instead be used to acknowledge common problems attendant upon certain sexual desires. And this schema results in a different conclusion: that perhaps there are elements of our character that can't be eradicated by the power of thought, that demand negotiation, not denial. The betas' problems were not just cultural constructs, but innate modes of behavior that needed to be acknowledged and addressed.

And so, as 4chan users groped with the central problem of defining their masculinity, they came into conflict with Tumblr as it reinvented identity politics around the central idea of dismantling gender roles as illusory ideas.

Traditional conservatives had come to deeply resent the left's postwar tradition of deconstructive analysis. The best example of this is the right's notion of "cultural Marxism," championed by loopy alt-right talkshow host Alex Jones and beta male self-help guru Jordan Peterson, who, as we will see in chapter 19, rose to prominence by opposing trans-rights legislation in a series of YouTube videos.

The term has various shades of meaning. Sometimes it indicates simply a suspicion of leftist deconstruction obscuring the traditional guidelines by which people should live their life. At other times it refers to the far wackier conspiracy theory that the Frankfurt School (of which Marcuse was a member) conspired to undermine concrete Western values by infiltrating American universities and teaching that all ideas were meaningless (and so bring about socialism).

And it was this range of conservative concepts that began to appeal to the betas. Cultural and economic liberalism, as embodied by Tumblr's new youth philosophy, was not liberating them from a prison of a narrowly confined gender roles but denying their complaint.

Hillary Clinton, with her army of experts, told them to be realistic and expect the status quo, while Trump, denier of all experts and even of reality itself, offered the liberating promise of infinite possibilities of political self-determination. Trump, by example, was willing to craft a personal world of self-definition. But he also offered the betas conservative guidelines for being men based on the archetype of "alpha male."

So from these two dueling adolescent image-sharing sites, two new forms of politics attempted to step into real life. And just like in the movies, when the magical creatures attempted to abandon their fantasy realms and remain in the human world (or vice versa), the results were inevitably disastrous.

Politics Steps Through the Looking Glass

When this is over, you will walk out of this room to the real world and your own concerns and leave me here trapped in a world I know to be nothing but illusion. I cannot bear that. I must leave!

—Holographic Professor Moriarty, from the 1993 *Star Trek: The New Generation* episode "Ship in a Bottle"

Identity-driven coalitions had made great political strides along with the counterculture. Indeed, the 1964 Sproul Hall protest had been inspired by the solidarity of the civil rights movement. And the 60s protests were followed by a cascade of very successful women's rights movements. But by the early 90s, when a new wave of identity politics swept U.S. youth culture, it became weirdly entangled in marketing and capitalist co-optation.

Early 90s identity politics coincided with the end-of-history nadir of counterculture, when capitalism seemed so victorious it was unassailable. At the time, the corporate hegemony did not even appear to be a hegemony, but like water to a fish, an element that was so ubiquitous it was invisible. Radical efforts in the 60s to dismantle capitalism were succeeded by countercultural efforts in the 90s to beseech it for justice. As Naomi Klein described in her 2000 book *No Logo*, "In the absence of a clear legal or political strategy [in the early 90s], we traced back almost all of society's problems to the media and the curriculum, either through their perpetuation of negative stereotypes or simply by omission . . . So outraged were we media children by the narrow oppressive portrayals in magazines, in books and on television that we convinced ourselves that if the typecast images and loaded language changed, so too would the reality."[1]

However, the strategy was an utter failure. Not for lack of trying, but because of poor aim. Corporations were delighted to accommodate youth demands to modify their products. Responding to feedback and reissuing merchandise was their central activity, typically bought at a premium from market-research firms. But thirty years of youth marketing was finally paying dividends: a whole generation of children thought of themselves principally as consumers who needed to agitate for better products.

This had been the mad dream of marketers when they first began co-opting counterculture in the 60s. In their wildest hopes, they imagined protest movements in which youth fixated not on foreign wars or socialism, but the consumer-manufacturer relationship.

In commercials, people center their lives around products. They think obsessively about chewing gum, cars, or flatware. As much as this demonstrates absurd behavior marketers hope the viewer will model, it also represents the aspirations of the marketers themselves laid bare by their creative act. Through their art, we get a glimpse into their psyche and can see how they wish people *would* behave.

Nineties identity politics produced just such a scenario. Why couldn't protests, marketers wondered, be about creating the perfect product? Why weren't the kids upset about that? And remarkably in the 90s, for a few brief, embarrassing years in my teens, they were. Counterculture morphed into youth movements asking corporations to change their marketing campaigns. Eventually, the strategy was abandoned since, in Klein's words, "the victories of identity politics . . . amounted to a rearranging of the furniture while the house burned down."[2] As ads and films filled with diverse models and actors, the larger problems of globalization were growing. By the end of the decade, "massive re-distribution and stratification of world resources: of jobs, goods and money" was occurring at an increasing pace. "Everyone except those in the very highest tier of the corporate elite [was] getting less."[3]

As economic inequality steadily worsened, identity politics also faced another problem in the mid-90s: it created strife. "The basic demands of identity politics assumed an atmosphere of plenty," Klein wrote. In the "New Economy nineties, however, women as well as men, and whites as well as people of color, were now fighting their battles over a single, shrinking piece of pie."[4]

Identity politics' vision was fundamentally radical. The world would have to be rebuilt to treat women and historically marginalized minorities as equals. However, the basic difference between late 60s counter-

culture and early 90s identity politics soon mirrored the difference
between radical and liberal. A liberal mindset accepted the status quo of
capitalism but asked for minor modifications. Demands for better representation in the media were like the modest tweaks liberal governments
demanded of corporations (pollute less, pay overtime, etc.) that didn't
tackle the systemic problems. In fact, by enacting small changes liberals
allowed corporations to endure by appearing to address the problem of
increasing corporate dominance.

Similarly, efforts for women and minorities to be treated equally in
society often cited systemic problems that would require dismantling the
inequities of capitalism to solve. But these requests were frequently co-
opted by neoliberals who promised that minorities did not have to eliminate the bourgeoisie because they could ascend to join them. For example,
the image Hillary Clinton employed during her 2016 campaign to display women's rights and female empowerment was the corporate business suit. Just as Trump did, she equated the government with a giant
corporation. Her presidency would "break the glass ceiling" of what she
framed as the largest corporation of all, the government. And her personal promotion would be a victory for all women everywhere, a signal
that they too could join the establishment.

Dangerously, centrist Democrats began substituting identity politics
for third-rail topics like meaningful economic reform. For example, in a
story on *This American Life*, when Bernie Sanders–style Democratic primary candidate for congress in New York Jeff Beals rose to speak at a
party of Clinton staffers and financiers with deep pockets in 2018, his
themes of income inequality, a "rigged economy," and socialized medi-
cine were met with an unhappy silence. "Why didn't you speak about
LGBT?" his host complained to him afterward. "You left the money on
the table."[5]

And the result was a hateful fascist backlash against both "the global
elites" and the LGBT community.

When identity politics reemerged on Tumblr in the late aughts, it
wasn't only because teens were mirroring the habits of the identity-
focused corporate software, but because the dynamics that had produced identity politics in the early 90s had never disappeared. In fact,
they'd continued to grow. Youth were more media saturated than ever.

When Hannah Arendt studied the extreme wealth inequality of
the 1920s and 30s, she noted how all the marginalized have-nots of

capitalist society did not form a solid political bloc agitating for a shared agenda as Marx had predicted would happen. Rather, they fragmented into groups that held the competitive mindset of capitalism, each frustrated that they were getting shuffled to the bottom of a perceived hierarchy.

As wealth inequality reached 1930s levels at the start of the twenty-first century, a panoply of young people, all feeling marginalized, also began to perceive society as a hierarchy of privilege.

However, the one salient difference between the identity politics of the early 90s and the new Tumblr iteration was the expansion of screen-mediated fantasy worlds.

Just as screen fiction had reconfigured 90s nihilism into ultra-nihilistic, meme-spouting 4chan culture, so too did it reconfigure the demands of early 90s identity politics. With the growth of increasingly elaborate escapist worlds, political demands began to bend inward into fantasy.

In an early 90s episode of *Star Trek: The Next Generation*, crew members of the *Enterprise* become trapped in a simulation of a Sherlock Holmes novel. When they attempt to leave the virtual reality "holodeck," a virtual Dr. Moriarty tricks them *by simulating an exit back into reality* on the holodeck. What follows is a game between the crew members and Dr. Moriarty in which each side tries to convince the other a false world is real. Several times during the episode, each side believes they have escaped the simulation, when in fact, they remain trapped.

By the 2010s, the internet-generated politics of radical youth culture was caught in a similar set of cascading simulated worlds. Each side was playing a game of trapped in the holodeck. The game was won when one side convinced the other that fantasy was in fact reality.

Those agitating for radical change believed they were affecting reality, when in fact they had received (and were often satisfied with) radical change only within the confines of a simulated fantasy world.

Perhaps the best example of this is the recent blockbuster in the Marvel franchise, *Black Panther*. The film explores the problem of racial injustice in America by presenting the story of an African superhero who works with the CIA to prevent a black radical from fomenting revolution. In this sense, it is an upside-down retelling of the story of the radical 1960s Black Panther movement.

At the end of the film, the problem of racial inequality is addressed by the victorious hero, the conservative Black Panther. The penultimate scene shows the superhero establishing schools and mentorship programs in underserved black communities in Los Angeles, just as the real Black Panthers did in the 1960s. In doing so, Black Panther decides to share the wealth and fantastical technology from the secret realm from which he hails, an African Shangri-la called Wakanda. Thus, in both the fantasy of the film and in real life the problem is addressed and solved *within the confines of the fantasy world*. The movie's solution to America's racial inequality is to apply healthy gobs of unreal fantasy (the wealth and technology of the mystical realm Wakanda) to the problem.

Just as with so many other fantasy products, *Black Panther* took people's unhappiness and frustration and sold it back to them as a brief snippet of relief. Viewed from one perspective, *Black Panther* was a victory for representation. But zoom out and it might be better regarded as *a simulation of a victory*.

In Baltimore, where I taught in predominantly black, underserved public schools for years, only a slim minority of my students would ever have the chance to enter the middle class. Against this grim backdrop, *Black Panther* was welcomed with a wave of euphoria. Local campaigns (#BlackPantherChallenge) were organized to bus children from their underserved areas to see the film.[6] It was hard not to delight in the kids' joy. But it also felt like a trapped-in-the-holodeck moment; the film fooled people into believing they had won a victory at the cost of a $14 ticket. Or more simply put, *it was a play*—a moneymaking scheme. It took something popular—Americans' desperate desire for racial equality—repackaged it, and sold it as a commodity that audiences could buy by the hour.

Indeed, using fantasy to sate the very real and desperate longing for social justice worked a little *too* well for *Black Panther*'s owner, Disney. Whereas in so many other entertainment products this dynamic goes ignored, the film's runaway success made the shocking disparity between the real and fake embarrassingly visible. People noticed that the corporation had pocketed $700 million worldwide selling a fantasy of social justice. In response, an embarrassed Disney hastily announced on Twitter that it would donate 1/700th of their $700 million to "advance STEM programs for youth, especially in underserved areas of the country."[7]

In Tumblr-style identity politics, now doubly focused on screen fantasy and representations, the complex dialogue between fan communities and politics gets even stranger. The trapped-in-the-holodeck strategy of shunting your foes into a world of illusions does not always result in simple cases like *Black Panther* in which an audience watches a super-hero solve all the problems they wish were solved in the real world.

The cutthroat competition for entertainment products to scratch the itch of their audience's deepest dissatisfaction has forced filmmakers to evolve. Once an audience *recognizes* that a filmmaker is playing this game, the spell is broken. The characters realize they are still on the holodeck.

Therefore, what occurs in the most cutting-edge films is a recursive play-within-a-play strategy in which concepts of real and fake are tied into a knot. Heroes and heroines of the latest films must first fight their way out of an elaborate simulation and *recognize it is as fake* before they can set the real world right. Oddly enough, these contortions give the fiction a gloss of reality. Since, like the audience, the film's hero must con-stantly fend off the manipulations of a fantasy world (in the case of the audience, these struggles are against other movies, TV shows, video games, advertisements, etc.), this allows the audience, who are already be-numbed to the ordinary techniques of escapist fantasy, to once again suspend disbelief and regard the fantasy as credible.

This technique was first employed by *The Matrix*, which plays on the gnostic themes of a cascading series of simulated worlds and the recur-sive logic of computers themselves in which functions are placed inside functions and so forth. Thus, when the alt-right emerged from 4chan's media-saturated betas on /pol/ in 2014, they expressed their philosophy in terms of "taking the red pill" and invited others to be convinced by the elaborate fictions that have been generated inside the world of com-puter screens.

The same dynamics occurring on Tumblr are perhaps best shown in its relationship to an episode of the dystopian science-fiction TV series *Black Mirror* titled "San Junipero." In the piece, a young interracial couple fall in love in a montage of hyper-real retro settings, pitch-perfect replications of the glamorous backdrops from classic movies of the 70s, 80s, and 90s. And here's the twist (spoiler alert!): they are meeting in a networked virtual reality simulation. Though they appear as teenagers, in real life they are very old and using the fantasy realm to explore their sexuality in ways that were not possible in their own lives. The story ends when the two lovers, facing death, upload a copy of their consciousness into the simulation. There, the computer replicas of their brains endure together forever, dancing and partying in paradise. To inform us the couple are enjoying an afterlife of truly eternal love, the 80s ballad "Heaven Is a Place on Earth" blasts over the scene.

Or so it seems at first. The last shot is terrifying. The camera pans across the vast reaches of a humming computer, where, beneath an in-human blinking node, we view how their souls are stored in a corporation's mainframe. As much as the creators would like us to believe the ending is happy, this last image presents an equally likely scenario: that the uncanny replication of the lovers in a false world is the fate of nightmares. The characters might be trapped in an unreal purgatory that will eventually be erased or glitched into oblivion when the corporation decides to pull the plug.

But in the Rorschach test of interpretation, the Tumblrverse rarely acknowledged this second possibility. When the episode premiered in 2016 it was celebrated across Tumblr in a cascade of reblogged fan art, quotes, screenshots, and gifs. And as usual, the media began to echo the memes. *Vulture* wrote that the episode "interrupts . . . the cynical gloom of the rest of season three of *Black Mirror* like sunshine breaking through the clouds (or rants about the Cloud)."[8]

That the disturbing ending was ignored underscores what is so unsettling about Tumblr. As long as carefully cultivated corporate fantasy worlds accommodated demands for racial and sexual parity, users rarely noticed the downside of being dumped into a fantasy world for all eternity. Moreover, if *the values of the fantasy world were just* (if the simulation accepted your sexuality, identity, and so forth), it often didn't matter that the real world was run by morally ambiguous technocrats who accommodated each person by assigning them a slot on their fantasy-generating servers.

Similarly, Steven Spielberg's *Ready Player One*, adapted from a science-fiction novel written by a nerdy Redditor, tells the story of a nightmarish near-future in which vast corporations rule over the United States while the majority of the population languishes in poverty. People no longer use TV, video games, and the internet to escape from a miserable and unjust world, but a new-and-improved, hyper-real networked virtual reality simulation called "the Oasis." Like the internet, the Oasis is populated with the scraps of decades of escapist pop culture: superheroes, sword-and-sorcery fantasy, giant robots from Japan, 80s movies, and so forth ad nauseam.

In the story, a young, impoverished hero named Wade Watts enters the virtual world to battle an evil corporation that is trying to take control of the Oasis, attempting to break the corporation's grip on not only the simulation but the real world. And along the way he learns a lesson: he ought to abandon the simulated world for the real one and use his newfound power to repair it. And so, in a similar, "*The-Matrix*-is-the-sort-of-movie-the-matrix-would-make" way, *Ready Player One* justified to the audience why the fantasy-saturated audience (who like Wade is sickened by the excess of fantasy) should indulge in yet another fantasy and believe it.

By diving headfirst into the simulation, Wade breaks the spell and finds his way out. But all of this is portrayed to convince the viewer the movie is presenting a "realistic" world so that we might indulge in the fantasy *just once more* when we see the tired old formula trotted out again—a hero breaks the grip of corporate manipulation on the populace!

In this, *Ready Player One* admits an odd truth: the world is now *so full* of escapist fantasy that characters and plots from one product spill over the brim into others, just as they do in so many human interactions.

Ready Player One was met with derision on social media partly because its formula was a little too on the nose. But nonetheless, it reflected the central values of social media–inspired identity politics and the alt-right ideology of "red-pilling": political change can be effected by simultaneously rejecting screen fantasy as unreal and indulging in it completely, whether through social media or the scraps of pop culture.

And so, by 2016, this new sort of politics, debated on social media largely through the mediums of franchise films and the content of video games, stepped out into the real world when Milo Yiannopoulos started to spend Robert Mercer's money to stir up online controversy in real life. And it didn't take him long to get the tornado whirling.

Tumblr Goes to College

We're a culture, not a costume!
—2011 University of Ohio student-run poster campaign / Tumblr post
transformed into a wildly popular meme on 4chan and Something Awful

By 2015, the rivalry between Tumblr and 4chan was years old. One of anonymous' largest hacking operations in 2010, titled "Operation Overlord," was an attempt to DDoS Tumblr. This resulted in a meme called "4chumblr," in which it was suggested the two sides begin dating to settle their differences, since, according to /b/, both sites were "filled with desperate virgin[s]."[1]

But as with so many other lighthearted ideas on 4chan, by 2015 gamergate and its hatred of social justice warriors and Quinn's Tumblr-style game had turned the innocent rivalry into a bitter dispute (at least on 4chan's end).

This meant that when Milo Yiannopoulos was tasked by Steve Bannon and Robert Mercer to reignite the 4chan-Tumblr culture war in real life in 2016, he needed to find Tumblr culture IRL.

This task proved easy. Tumblr had gone to college.

By 2016, all those smart, artistic, literate, nerdy teens who used Tumblr between 2008 and 2014 to teach themselves a very specific and rigid set of internet ethics were now mostly in universities, eyeing their campuses, classes, and the curricula with the same judgments they applied to a lifetime of perusing internet comments sections. And that's where Yiannopoulos would go. The strife Yiannopoulos sowed during the Dangerous Faggot Tour was so great it ultimately outlived his fame. Though it was not all his doing.

Much of the political landscape in the latter half of 2014 was defined by the protests in Ferguson, Missouri, following the police killing of an African American teenager named Michael Brown for allegedly stealing cigars from a convenience store. Brown's death had only been the latest in a series of high-profile police shootings of African Americans. And in the spring of 2015, similar protests erupted in Baltimore when a local named Freddie Gray died from a broken neck while in police custody. By mid-April, Baltimore had broken out in riots, first at its Inner Harbor, then at one of the city's public high schools the next day, before spreading to much of the city. According to anxious school administrators monitoring Twitter and Instagram, the students had been planning a day of shoplifting and mischief based on a B-movie version of *The Hunger Games* called *The Purge*.

But beneath this hash of social media and pop culture were the concentrated symbols of America's refusal to reckon with its past. Though participants in the Inner Harbor brawl didn't realize it at the time, their conflict began on the exact same spot as the riot that had drawn first blood in what became the Civil War. The high school where the race riots started the next day, Frederick Douglass, was the alma mater of Thurgood Marshall, who had argued for an end to the "separate but equal" Supreme Court ruling. When the National Guard was brought in to pacify the city it was hard not to make comparisons to the last time this had occurred, the riots of 1968 following the assassination of Martin Luther King Jr.

Ferguson's and Baltimore's complaints were the same: things had gone on too long. Conditions in the inner city, untenable half a century ago, had not changed, but rather endured in a permanent state that always seemed to be on the cusp of change. America's reckoning with its legacy of slavery, not only social discrimination but the long-standing economic disparities, was overdue.

Ironically, the teens at Frederick Douglass used social media just as the 80s and 90s prophets of the internet imagined the networks could be used, as a force to shatter an oppressive situation, in this case living as a black teenager in Baltimore City. However, this wasn't a result the liberal order welcomed. After the uprising, I spent time teaching at Frederick Douglass and watched as the city quickly snapped back into its old routines. School and city officials offered the same bromides: though social conditions had declined for decades, now was the time when students and city residents would see slow, steady improvement gained through legal and social channels.

Though it wasn't recognized at the time, the internet's power for social mobilization was intersecting with all the places where decades of American promises of prosperity and improvement had never been fulfilled, a growing number of nodes, as it turned out.

A few months after the events in Baltimore, Dylann Roof, an impoverished white teen in South Carolina living on the margins of American society, shot and killed nine parishioners in a prominent black church in Charleston during a prayer meeting. Roof, semi-homeless and undereducated, had self-converted to white nationalism via the internet. One of his favorite sites was Andrew "weev" Auernheimer's the *Daily Stormer*, where Roof posted frequently as "AryanBlood1488." Having dropped out of school in ninth grade, he spent the rest of his time drinking and playing video games. In his manifesto, Roof explained that he intended to incite a race war with this act, angry at what he saw as anti-white sentiment after the shooting of Trayvon Martin and the protests in Ferguson and Baltimore.[2]

Roof had obviously sopped up some of the *Gone with the Wind*–style mourning for the vanished glory of the antebellum South that had soaked into every cobblestone in the city where the Civil War began (unless one counted Baltimore). The old quarter of town, where Roof perpetrated his massacre, was dotted with museums on the theme.

But this was only half the story. Roof was a weird amalgam of the typical neo-Nazi, a poor white southerner, and the new underemployed populations of young men immersed in video games and message boards looking from the outside in at happy, healthy adults. The church had been his second choice. At first, he had wanted to shoot up the preppy College of Charleston, but he changed his mind at the last minute because he thought there would be security guards there.[3] His archaic Civil War fantasies incorporated the spree-shooter vision celebrated on 4chan in James Holmes Joker memes and Elliot Rodger beta uprising jokes. His abandoned target was similar to Rodger's—kids his own age who were doing fine at college.

By the end of the month, many of the problems evoked by Roof's massacre had condensed into the question of the Confederate monuments that peppered Baltimore and Charleston. When school started in the fall of 2015, this campaign moved from the most impoverished and neglected places in America into the wealthy centers of the powerful elite—high-end liberal colleges. Rigorous student campaigns rooted out statues, plaques, and buildings dedicated to once-celebrated historical figures whose legacies did not accord with contemporary values.

Princeton students conducted sit-ins to remove former Princeton and American president Woodrow Wilson's name from dormitories because of his policies supporting racial segregation.[4] Yale students protested to remove the slave owner John C. Calhoun's name from campus buildings.[5] Racially charged protests organized over social media occurred at Georgetown, Harvard, Ithaca College, and the University of Missouri, among other places.[6] And the trend was not confined to the United States. In the U.K., Oxford students demonstrated against the presence of a statue of the infamous imperialist Cecil Rhodes, echoing a similar campaign in South Africa.

Several deans and faculty members wrote op-eds in major newspapers opposing the students' demands. And according to the *New York Times*, liberal administrators struggled to respond to the "fluid, fast-moving protests on campus and the heated debate on social media."[7]

Professors were overwhelmed by the demonstrations because history and politics had melded with social media in bizarre new combinations. As wealth inequality reached new heights in the United States, so too had the historical fissures that separated rich from poor widened, despite decades of promises that the neoliberal order was collaborating with capitalism to lessen these divisions.

Students were naturally angry about all this inequality as it bubbled to the surface in places like Ferguson, Baltimore, and Charleston. However, capitalism's influence had extended not only over political power in Washington but cultural power as well. Students entered university with patterns of consumer-minded thinking that they had learned by channeling nearly all of their interactions through social media companies, the same places where they were now organizing their demonstrations.

As Angela Nagle pointed out in *Kill All Normies*, this new Tumblr version of identity politics duplicated the splintering of the left in the early 1970s.[8] Since the beginning of the nineteenth century, social justice causes in which minority groups worked to gain parity with other citizens had been a key part of the Enlightenment effort to build an equitable society. However, by the late twentieth century, identity politics was often seen as conflicting with the traditional Enlightenment vision of all human beings united in a coalition to wrest power away from a small elite.

In the late eighteenth century, the original Enlightenment thinkers in Europe extended a vision of *liberté, égalité, fraternité* around the globe. As Tocqueville put it, the Enlightenment "believed in the variety of races but in the unity of the human species."[9] Late twentieth-century identity politics broke with the late eighteenth-century ideal of a worldwide co-alition organized against the consolidation of power in the hands of the few, arguing that the needs of certain minorities could never be met us-ing this method. To its critics, this fragmented coalitions based on class into smaller factions, which diluted people's power to organize and chal-lenge an elite (and as a result benefited the elite).

As a resurgent, internet-inspired identity politics swept college cam-puses in 2015, these old fissures between identity politics and the eco-nomic left reappeared. A new generation had revived identity politics partly because they were frustrated by the half-century-long holding pat-tern that had left the lot of minority groups unimproved. As global in-equality rose in late-stage capitalism, these groups were only getting more marginalized. Thus, it appeared the left had to double down on its devo-tion to uplifting marginalized elements in society. But viewing the revolution as an alliance of interest groups aspiring to seize power from another identitarian group naturally increased factionalism. This zero-sum think-ing ran contrary to the older Enlightenment vision of people working together collectively as nation-states to better their lot.

Young people had also revived identity politics because it accorded with their experience on corporate social media, where they were encour-aged to treat their lives like advertisements, cultivating personally tai-lored worlds of interests, beliefs, feelings, and likes that floated above reality in the realm of texts, photographs, and video clips. As we saw in previous chapters, consumerist ideology orbited around constant buy-ing to not only accommodate self-centered needs but *to continually de-fine one's increasingly fragile identity*. So, it was no surprise that corporate social media, which ran on the fuel of advertising, focused a new gen-eration on self-definition and accommodation.

On social media, young people had beseeched corporations for more friendly environments and improved products, such as better representation in fantasy games, movies, and books. Now they simply swapped their schools into the familiar role of manufacturers that had to listen to the demands of their customers. And conveniently for those interested in maintaining the status quo, demands for personal accommodations were easily granted and often deflected radical attention away from structural inequality.

Students were paying approximately $55,000 a year (at a four-year minimum) for access to the upper echelons of this power hierarchy: a degree that, if they were lucky, acted as a passport to the dwindling number of slots in the middle class. Both sides had stipulated that the $220,000 contracts included a comfortable four-year stay at the universities. And so, the protesters argued from the role of customers that they were not comfortable with statues of or the names of certain historical figures on campus buildings.

The countercultural revolution of the 60s had been sparked by high-end American universities positioning themselves as toll collectors for the Corporate State hierarchy. In 2015, this assumed role was evoked as a bargaining point in the protests. Student protesters were not challenging the consolidation of power into the hands of the wealthy elite this half-century-old structure was supporting. Rather, their protests began as a contract dispute over the decor in their accommodations.

And as things progressed, the vague twinkle of unreal fantasy that spilled in from the virtual world began to turn into a shimmer. The location of protests shifted away from Baltimore and Ferguson toward Tumblr.

In November 2015, a professor of early childhood education at Yale named Erika Christakis questioned the merits of an email directive sent out by the Intercultural Affairs Committee warning students to be careful about offending minorities with their Halloween costumes. The result was a confusing controversy that exploded onto the national stage, and that was also, uncoincidentally, pure Tumblr culture. When Christakis mused whether "blond toddlers should be barred from being dressed as African American or Asian characters from Disney films," she blundered into a hot-button issue on millions of teen blogs: cosplay, fantasy, and representation. In fact, by putting her objections in a reply-all email, she had unwittingly replicated the experience in both form and content.

Many Yale students knew the ruling on cosplay that was settled years ago on social media: culturally insensitive cosplay was wrong. And they had learned what to do next: call her out. This produced a set of comical videos posted to YouTube in which the young students screamed and cursed in the face of compliant Yale professors and administrators, most notably Nicholas Christakis, Erika Christakis' husband, a so-called Master of student life.

The press, like the administration, didn't know quite what to make of a demonstration possessed of the histrionic quality of a family quarrel, in which an apparently insignificant quibble stood in for a world of inherited grievances. Were the future leaders of the United States who had won coveted tickets to the highest echelons of the neoliberal meritocracy—the ones who were supposed to take over the newspapers, high political offices, and corporations—really demonstrating in the quads not about the military-industrial complex, wealth inequality, or America's endless foreign wars, but cosplay?

Unlike previous generations of university students who had objected to these larger systemic issues (and lost), this new generation did not regard themselves "unto gods," as the 60s generation had described itself, able to remake the world in their image. Rather, their identities and requests were much reduced. They had long ago turned inward to parse worlds of fear, anxiety, and depression until their safety became the subject of their external demonstrations. Their objections were rooted in the assumption that they were powerless and marginalized. They weren't interested in shattering what had proved to be unbreakable institutions that had made universities into funnels for computer-assisted meritocracies. Instead, they were focused on battles they could win, which generally meant consumer-style demands. And so they were asking yet another immortal institution (Yale) in its great power as a supplier for a small accommodation. As in Tumblr's interpretation of the *Black Mirror* world in "San Junipero," getting assigned a place in the technocratic hierarchy was a given, but there was a perceived right to identity politics–style accommodation.

The tech prophets of the 80s and 90s had successfully predicted the internet would function as a free-speech zone of infinite debate and exchange of ideas. But they had not imagined it appearing in this America, where large institutions only consolidated more power while vast groups of disenfranchised people were being told, contrary to their experience, that their lives were improving.

And outside of its capacity as a public forum, the internet had also created another unforeseen cultural phenomenon: the online world had balkanized into genre-organized echo chambers of solipsism. Wholly un-interested in debate, these groups sought the right to have their beliefs, however self-contained, acknowledged. This dovetailed with the way so-cial media encouraged cultivating a small personal reality. Just as the platforms encouraged users to take a variety of photos and upload only the pictures that best accorded with their ideal image of their life, so too could ideas be treated this way, in which a chosen personal viewpoint was valid in and of itself.

The student protests were operating under new internet-generated as-sumptions. Could Woodrow Wilson's name make a student feel unsafe? What about a blond baby dressed as Mulan? To the culture-shocked pro-fessors, these were questions to be debated. The faculty members were, after all, academics accustomed to constantly shifting their perspective on issues like morality, politics, and history by employing a variety of nuanced approaches, each interpretation casting doubt upon the last. And perhaps up until that moment, they had imagined it was their job to teach students this practice.

Now they encountered a new generation of young people infuriated that individual beliefs, feelings, and perspectives were not acknowledged as correct simply because they were deeply felt. Instead, the professors adopted an attitude that enraged the students. They assumed that the students, being young and naive, didn't know their own minds.

"It's not a debate!" the students screamed at their "Master" Nicho-las Christakis. "It's not about creating an intellectual space!"[10] And to them it wasn't. To the students, the Halloween costumes made them feel unsafe. The proof? They said they felt unsafe.

Universities like Yale looked even more ridiculous for the role they played in the drama. In videos, Nicholas Christakis stands in a circle of students, hands clasped receptively, nodding vigorously, interested in hearing his students out as they yell things like "You should not sleep at night! You are disgusting!"[11]

In the mid-60s, students had protested that their schools were becom-ing leadership factories for the status quo, selling what Charles Reich had successfully argued in front of the Supreme Court was a form of "new property," degrees that earned the student a high place in society's hierarchy. And after decades of colleges reinventing themselves as brand-name degree factories, professors were no longer "Masters" willing to offer their expertise to humble students, but clerks nodding vigorously as their customers sent back their overpriced education like it was an imperfect Frappuccino.

On Tumblr, a generation had learned to agitate as consumers for better representation in entertainment products. And it was only natural that the question of who got to dress as a Disney princess transitioned seamlessly into a list of complaints about how the university could do a better job.

In this, the Yale controversy reflected a conflict the previous year at Oberlin College, in which students argued that because the dining hall's Vietnamese sandwiches and Japanese sushi were not "authentic" (rather poor replications made by low-wage workers in the dining hall) they were evidence of "cultural appropriation."[12] The crisis was resolved when the catering company held a meeting with the students and promised to fix all of their customers' issues with the food. Here the real issue was the slipshod service of a class of servants to a new youth culture that was full of wounded anxiety about their own status in the immense hierarchy of society. And just as the most expensive coffee is labeled "fair trade," so too were students allowed to purchase along with the product the self-satisfied feeling that they were exploiting no one. In fact, by buying the fanciest coffee or, in this case, eating the best sandwiches, they were somehow *helping*.

The 4chan far right reveled in the YouTube videos of the Yale debate because they appeared to display young, privileged people throwing tantrums about their "feelings" and their lack of "accommodations" in a setting that was as far from the backwaters where 4channers dwelled as possible, a garden of wealth, patrolled by private security, whose every exit led to a lifetime among the ruling class. Nor was it difficult to imagine that all that smart, radical energy would eventually be channeled to maintain the status quo in the corporate hierarchy of foundations, non-profits, and teaching positions at liberal universities.

To express their contempt, the betas borrowed a phrase from the movie *Fight Club*, "You are not a beautiful and unique snowflake."

But as the student protesters saw it, they were urgently sounding the alarm about a difference to which privilege was blind—the difference described by Margaret Atwood when she said, "Men are afraid that women will laugh at them. Women are afraid that men will kill them." To minorities, women, and trans people who faced the daily threat of physical harm, matters of justice began with feelings, accommodations, and safety. For example, despite all the private security, campuses were often the setting of sexual assaults, an issue that was only just then getting increased attention with the introduction of Title IX (a law that prohibits sex discrimination in any institution receiving federal financial assistance).

By defining and advocating for an increasingly diverse array of marginalized groups, students felt they were simply completing the long-overdue Enlightenment project of setting everyone on an equal footing. But their generation's obsession with hierarchy and cataloging a diverse array of individual frustrations spoke to a much larger overriding theme: fear—the same immense sensation of powerlessness in twenty-first-century capitalism that had defined the rival youth movements on 4chan.

Around the same time, two older leftist activists, Morgan Page and Sarah Schulman, were heavily criticized online in what was now a familiar dogpile of social media for giving blunt eulogies at the funeral of a trans person who had committed suicide. In a subsequent talk on the internet controversy, Page spoke about how the explosive anger she witnessed online emerged from a feeling of frustration that everyone, particularly those with marginalized identities, faced. "[There's] so much garbage 24/7—we're dealing with it from people on the street, we're dealing with it trying to access medical institutions, from trying to deal with the government on any level in any way, and we have basically zero power to change that, or at least we feel that way, most of the time." For this reason, she argued, online dogpiling reflected a deep frustration at not being able "to hurt an institution" or "get an institution to empathize with you." Schulman and Christakis stood in for the frustration that accompanied living in the margins of a world dominated by monolithic indestructible institutions.

The bottom-dwellers of 4chan resented how privileged groups at Ivy League schools palliated their privilege by obsessing over hierarchies of privilege. But this conflict spoke to an odd reality. The sensation of being on the bottom of an immense hierarchy was so pervasive that *even those at the ivy-coated gates of power felt it keenly*. This reality echoed Reich's observation at Yale in the 60s that in the tangled hierarchy of the modern Corporate State, even CEOs (or, in this case, likely the children of CEOs) felt they were powerless to fundamentally change society.

Naturally, a Corporate State hierarchy composed of narrowly focused "experts" only allowed to offer their opinion in the pigeonhole of their expertise has culminated in a pervasive feeling of impotence. Part of this sensation was personal impotence; Hannah Arendt's "cog" in the power-accumulating machine. But there also existed the larger dread that defined the 2016 election, of a totally rudderless ship of state, that everyone, even those at the top of the immense apparatus, was still somehow merely a minor mandarin functionary, unable to steer the thing as a whole. Even a highly efficient cog at Yale could not change its output.

What counterculture emerged after the punk disaffection of the 90s? In retrospect, it seems almost inevitable: an endless, neurotic labeling project.

Counterculture, after numerous escape attempts, was still in the same prison. And now the prisoners had become a little unhinged. For decades they had tried to gnaw their way through their chains. Now they began to gnaw on themselves.

The new generation focused on cataloging all the ways they felt impotent.

Young people now assumed they were more grist than mill builders, let alone mill destroyers. They didn't expect that they would rebuild the structure of society. Rather, they saw themselves as trapped inside an indestructible system and hoped that they would simply be treated mercifully by its chutes.

Both Tumblr identitarians and the betas on 4chan felt the keen frustration of the gap between fantasy and reality. For betas it was the difference between pornography and intimacy, video games and actual accomplishments. And young people on Tumblr tortured themselves with the gap that existed between how we imagine ourselves to be and how we are. Or, as Mark Fisher put it in his 2014 book on depression *Ghosts of My Life*, "It's miserable for anyone at all to *be themselves* (still more to be forced to sell themselves)."[13] In an uncertain world, what could be a worse anchor than what philosophers like Judith Butler discarded as so fluid it was meaningless—identity?

At the core of both youth cultures was the disease of the twenty-first century: depression and anxiety. Fisher's book was about how depression was better regarded as a cultural malaise than an individual sickness. The center of gamergate was *Depression Quest*.[14] Likewise, in Page's talk regarding her friend's suicide, she noted that there was an "epidemic" of suicide in the trans community. And Schulman explained that her friend died from the same problems that afflicted all marginalized millennials: depression and isolation. Ultimately, she decided, her friend had "died of poverty."

Both 4chan's anonymity and Tumblr's obsession with identity spoke to that isolation. An anonymous existence on message boards created crises of identity. Likewise defining oneself via social media was the opposite of real self-confidence, in which a person received their self-worth from themselves alone (unmediated by the likes of strangers). It was also the opposite of an alternative theory for selfhood in which a person derives their sense of value from their community. Not the ersatz communities of the internet, but real and actual people with whom one shares a direct and personal bond. Young people, lacking either the confidence to self-define in isolation or in a real-life community, often turned to the internet, where false subsitutes for confidence and communities made their problems worse.

Ironically, both 4chan and Tumblr users used their respective anonymity and self-definition *as ways to find context in a group*. 4chan began to glom together as Anonymous, then anonymous, then betas, incels, NEETS, etcetera. And like the original otaku, Tumblr users found their identities by connecting over the products they bought in interest groups. At the root of both youth movements was a strange interplay between isolation and group membership, one that would be exploited in the 2016 presidential election to great effect.

2016: Ejecta Assemble

I've wasted tiiiiime,
I've wasted me!
So say I'm slow for my age
A late bloomer
Okay, I agree!

—"Proud of Your Boy," from the Broadway
musical adaptation of Disney's *Aladdin*

It was into the chaos of the university protests that the newly knighted Mercer-nary Milo Yiannopoulos would step from the pirate-themed yacht at Cannes to stir the brew.

If gray-haired, liberal Yale professors offering dialogue and reconciliation could "trigger SJW snowflakes" into creating viral videos, then what mischief might the self-described "Dangerous Faggot" effect make? The answer, it turned out, was a lot. At Yiannopoulos' first speaking event, at DePaul University, to discuss his 4chanian view that "feminism is cancer," he was surrounded by a swirling storm of protesters, and in the melee two rushed the stage to accost him physically.

To help all of this along, Yiannopoulos hired an entourage of, as Bannon had promised, "the best people." One of his first assistants was another clownish alt-right Twitter personality who out-garished his new boss, though his version was more backwoods, monster-truck aficionado than Yiannopoulos' "Like a Virgin"–era Madonna. Tim "Treadstone" "Baked Alaska" Gionet favored camouflage prints, neon tank tops, and humongous sunglasses. Also like Yiannopoulos, Gionet desired more than anything to be famous. His profusion of names spoke to his various efforts to promote himself. The son of a proselytizing Christian minister in Alaska, Gionet had sought first to become a rapper in L.A., before moving to New York to produce viral videos for *Buzzfeed*.

Now he had achieved his dream of internet fame on alt-right Twitter. Sort of. It was hard to say whether Gionet was more LOLcow or celebrity, since part of his appeal was an oafish display of stupidity on selfie-stick livestreams. Online, Gionet had asked a thirteen-year-old girl whether he could "grab her by the pussy," meditated on the "JQ" ("Jewish Question"), and threw up Nazi salutes, habits that got him a headlining spot at Charlottesville's Unite the Right rally. But he would frequently get huffy when people suggested he was a Nazi.

Two weeks after the visit to DePaul, Yiannopoulos was joined by another media personality for a trip to Florida to give a speech outside Pulse Nightclub after the massacre there. As Yiannopoulos spoke about the dangers of Islam in the parking lot, a man in a fancy gray suit and an old-timey beard named Gavin McInnes appeared beside him. Echoing Yiannopoulos' sentiments, he spoke of society's "phobia of Islamophobia."

Twenty years ago, McInnes had cofounded *Vice* magazine, which earned him the (mostly self-applied) label "godfather of hipsterdom." McInnes eventually split with *Vice*, which morphed from a magazine into a media concern covering anything grotesque and postmodern, from child soldiers in Congo to dragon dildos sold on e-shops.

Though *Vice* had been on the far left from the very beginning, the core of McInnes' work remained remarkably unchanged as he transitioned to the hard right. He told men how to be men. Like *Playboy*, *Vice* hoovered up counterculture and resold it as products that defined a reader's status and gender, offering tips on how a man might advertise himself in the subtle language of fashion. (Technically, the magazine was unisex, but it was full of mostly female nudity.) McInnes began his career writing such advice pieces. Indeed, the term "hipster" embodied this process, since it referred to two radically different groups: anti-consumerist, far-left artists and a new generation of young urban professionals who buy the artists' avant-garde work, sold by marketers like McInnes who peddled them as must-have lifestyle choices.

In those days, *Vice* was distributed free in New York City and made its money solely on advertising. The Hefnerian equation it sold hadn't changed in half a century: buy to be happy; buy to be sexual. Men could win women by becoming economically successful, then advertise their economic victories by acquiring products that defined their masculinity.

As Marcuse had written in the 60s, sex was employed as a mechanism to maintain the status quo, a reward for societal conformity. And *Vice* was the last in a long line of magazines that pretended that transgression and sex were anti–mainstream culture, rather than the inverse, a reward for being a loyal wage-earner.

But each year, the trick was getting more difficult to perform. In order to be credibly anti-mainstream, *Vice* had to keep getting weirder and more vulgar. The results were predictably grotesque.

Vice's imperatives to buy were blended with successive waves of anti-capitalist, anti-consumerist youth culture. And some sixty years of marketers joining bright opposites had produced a brown sludge. McInnes' early articles in *Vice* spun on this dizzying point of this contradiction, which, by the late 90s, had reached a whirling madness. Like a Xerox of a Xeroxed zine, the ideas became murky black passages of fatalistic 90s self-loathing.

Vice employed the language of profanity-laced youth culture that had originated as a defense strategy against magazines and marketers. And with this blunt instrument, it offered to guide readers through deep philosophical and political issues by peering into what was cool and uncool, an attempt that reads like trying to repair an engine with a Fisher-Price tool kit.

"Being rejected sucks ass," McInnes wrote in the "Nobody Wants to Fuck Me" section of the 2003 "*Vice* Guide to Happiness." "Trying to suck someone's ass and being told 'no' sucks even bigger ass. Fooling around with some chick with a big ass and trying to go down on her ass and getting rejected sucks HUGE ass."[1]

However, as McInnes grew older, his ass-based philosophy became less appealing to him. When the alt-right appeared in 2015, he had recently moved out of Williamsburg to raise a family in the suburbs, which allowed him to switch lanes. He would drive all the way around the American cul-de-sac, back to the place Hefner fled when he began *Playboy*. Instead of purveying a *Playboy*/consumer/hipster variety of masculinity, he would sell the only cultural alternative—the 1950s breadwinner.

This was his new secret formula for happiness: No longer should a man wander the streets of Williamsburg meditating on how everything "sucks ass" while calculating what brand of whisky, skateboard, or sunglasses might best attract women. Rather, the new boss was the same as the old old boss. All a man needed to do in life to be happy, according to McInnes' new slogan, was "to venerate the housewife and glorify the entrepreneur."[2]

In some sense, McInnes had independently anticipated the migration of youth counterculture that had occurred on 4chan, where, in the darkest corners of unyielding consumerist nihilism, one suddenly discovers, in desperate groping, a small door that leads to the instructive safety of fundamentalist traditionalism.

McInnes had also found 90s nihilism's final bedrock. Young people were adrift in the shreds of a counterculture that had been consumed, then re-consumed, until everyone became bottom-dwellers, sorting through the scraps on places like 4chan.

This presented the same question: How long can you believe in nothing? What is beneath nothing? How long can your "guide to happiness" be couched in the language of "sucking ass"?

As a marketer who had profited immensely from working edgy youth culture into ads, McInnes was keenly aware of how the whole thing was teetering on the edge of a crash. His job was to stay ahead of the curve. And it hardly seemed likely that the counterculture would remain frozen in 90s nihilism for yet another decade. A marketer needed to catch the next wave before everyone else noticed it had crested.

One solution, of course, was to go in the direction of Tumblr along with the rest of *Vice*, in which youth culture became about crafting a unique identity, being ultra-polite, and respecting everyone's self-defined reality. Such a culture of "self-care" was profoundly important to a new generation that existed in a state of constant anxiety that accompanied extreme economic precariousness.

On the left, shrugging powerlessness was transcended by a new grander realm of powerlessness—a quivering, restless impotence born of the fear and depression that resulted from being confined to the bottom of society; your only power is a modicum of buying power measured out to you from above and generally directed toward digital escapism.

In this environment, Tumblr counterculture drew up a peace treaty with its predator, corporate consumer culture. The two would align in an illusory synthesis. Youth rebellion and social justice would be about prevailing on vast institutional forces for small, consumer-style accommodations. A layer of fantasy would be superimposed over reality. Just as social media encouraged the creation of an imaginary self layered over one's real life in the form of curated selfies and posts, so too the new left would be about respecting whatever world a person chose to create.

But preferring the raucous, offensive, punk, and deeply misogynistic elements of 90s nihilism, McInnes pivoted in the opposite direction, setting himself up as the nemesis of identity politics. He would form an open alliance with counterculture's age-old enemy: straitlaced, corporate mainstream culture.

In this sense, Yiannopoulos and McInnes were the final demented regurgitation of youth counterculture, which had passed through a fifty-year-long digestive track of corporate co-optation. The weird creatures that emerged were Frankenstein's monsters—stitched-together abominations, abhorred by humanity and holding together pieces of themselves that would never mend because they were already dead.

Freakishly, McInnes was a punk venerating the square suburban values of the 1950s. Even weirder, Yiannopoulos channeled 1980s gay counterculture to teach hordes of young straight men who couldn't find girlfriends that they should give up on life and play video games all day. Gionet was a pot-smoking, Christian rural racist who aspired to be a cool urban rapper, a sort of bludgeoned copy of the black gangster-rap culture adopted by poor young whites prior to the advent of the alt-right to express their own voiceless societal marginalization under capitalism.

To McInnes, Yiannopoulos' Dangerous Faggot template of offending those easily offended and feeding off the media attention must have come as a revelation. A few weeks after his speech in Florida, he inaugurated the first meeting of a new "fraternal organization" at a fashionably seedy bar in Greenpoint, Brooklyn.[3]

He called his fraternity the "Proud Boys."

Like Yiannopoulos' columns and the far-right neo-Nazi movements, the Proud Boys offered what disenfranchised young men longed for—solidarity, identity, and pride. The Proud Boys' escape hatch fled the same mental demons afflicting youth on the left—the anxiety and loneliness that came with living on the edge of personal, financial, and psychological collapse, when the rent wasn't paid, your savings had run out, and your dead-end job siphoned away the last of your meager hope into your student loans.

Ever the canny marketer, McInnes simply copied the competitor's product. Just as anxious, isolated young people on Tumblr found communion online through their identity groups, so too would the Proud Boys offer pride and belonging to the market demographic Tumblr neglected: cisgender white males.

McInnes reveled in his role as patriarchal lawgiver, no longer dispensing anything so pedestrian as advice in a magazine column, but a formula for living. He did not encourage young men to keep retreating, as Yiannopoulos' incel-inspired message did. Rather, his personal brew was a pickup-artist-flavored concoction. His attitude toward women was anti-feminist, suggesting men behave in the old-timey dominant and manipulative manner that had served them throughout the centuries.

"I learned [women] want to be downright abused," he opined in an interview. "When I stopped playing nice and began totally defiling the women I slept with, the number of them willing to sleep with me went through the roof."[4]

But unlike among the pickup artists (PUAs), women were not the focus of the Proud Boys; boys and pride were. As McInnes did when he sold suits, shoes, and beer via glossy magazine ads, the marketer would model manhood for men, showing his boys how to sift through the pools of nihilistic accumulation by developing, like the Nazi-worshipping alt-right, a rigid set of man codes he styled "alt-lite," a term meant to distinguish how his moral system did not condone racism.

These revelations did not come to him on a mountaintop via God, but rather while watching a stage production of the musical *Aladdin* at his daughter's school. In a scene that was cut from the film version, Aladdin sings to his mother about how, though he once was a scoundrel, he would soon make her "proud of your boy."[5]

Listening to the song, McInnes was disgusted. It is the natural capacity of men, he reasoned, to be scoundrels. They shouldn't be taught by modern culture to be prancing corporate Aladdins to please their moms.

And thus, the Proud Boys were formed quite literally from the scraps of pop culture on the cutting room floor. The rules were simple and built for men with the mindsets of prepubescent boys desperately wanting to know how to be men.

The first rule was a jingle: "The West Is the Best!" No more viewing the past as a succession of crimes perpetrated by white men. Instead, Western culture and innovations were to be celebrated—a point of pride rather than penitence and guilt. Another rule dictated that to join the Proud Boys, an initiate would be beaten (in practice, generally lovingly and lightly) by the rest of the boys until he named five breakfast cereals. And in a nod to the dissipation of media and the internet that had brought so much of Yiannopoulos' fan base into being, McInnes imposed the ultimate patriarchal injunction upon his boys: no masturbating more than once a week. A man's vital energy, he argued, was better spent trying to free oneself from indulgent fantasy. Proud Boys needed to step out into the real world and attain women in the flesh.

And as for the spiritual emptiness that he had railed against since the 90s, the pop in the center of pop culture. There too his alt-lite alighted upon the same biblical answer as the Evolian alt-right: traditional conservative values. A wife and family would answer the big existential questions. Modernism and economic marginalization were granting lonely people cramped in apartments the company of "cats and dogs," as McInnes liked to say, instead of children. Only by adhering to the traditional standards of the past, the tried-and-true formulas for happiness, would one find genuine contentment.

This message appealed to so many young men because they had lived very different lives than their parents (or as the *Aladdin* musical put it, "I wasn't born perfect like Dad or you, Mom!"). Instead of ascending into the middle class, they'd endured an existence of low-income jobs and high rents that left them with the vague suspicion that society must have been built for someone else. For this reason, they deeply resented the left's increasing focus on the notion that white men enjoyed special privilege. Their experience was the opposite. They felt like they were on the bottom. Marginalized, they wanted to feel accepted. Debased, they wanted to feel proud. And ill-equipped to deal with life, they fashioned answers for themselves that were puerile and crude, pieced together like folk art from pieces of garbage in which YouTube videos and breakfast cereals were repurposed into an illuminated codex of brotherly ideology.

For all its hate, there was something touchingly naive about uncultured men venerating tradition and ancient values they had never experienced. What could be more deranged and quixotic than building the foundation of your philosophy on outtakes from a Disney musical? It was also inherently comedic, like the monster Caliban in *The Tempest* imagining that the drunken sailors who visit his remote isle are kingly liberators. And indeed, most of the Proud Boy meetings involve heavy drinking.

However, almost immediately after their founding, McInnes would have a difficult time distinguishing his Proud Boys from the white nationalist organizations that were forming in the wake of Yiannopoulos' tour.

At the end of June, in between his speech with Yiannopoulos and the first Proud Boys meeting, one of the first of a series of violent clashes between the alt-right and counterprotesters would occur.

In Sacramento, California, a neo-Nazi march was met by an antifa counterprotest. The result was a tremendous street brawl involving three hundred people. Seven participants were stabbed and nine hospitalized. The march had been organized by a new group of fascists called the Traditionalist Worker Party, whose membership had been growing in the summer of 2016, emboldened by the success of Trump. Like Richard Spencer's New Century Foundation, the group advocated for a "white ethnostate" and attracted the traditional neo-Nazi crowd of poor, uneducated whites.[6]

Despite Yiannopoulos' attempts to stir up press coverage with his tour, much of his power was still virtual. The main battlefield for clashes between left and right remained online in squabbles over entertainment products. In July, the largest clash centered around the gender-swapped *Ghostbusters* movie, condemned as a disgrace by nerdy young men on the alt-right and lauded as a political victory on the left.

In July, /pol/ began harassing one of the film's stars, African American actress Leslie Jones, deluging her with pictures of monkeys and apes on Twitter. As usual, Yiannopoulos followed /pol/ into the fray, which earned him a permanent ban from Twitter. However, all of the press coverage Yiannopoulos received for his *Ghostbusters* Twitter ban paled in comparison to the profile boost he received the next month.

In mid-August, Trump's campaign manager Paul Manafort resigned when a secret ledger surfaced detailing alleged bribes he had received while working for a corrupt Kremlin-backed regime in Ukraine. Bannon, of all people, was tapped to replace him. And on August 17, he departed *Breitbart* to become Trump's chief campaign strategist.

In this, Clinton saw an opportunity. Bannon had recently told reporters from *Mother Jones* that *Breitbart* was "a platform for the alt-right."[7] Clinton delivered a speech specifically naming the alt-right and condemning Trump for his association with such unseemly elements. At the rally, she explicitly mentioned the then obscure site *Breitbart News* and Yiannopoulos- (and 4chan-) themed articles such as "Would You Rather Your

Child Had Feminism or Cancer?" However, the speech is not remembered for Clinton's strong words, but a meta-media moment. When Clinton uttered the word "alt-right," somewhere in the crowd a man shouted, "PEPE!"

Both Yiannopoulos and Bannon were delighted. "I've never laughed so hard," Yiannopoulos wrote his old boss. To which Bannon replied, "Dude: we r inside her fucking head."[8]

Not long after, on September 7, at a fundraiser in New York City, Clinton described Trump supporters as a "basket of deplorables." Though "deplorables" was picked up and memed, the choice of the word "basket," plucked seemingly at random from the unconscious drawing room of Clinton's mind, was the more damning half of the statement, evoking not only her patrician taste for East Coast, Martha Stewart–style luxury, but the other reason the alt-right resented her: she was the mom in the *Aladdin* musical.

The basket metaphor condensed the idea into a single image: Clinton was trying to safely ensconce their rebellious/deplorable/scoundrel/proud-of-yer-boy masculinity into her womblike world of decorative baskets, shaming them into toeing a polite line of liberal moral rectitude. Like a mom catching boys romping through the house, Clinton told the young men to obey, to defer to her stern expertise, or in this case her pile of experts (a list that, much like the ill-fated catalog of ships in *The Iliad*, ran on for several pages in her post-campaign memoir *What Happened*). By contrast, Trump represented rude freedom, defying Corporate State experts, and creating one's own hyper-masculine reality.

The young people of the alt-right delighted in the "basket." Soon a meme was generated out of the poster for a Hollywood action movie. Trump, Pepe the Frog, and his team of associates, including Yiannopoulos, Alex Jones, Ben Carson, Roger Stone, Chris Christie, and Trump's sons, were superimposed over the faces of old media hyper-men like Sylvester Stallone, Chuck Norris, Arnold Schwarzenegger, and Bruce Willis. The meme was shared on social media by several of those depicted in it, including Donald Trump Jr.

Then things got even loopier. In response, Clinton's campaign released a statement condemning Pepe the Frog. In what *The Verge* called the "death of explainers," Clinton's team described how Pepe, "an innocent meme enjoyed by teenagers and pop stars alike," was now a hate symbol.

To young people, the idea that Pepe, the symbol of idiotic internet trash, now took center stage in U.S. election coverage only confirmed their suspicion that the whole affair was so much tawdry refuse.

Weirder still, as the election drew to a close, the endless drama of computer breaches merged with the memes. A few weeks before the election, the hacked emails of Clinton's campaign manager John Podesta were released by WikiLeaks, which had most likely obtained them via the Russian government. WikiLeaks published over 20,000 pages of emails. In 2018, the *New York Times* reported that Steve Bannon directed a former Trump campaign adviser, Roger Stone, to keep tabs on WikiLeaks' efforts. And Stone's possible coordination with Trump's campaign and WikiLeaks is now a subject of Special Counsel Robert Mueller's probe.[9]

But in 2016, the emails were simply more fuel for the dumpster fire and /pol/, like many others, went digging through them looking for dirt. The correspondence contained excerpts from Clinton's infamous paid speeches to large Wall Street financial institutions, which she had refused to release. However, other than this, there wasn't much to be found. Clinton's emails were terse, mostly grandmotherly hellos to old acquaintances. But this did not stop the fantasy-prone hordes who had spun gamergate from nothing. In fact, the experience had taught them a valuable lesson: "gates" were not discovered but made.

The effort was led by the old gamergater Mike Cernovich. During the election, Cernovich had made a small business around the idea that men would welcome treating real events like a digital fantasy product that can be toggled and manipulated as if they were in their favorite video game. He began performing in weekly livestreams in which he asserted his independent masculine right to think as he pleased, selling books and soliciting donations to fund the fight against his new bugbear, the mainstream media.

As part of a profile, the *New Yorker*'s Andrew Marantz had watched as Cernovich spun news into lies (in that case, that Hillary Clinton was seriously ill) by spreading the falsehoods on social media to an audience of men willing to multiply the rumors online in the style of 4chan trolls.[10] This process was helped along by a new online audience: credulous older newcomers to the internet who weren't practiced in critical reasoning but would certainly indulge in 4chan-crafted fantasies as they spawned in the swamps of /pol/.[11]

A few days before the election, on November 4, as /pol/ sifted through the Podesta emails, they found a few related to an event he had organized at a hybrid show venue/pizza parlor in D.C., Comet Ping Pong.

Ever since 4chan's founding, child pornography had been the subject of frequent jokes on the site. Disaffected teenagers' compulsion to outcompete each other with transgressive humor mingled with a desire to make fun of the perverted otaku who visited the anime sections looking to share sexualized drawings of young girls. (In 2016, the running joke on all boards was that the pedophiles would finally leave, since now that 4chan had turned thirteen it was "too old.")

4chan's slang for child pornography was "CP," and from 2004 onward it was spun into memes about other things that started with the same initials, most notably images of Captain Picard and cheese pizza. When the denizens of /pol/ saw references to cheese pizza in Podesta's email in 2016 and noted the initials of Comet Ping Pong, the rest of the tale wrote itself. Clinton and Podesta, they asserted with deadpan earnestness, were running a child sex dungeon out of Comet Ping Pong. The emails were obviously in code (coincidentally, the same code that perverts and trolls on the chans used for child pornography).

To anyone remotely familiar with chan culture and its winking meme signals, it was clear that the "pizzagate" conspiracy theory was a joke generated on 4chan. But remarkably, in a post-fact world, in which conspiracy was more fun and useful than reality, the report spread like all the other Clinton "scandals," the capstone of years of Clinton conspiracy theories purveyed by Republicans like Bannon and David Bossie. In this environment, it was easy for Cernovich to pick up the banner on Twitter and insist that pizzagate was real. "Some truly sick stuff going on in #PodestaEmails. It's some sort of sex trafficking ring," he tweeted a week before the election. "The Clintons are running a pedophile ring."[12]

Practically, pizzagate functioned as gamergate had. Reality-challenged kids and adults collaborated with nihilistic trolls to play the internet like a video game. They set up subreddits like /r/pizzagate, which were a combo of /pol/, the old gamergate subreddits, and 4chan's paranormal board /x/. The goal was to make a role-playing game out of the internet by e-stalking anyone associated with the topic and digging through social media and public records for "clues" to build the fiction.

Far from disappearing as part of the 2016 campaign dumpster fire, pizzagate instead became a template for alt-right hijinks. The central con-spiratorial fiction behind pizzagate was that the pizza parlor sex dun-geon held children who had been purchased by high-ranking left-leaning politicians and their Hollywood donors. Cernovich spent the next two years accusing various left-wing enemies who criticized him of being pe-dophiles, charges that were echoed by his online hate mob. "Is there a massive pedophile ring involving members of Hollywood, the media, and Congress?" he speculated on Twitter in November 2016, apparently building on a tweet from a few days earlier in which he had declared, "Pizzagate is not going to go away, this story is huge!"[13]

And in fact, pizzagate didn't go away. By 2018, it had been folded into the larger and even more ridiculous "Q-Anon" conspiracy theory, which began in October 2017 when an anonymous user on 4chan's /pol/ claimed that as a member of the deep state, he knew a great secret: Rob-ert Mueller's investigation of Trump was in fact a covert sting operation to catch not Trump and his campaign advisers, but Hillary Clinton and John Podesta.

As the meme-spiracy spread to 8chan and Reddit, the theory was soon championed on Twitter by none other than Roseanne Barr, just as her pro-Trump sitcom on ABC aired. By August 2018, Q-Anon had hit the front page of the *New York Times* after rabid "Q supporters" appeared at a Trump rally in Tampa, Florida.[14] Earlier, a Q-obsessed shooter had created a standoff with law enforcement at the Hoover Dam. The growing number of unhinged and credulous non-chan-going normies willing to drink the Kool-Aid surprised everyone, even 4chan.

Moreover, the evolution of pizzagate into Q-Anon represented a new low for both the chans and post-truth political discourse.

For a long time, the insider claiming to be "Q" didn't bother to log in with a password to the boards in which he posted. In other words, anyone could be Q.

All one had to do was write in Q's easy-to-replicate style of second-tier spy movie (though with more grammar mistakes) and then hit "post." (E.g., "HRC's mentor is who? / What happens if the truth about Haiti is released? Through the looking glass.")

Any anon could add to the official canon of insider knowledge com-ing directly from the deep state. Just as with gamergate, most people consumed all of this 4chan and 8chan content secondhand via self-appointed YouTube pundits profiting off the view counts.[15] So most Q-Anon subscribers didn't see how the sausage was made.

Before Q was known as Q, he was referred to as "that larper guy" (LARP, or live action role-playing). And anons begged for him to "come back," that is, for someone to write in his style (much like a child begging a parent to read them a bedtime story).

Soon, even /pol/ users believed the fiction, even though they were the ones making it up. Except "belief" wasn't really the correct term anymore. There was no word for this new sort of naiveté, in which the distinction between reality and fiction, trolling and trolled, identity and anon erased itself as people made a sport out of their politics and the discontents it bred.

Did Cernovich truly believe in pizzagate or the Q-Anon theory?

The answer was that words like "truly" weren't really relevant to him. Truth and reality were unseated by unhappy grievances that cried the sense out of everything.

And now many in the country marched to the discordant beat of his caterwauling.

And all of this, of course—the dumpster fire eternal—was made possible by an event that surprised everyone: Trump won the 2016 presidential election.

2017: The Alt-Right Implodes

What a time to be alive.
—Traditional meme expressing how it is in fact a disappointing time to be alive

When Trump was elected, Yiannopoulos' campaign tour and the demonstrations didn't end. They intensified. Even pizzagate ramped up. Comet Ping Pong became the target of harassment not only by wackos, but by self-described online journalists like Lucian Wintrich, who had also just been invited into Trump's White House press briefings. Finally, a twenty-eight-year-old man named Edgar Welch put an end to the affair when he drove to the restaurant on December 4 and fired an assault weapon into the ceiling in an attempt to free the fictitious children trapped in the basement. Welch had heard about the pizza-themed sex ring on Alex Jones' conspiracy-laden internet talk show, *InfoWars*. No one was harmed. And Welch was sentenced to four years in prison.

Meanwhile, as the left mobilized to protest Trump's ascension it split along similar lines as in the primaries. Generally young, leftist radicals (a mix of socialists, anarchists, and "libertarian socialists") who wanted profound if not revolutionary change to the status quo organized in the J20 (January 20) to disrupt the inauguration. Unwilling to protest the inauguration directly, older, centrist liberals, in the imprint of Clinton, organized an identity-themed march for the day after the inauguration, on the twenty-first, which was billed not as an explicitly anti-Trump march, but as a Women's March.[1]

This schism resulted in two dramatically different scenes. On January 21, millions of women in knitted pink pussy hats flooded the streets with their daughters and granddaughters, milling about peacefully. The previous day, the more radical protesters had been left exposed, wandering in loose packs in the streets around Trump's sparsely attended inauguration; those who came to protest nonviolently mixed in with groups who smashed shop windows, set fires, and set off fireworks.

Beneath overcast skies, D.C. police scooped up groups of marchers indiscriminately. There were 230 people "kettled" between Twelfth and L Streets. The authorities charged anyone caught in the dragnet, including some journalists and legal observers, with felonies under the Federal Riot Statute, alleging that they were conspirators of those who caused property damage and thus subject to answer for their crimes.[2] Most of the cases were eventually dismissed.

Amid this chaos, the white nationalist Richard Spencer was wandering the streets, dressed in a tweed suit, followed by an Australian documentary crew. He too was a refugee from a political schism, this one between the alt-lite and the alt-right. The day before, Cernovich had organized a "DeploraBall," explicitly disinviting not only Spencer but images of Pepe the Frog. Recently, Spencer had been caught on camera by *The Atlantic* throwing up the Nazi salute and telling a group of men, "Heil Trump!"

Now, as he stopped on Fourteenth and K to answer questions from the filmmakers, the conversation turned to the Pepe the Frog pin on his lapel. Looking a little like Pepe himself because of the way his neck bulged from his ill-fitting collar, Spencer looked down, eager to explain his pin's significance, when a member of antifa leapt into the frame and landed two sucker punches in quick succession.[3]

This footage became a training video introducing citizens to the combatants in the new conflicts of 2017, the previously obscure anti-fascist group antifa (in this case, a Philadelphia chapter called the black bloc) and a new breed of frog-worshipping internet Nazis, drifting like Pepe in the liminal space between pop culture and hate symbols.

The clip inspired endless remixes, the creation of which all framed the same question: Is it okay to punch Nazis parading in the streets after Trump's surprise victory? The consensus, reached through meme-ified mash-ups of clips from Nazi-socking movies and comic books, was yes. That's how it played out in Quentin Tarantino films, on *Captain America* covers, and in history itself, the reasoning went.

Meanwhile, Yiannopoulos, less interested in politics than self-promotion, kept his act rolling. During the inauguration he spoke at the University of Washington in Seattle, where one of his supporters came prepared to shoot protesters, which he promptly did when the speech began. (The attacker was arrested and the victim survived.)[4] Then a few days afterward, Yiannopoulos led his Dangerous Faggot Tour to Berkeley.

The events in D.C. and the violence in Seattle had brought the situation to a boiling point. Roughly 1,500 people filled Sproul Plaza to protest Yiannopoulos' planned speech. Among the counterprotesters were a smaller number of black-clad protesters from organizations like antifa, black bloc, and By Any Means Necessary, who sowed chaos: lighting fires, throwing rocks, and shattering store windows. Eventually, the riot spilled out of the campus, as demonstrators attacked Yiannopoulos' supporters and, in some cases, people who simply "looked like Nazi[s]."[5]

Meanwhile, fleeing the violent mob on the tour bus, Yiannopoulos' entourage of naive young men, almost exclusively teenagers, ate ice-cream bars and drank root beer.[6]

The event proved to be a high-water mark for Yiannopoulos. A year before, the blogger was promoting himself on obscure furry-themed fan pages and drifting around as the butt of jokes on Tumblr and 4chan. The riots in Berkeley put his name on the front page of the *New York Times*. But it was not to last.

When the Conservative Political Action Conference (CPAC), an influential annual meeting of conservatives, announced Yiannopoulos would be a keynote speaker at the event along with White House chief strategist Steve Bannon, the conservative establishment balked. In previous years, Bannon had held an alternative conference mocking CPAC titled "The Uninvited." Now, it appeared, the conservative party was being consumed from within by Trumpism, though no one was yet sure if it had first taken the trouble to die.

In response to the news, a sixteen-year-old Canadian girl dug up video clips of Yiannopoulos seemingly countenancing sexual relationships between young teenagers and adults, particularly homosexual ones, as he recounted his underage experiences with an older priest he called "Father Michael." "I'm grateful for Father Michael," he said. "I wouldn't give nearly such good head if it wasn't for him."

Though Yiannopoulos sounded sincere when he argued "Pedophilia is not a sexual attraction to somebody 13 years old who is sexually mature," when the news broke, he began to backpedal on his Facebook page, claiming the remarks were edgy satire, which allowed him to speak about his own abuse.[7]

In disgrace, Yiannopoulos lost his invitation to CPAC, then his job at *Breitbart*, and finally his six-figure book deal with Simon & Schuster. He would spend much of the next year unsuccessfully suing his former publishing house for breach of contract. Robert Mercer would eventually disavow him too, though only after his role in the tour was outed by Yiannopoulos' leaked emails, an act the billionaire would soon repeat with Bannon after the disastrous events in Charlottesville. Though Mercer never denounced Trump or his administration, which was stocked with Mercer confidants like Kellyanne Conway and John Bolton.[8]

By 2018, the only news Yiannopoulos generated was when he appeared on *InfoWars* to sell health supplements. However, the conflicts he inspired didn't end with the tour.

In the first months of Trump's presidency, other visitors to college campuses received the Yiannopoulos welcome. On March 2, when a liberal professor of political science named Allison Stanger attempted to interview the controversial conservative policy wonk Charles Murray at Middlebury College in Vermont, the students tried to tear both limb from limb, leaving Professor Stanger concussed and in a neck brace. Murray coauthored an infamous early 90s book, *The Bell Curve*, which made a statistical argument that blacks were genetically predisposed to lower intelligence than whites based on IQ scores. The idea was roundly dismissed as spurious by the scientific community, most notably by the Harvard evolutionary biologist Stephen Jay Gould, who, in addition to various statistical critiques, noted a mistake that could be observed by any layman: the thesis reflected the ideological fallacy that intelligence is defined by a standardized test that flattens an individual into a series of metrics. Only in the modern era of industrialized hierarchy would intelligence be considered how fast a person can grind through a series of tasks for someone else. Nonetheless, the book found traction in conservative politics.

In an interview with C-SPAN and an op-ed in the *New York Times*, Stanger said the students attacked her because of their failure to "read for themselves."[9] Instead, they simply credited the online definition provided by the Southern Poverty Law Center (SPLC) of Murray as a racist. If Stanger's students were guilty of consulting their phones instead of the text, Stanger was guilty of failing to include internet spaces in her study of politics.[10] She saw a contradiction in students attacking a Never Trump conservative like Murray as a stand-in for Trump, unaware that Murray was in fact a stand-in for Spencer. The reason Murray landed in the SPLC's glossary was that his work had laid the foundation for self-declared "scientific," "intellectual," statistics-obsessed white supremacists like Spencer and Jared Taylor, who were now at the center of the alt-right campus conflicts.[11]

Similarly, on March 17, a controversy broke out at Canada's McMaster University around Jordan Peterson, a once-obscure psychology professor who had recently risen to internet fame on account of a YouTube video he had posted in September 2016, at the height of Yiannopoulos' campus-baiting tour. In the video, Peterson stated he would not address students by their preferred pronouns and criticized a recent Canadian bill, C-16, that would render his refusing to do so illegal. The hit YouTube videos of Jordan Peterson at McMaster echoed those produced at Yale a year earlier. Once again, a lone white professor was surrounded by a young, diverse group of students. The students screamed and yelled at Peterson, who always kept his cool, for something that, at least on the surface, seemed insignificant.

Meanwhile, the memes and news articles about the left attacking the right had not gone unnoticed by /pol/. The Spencer punch drew out a consensus; if the left preferred violence, it was violence they would get. Organizing on social media, in chat rooms, and on message boards, anarchists and Nazis drove in from out of town to clash at Berkeley on March 4 and April 15. And on March 25, a brawl broke out in Huntington Beach, California, between pro-Trump marchers and counterprotesters. In the middle of the fray was a local group of street-brawling neo-Nazis, Identity Evropa (pronounced Europa), founded two years prior by a thirty-year-old ex-marine and ex-convict from the Bay Area named Nathan Damigo. Though Damigo's brand of fascism was classic neo-Nazi, he didn't fit the profile of southern, uneducated, and impoverished. Rather, his white pride stemmed from his humiliating failure to succeed in adult life. Before his stint in the military ended in a drunken assault, he had been a poor student at a high-end private high school in Silicon Valley.[12]

After the fights, /pol/ was eager to invent a meme to counter the Spencer punch. Sifting through grainy footage from April's brawls, they picked out what they thought was a moment comparable to the Spencer blow, though the video had to be slowed down, enhanced, and cropped considerably for it to be noticed.

In the sequence, a man breaks a long wobbly stick over the head of a member of antifa as the two sides surge at one another then sheepishly recede. The stick-wielding man is sporting a motorcycle helmet, a gas mask, and a tabletop decorated to look like Captain America's shield. As a riposte to all the memes of Captain America punching Spencer, /pol/ dubbed the figure "Based Stickman" or the "alt-knight" and began remixing the clip with songs and images. Fittingly, the character /pol/ elevated turned out to be a forty-one-year-old repeat felon named Kyle Chapman, with a history of drug abuse and, according to his lawyer, "severe psychological problems." Delighted, Chapman dove into the role, founding an "order of alt-knights," traveling the country to brawl, and participating in a *Vice* documentary, though all the activity would eventually land him back in jail on parole violations.[13]

Wanting in on the action, Gavin McInnes and Ann Coulter announced pilgrimages to Berkeley to speak, but unfortunately for them, no one cared to shed any blood. After extensive negotiations with the police, their event at Sproul, which in the end featured only McInnes surrounded by some seventy police officers and 150 protesters, went off largely without incident.[14]

However, elsewhere emotions were beginning to boil over. On May 26, a white nationalist in Portland, Oregon, named Jeremy Joseph Christian began shouting racial slurs at two teenage girls on a crowded train car on the local light rail. When three passengers intervened, Christian pulled out a knife and slashed at their necks, an attack that only one of the three survived.

A month earlier, on April 29, Christian had been filmed at an alt-right political rally in Portland wearing an American flag like a superhero cape, throwing up Nazi salutes, and screaming racial slurs.[15]

In response to the stabbing, the right organized another "free speech" rally, which was met by a large counterprotest. Though much of Portland was on the far left, Oregon had a long history of systemic racism that had driven out much of the state's African American population. For this reason, /pol/ and the rest of the white nationalist movement held it in special regard. When the United States collapsed, they imagined, it was the Pacific Northwest where they would found their new "white ethnostate," since it was the most suitably homogeneous area of the country.

Once again, young white nationalists and far-left activists drove in from surrounding areas to brawl. Among those in attendance were the familiar roving band of /pol/-anointed costumed warriors, including Based Stickman and Tim "Baked Alaska" Gionet.[16] But it wasn't just the right interested in a fight. By this point, both sides were eager to draw blood. I had been in Portland the week before the stabbings and was surprised to encounter young people who spent most of their afternoons training with black-clad, far-left protest groups, preparing for the next conflict. When the day of the protest arrived, the police made fourteen arrests before breaking up the event as it quickly degenerated into a street brawl.[17]

Meanwhile Spencer, now a famous punching bag, had not been idle. He had teamed up with a far-right activist in Charlottesville, Virginia, named Jason Kessler. Unlike the sharply dressed Spencer, Kessler was bland looking, with dark features and a round, perpetually unshaven face. Both had graduated from the University of Virginia in Charlottesville.

In his early years, Kessler had been a devoted leftist activist, camping out for a week at Occupy Wall Street. But after college, he had worked in a string of low-skilled jobs. Like Cernovich and Damigo, through a mix of behavioral issues, foolish ideas, and lack of trying, he was failing at real life despite his expensive education. And so Kessler retreated into a fantasy of self-justification, also known as blogging. He wrote science-fiction novels no one read and attempted to break into journalism. And in this, he eventually succeeded.

Quaint and picturesque, Charlottesville has been voted one of the best places to live in the nation several times. But those votes came at the expense of gentrification. As the D.C. sprawl continued to expand, Charlottesville's efforts to attract wealthy, mostly white yuppies caused friction with black populations whose neighborhoods were still suffering from centuries of racist policies.[18] In the wake of the Dylann Roof shooting in Charleston, South Carolina, the city was reckoning with its Confederate monuments, specifically a statue of Robert E. Lee in the center of the city. Other than being in Virginia, the town had no ties to the commander of the Army of Northern Virginia. The monument had been erected with a set of other American historical figures by a local businessman in the 1920s.[19]

One of those leading the charge for the statue's removal was a young

African American city councilman named Wes Bellamy. Amid the debate over the statues, Kessler dug through Bellamy's voluminous Twitter history and unearthed a large quantity of anti-white and misogynistic tweets.[20] These inspired Kessler to organize a set of protests to counter Bellamy's.

In June, fresh from marching in Charlottesville, Spencer and Kessler demonstrated on the mall in Washington, speaking at a free-speech rally organized by a Baltimore teenager. Beside them was the neo-Nazi street brawler Nathan Damigo and another alt-right character named Augustus Sol Invictus, a 2016 Libertarian candidate for the U.S. Senate in Florida.[21] Inspired by the /pol/ meme, Invictus, whose adopted Latin name translates to "majestic sun unconquered," had collaborated with Chapman to form the Fraternal Order of Alt-Knights.

Only a hundred people attended the event. And across the mall, the alt-lite held a competing rally "against political violence" that wasn't much larger. It was composed of many of the speakers who had dropped out of the original event when they had heard Spencer was speaking. Among them were Roger Stone, Mike Cernovich, and Jack Posobiec, a pizzagate conspiracy theorist who had praised Spencer as "indispensable" on Twitter less than a year before. Standing beside them was Lucian Wintrich.[22]

That the broken halves of the same protest were held so close together only seemed to emphasize the bizarre intimacy of the two pro-Trump camps, which, ever since they were born three years earlier, had tried and failed to separate from one another. At the alt-lite event, Wintrich told the *New Yorker*'s Andrew Marantz that the term "alt-right" "was adopted by libertarians, anti-globalists, classical conservatives, and pretty much everyone else who was sick of what had become of establishment conservatism. Then Richard Spencer came along, throwing up Nazi salutes and claiming that he was the leader of the alt-right. He effectively made the term toxic and then claimed it for himself. We all abandoned using it in droves."[23]

This account was in no way true. Spencer himself had created the term in 2010 when he registered alternativeright.com. And several years earlier, Yiannopoulos had acknowledged the alt-right was full of neo-Nazis in his failed attempt to marginalize them in the movement.

Less than two weeks later, the same fissures and loopy cast of characters would cause the alt-right, at least in its present form, to crumble catastrophically. Kessler had planned yet another protest around Char-lottesville's Robert E. Lee statue on August 12. Billed as the Unite the Right rally, it was headlined by Spencer and Baked Alaska.

On the eve of the event, Kessler and Spencer held a surprise march through the University of Virginia, where they were followed by about 250 young white men dressed in white polo shirts carrying tiki torches and shouting the same weird slogans, "Jews will not replace us," "You will not replace us!" and the old Nazi slogan "Blood and soil!" A similar march had occurred in June, when the participants also yelled, "Russia is our friend!"

The University of Virginia was miles from the statue of Lee. But it's easy to imagine why it was the focal point of Kessler's resentment. After graduating, Kessler settled into life as a low-wage laborer. The univer-sity from which he had earned a high-priced degree must have symbol-ized a great deal of disappointment for him.

The marchers met a smaller group of student protesters who had ringed themselves around a statue of Thomas Jefferson. A shouting match occurred: "White lives matter!" the fascists yelled. "Black lives matter!" the protesters rejoined.

According to the firsthand account of *ProPublica* journalist A. C. Thompson, the white nationalists were "really aggressive, really menac-ing. I mean, they told me, we're going to put you in a camp. They said that to myself and my camera person. They were incredibly hostile. And they just basically went crazy and attacked this very small group of anti-racist counter-protesters and students."[24]

The marchers flung their torches at the counterprotesters and threw punches. When the police arrived and the crowd dispersed, a group went to menace a local synagogue. Last time, only local press had covered the conflict. But now the entire nation, then the world, turned its attention to the bizarre spectacle of men parading in white polo shirts brandishing tiki torches.

Vice, the documenter of freakish postmodern subcultures, was on the scene to capture the whole event in HD. Though, oddly enough, *Vice* was on *both* sides of the equation. Kessler was not only an alt-knight but a member of *Vice* cofounder Gavin McInnes' "western chauvinist organ-ization" the Proud Boys. Sort of. He had been excommunicated by McInnes for associating with Nazis.[25]

But many Proud Boys attended the rally anyway. In fact, they were easily identified by the Proud Boys uniform McInnes had concocted that screamed "militant jock"—a black Fred Perry polo shirt with bumble-bee yellow faux–sergeant's stripes on the collar.

Possibly because it was at the end of a summer of heated campaigns, the Unite the Right rally was a magnet for all of 2017's brawlers. It attracted many of the veterans of the Battle for Berkeley, Portland, and the D.C. mall protests, including Chapman and his Fraternal Order of Alt-Knights, Damigo with Identity Evropa, the Traditionalist Worker Party, and, to the confusion of everyone, a self-styled militia from Pennsylvania dressed like the U.S. Army.

The morning after the torch-lit rally, they all marched into the center of Charlottesville in a sort of medieval pageant, decked out in sword-and-sorcery-inspired battle gear, including replica swords, homemade shields, Spartan brush helmets, ski goggles, and superhero paraphernalia. It was not a coincidence that they all held banners with elaborate insignia like in *World of Warcraft*. This was where the internet, video games, and the latency-period fantasies of warrior histories that had obsessed Julius Evola and Steve Bannon intersected in a ridiculous spectacle. Joining these newly minted organizations were the older generation of fringe groups. The Ku Klux Klan arrived in droves in their wizard's robes, as did many leather-clad biker gangs. So too came the nerdy boys of /pol/, easy to spot because most of them carried flags with 4chan's four leaves on them dedicated to Kek, the ancient Egyptian frog god of obscurity (now resurrected as a meme that resembled Pepe).

On 4chan's /pol/, some users delighted in the spectacle. But as the ridiculous images hit the news, users mocked the participants as LARPers. And indeed, the same poor reality testing and capacity to make bad decisions that had elevated frauds like Yiannopoulos to leadership roles were on display in Charlottesville. The tiki torches, the polo shirts, the absurd costumes all contained the quixotic dream of dragging internet fantasy into reality and imagining it would look normal. When, in fact, barely any of the alt-right's ideas could endure outside the matrix of the internet.

For example, when I spoke to some boys carrying 4chan flags during the summer protests, they explained to me that they were *opposed* to white supremacy. "But your Kek flag is based on a neo-Nazi flag," I countered. "And you're marching with neo-Nazis."

"It's parody," one boy insisted. Partly this was true. In addition to being 4chan's newly appointed patron god, Kek was another way of saying LOL. The boy was marching for nothing, but the loopiest form of nothing I had ever seen. He was dressed in bright Pepe-green ecumenical robes. Around his neck hung a large gleaming pendant I recognized as the snaky symbol of Scientology. It was simply a nod to tradition; he couldn't have been older than twelve when the 2008 protests occurred.

He didn't buy my argument that no one understood what he was doing. Instead, he expounded on the political philosophy of one of the lesser-known gamergate YouTube personalities who had pivoted to right-wing politics with Trump, Carl Benjamin, a plump British vlogger in his late thirties who called himself "Sargon of Akkad."

"He's really funny," the boy explained to me.

The spectacle the alt-right created was not the one they desired. They wanted a show of strength, but they created a horror movie. Like at the end of Alan Moore's graphic novel *Watchmen*, it appeared as if a monster had been transported into our world from another dimension, and here it could survive only long enough to writhe in dying, murderous agony.

Though the crowds seemed large on TV as they crammed into the narrow streets of Charlottesville, the Unite the Right rally drew only between five hundred and a thousand protesters and a similar number of counterprotesters.[26] Antifa had come, which around the D.C. metro area generally consisted of college students dressed in theatrical black. But many anti-alt-right demonstrators were locals, including a variety of church leaders, angry that Kessler continued to bring far-right elements like the Ku Klux Klan into the town to demonstrate.

The offical Unite the Right demonstration was scheduled to begin at noon. But the fighting had grown so intense by midmorning, police declared the event an unlawful assembly and cleared the area around the statue.

Among the out-of-state alt-righters was an awkward nineteen-year-old boy named James Alex Fields Jr. Earlier in the day, Fields had been photographed standing among a fascist militant group called Vanguard America, which bills itself as "the face of American fascism," holding a toy shield with the group's distinctive insignia. The group later claimed he was not a member.[27]

Up until six months earlier, Fields had lived with his mother. After graduating from high school, he had not done all that much but spend several months in the Army, departing after "a failure to meet training standards." He had driven to the protest from Kentucky in a new Dodge Charger he had purchased with inheritance money. Former classmates described him as a loner who spouted white nationalist rhetoric sympathetic to Hitler and questioning the Holocaust.[28] He was known as "the Nazi of the school."[29]

As counterprotesters celebrated driving the Nazis from the park, Fields went back to his car. He then barreled down an alley that the police had intended to close off. In the chaos, the barricade had been abandoned. Fields accelerated down the hill and rammed into a crowd of counterprotesters, wounding seventeen people and killing thirty-two-year-old Heather Heyer. Around the same time, a police helicopter monitoring the protests crashed, bringing the fatality count to three.

Where did Fields get the idea to drive into the protesters? As many noted afterward, ramming protesters had been a frequent joke in alt-right chat rooms and memes, tracing back to a decades-old episode of *South Park* in which hippie-hating Cartman bulldozes demonstrators he despises. And Fox News had recently run a segment on the legal right to drive through protesters blocking roads. Fields had, prosecutors showed at trial, shared this meme online.

But it's possible that Fields employed his sports car in this massacre because the purchase had been yet another failed effort to boost his confidence, as was the case with Elliot Rodger and his BMW. Fields' expensive Charger had not helped him fit in, even among his fellow racists. The muscle car must have been yet another symbol of dashed hopes.

Fields' Facebook profile contained only a few images. Besides a snapshot of him leaning awkwardly against his new Dodge, there were memes of Pepe the Frog, Wojak, and Bashar al-Assad. For /pol/, Assad memes were a celebration of Russia's proxy victories in Syria. As much as white nationalists fawned over Hitler and Nazi imagery, they found a less complicated modern embodiment of their ideal far-right "ethnostate" in Vladimir Putin's Russia.

When the Soviet Union collapsed in 1989, President George H. W. Bush's administration pushed a foreign policy that reflected popular conservative ideologies that imagined that Enlightenment inventions like modern democracy and civil rights arose from business transactions. Bush expected that the introduction of American-style free enterprise would lead naturally to Western-style freedoms in Russia. In reality, the capitalist model produced an autocracy, in which Putin ruled over a set of oligarchs. Drawing strength from the country's profits, Putin promoted a narrow-minded, traditional way of life based on myths of a single Russian people united by blood. This pro-capitalist, militaristic, ethnocentric model, which channeled earnings to a ruling class of privileged white people, was not all that different from Hitler's model. In Putin, ethnonationalists like Spencer and /pol/ found a living model of this ideal, one who outmaneuvered liberal Western Europe and the United States in real time.

After the disaster at the rally, Trump refused to disavow the alt-right participants. In a press conference, he condemned the "hatred, bigotry, and violence" on "many sides."[30] Encouraged by Bannon, he pushed back on critiques of the alt-right, arguing, "There's blame on both sides," "not all those people were Nazis," and that some on the alt-right are "fine people."[31]

"What about the 'alt-left'?" he asked, borrowing the term from recent Fox News broadcasts. "Let me ask you this: What about the fact they came charging—that they came charging with clubs in their hands, swinging clubs? Do they have any problem? I think they do."

But as the outcry grew, Trump walked back his claims and insisted that he had said something different in the first place. "As I said on Saturday, we condemn in the strongest possible term this display of hatred, bigotry and violence," he conceded, leaving out "both sides" this time. "Racism is evil, and those who cause violence in its name are criminals and thugs, including the KKK, neo-Nazis, white supremacists, and other hate groups are repugnant to everything we hold dear as Americans."[32]

By the end of the week, Steve Bannon had left the administration. According to the *New York Times*, Bannon's exit was planned before Charlottesville, but it was "iced" during the event, when he had advised Trump not to give in to public pressure to condemn the alt-right. These wild volte-faces and ejections reflected the dynamics of the Trump White House, as reported in two tell-all books later, both of which appeared to rely heavily on Bannon's spurned-insider account, *Fire and Fury* by Michael Wolff and *Fear* by Bob Woodward. In *Fear*, Woodward described a contingent of traditional conservatives undermining Trump's unconventional decisions. In Bannon's view, Trump was fighting an operatic *Gotterdammerung* ("final battle of the gods") against the globalists Trump had hired to advise him. Though Bannon pictured Trump as the ancient Roman populist Tiberius Gracchus, the portrait of the president these accounts painted was closer to a child king, whose whims were constantly undermined, spun, or manipulated by a circle of competing ministers. As with Yiannopoulos, Trump was a creature of the screen, powerful in two dimensions, but hardly effective in the third.

Thus punctured, the weird mushroom of the alt-right began to deflate. A No to Marxism in America rally planned for August 27 at Berkeley, billed with Chapman as a headliner, was canceled. Two days before the planned alt-right rally, approximately 3,000 people attended a Rally Against Hate counterprotest. McInnes had planned a rally in Boston shortly after Unite the Right, but canceled it in the wake of the catastrophe. Eventually, he would resign from the Proud Boys when his boys experienced another disastrous clash with antifa in New York City in 2018 after he spoke at the Metropolitan Republican Club. The ironically named Mother of All Rallies for Trump on the mall in September 2017 fell flat, with a tiny, sparse crowd of several hundred, overshadowed by the nearby March of the Juggalos for the goth-rap band Insane Clown Posse. At the end of September, Yiannopoulos attempted to reprise his rise to fame, organizing a Free Speech Week event back at Sproul Hall in Berkeley, but attendance was sparse.

Soon after, a speech by Spencer at the University of Florida sparked massive protests, with an estimated 4,500 demonstrators and some 500 law enforcement officers. The demonstrators quickly shouted him down. Spencer responded by calling the crowd "shrieking and grunting morons."[33] This turned out to be the last public speech Spencer gave. Thereafter, he resorted to clandestine meetings. But these were often embarrassing failures too. A month later, he was kicked out of a barn he had rented in rural Maryland for a "weekend conference" when the owners realized who he was.[34]

The underlying forces that had created the alt-right remained, but its first bizarre manifestation had crumbled.

2018: What a Time to Be Alive

Of all the peculiarities that monuments can claim, one feature stands out for sheer irony; the strangest thing about monuments is they're not all notice-able! Nothing in the world is more invisible.
—Giorgio de Maria, *The Twenty Days of Turin*

In the aftermath of the 2017 brawls, the most commonly cited explana-tion from the left was that the past was returning. In this version of events, Donald Trump was a pied piper drawing out the wicked elements from America's history. Unreckoned-with racism and sexism, which had long lain dormant, rose again.

From this perspective, the solution seemed to be to continue to, as the signs read, "resist racism, sexism, xenophobia, transphobia," etcetera. The project of building a better world was similar to the project to dis-card the statues. We had to look backward with a keen eye toward the past, recognize the numerous injustices in our society, and pluck them out. Social justice efforts to place everyone on an equal plane would squelch the ancient anima of racism and sexism. To young, disenfran-chised radical leftists like antifa, this would be accomplished by disman-tling society. To moderate neoliberals, the same idea of the hierarchy of privilege suggested we would need to merely modify the status quo.

The new right regarded the conflicts quite differently. It saw its move-ment as a response to an existential crisis in which society was crum-bling as a small global elite reinforced unfair power structures. In this, its outlook resembled that of the socialist left, with the exception that the new right idealized capitalism as the solution rather than recognizing it as the problem.

In response to the now half-century-old problem of the Corporate

State, both sides battling on the streets came down in favor of an alternative to liberal capitalism, either socialism or fascism.

As Hannah Arendt explained, race-based thinking and fascism are not perennial evils that occasionally well up from the ground. They are better understood as a very modern problem, an outgrowth of capitalism and industrialization.

If we regard the alt-right from this perspective, racism appears to be a symptom of deeper societal problems. It is similar to the newly resurgent belief in conspiracy theories. Both are wrongheaded concepts that flow from underlying societal unrest. The wild popularity of YouTube conspiracist Alex Jones does not come from his keen reasoning, but from his angry rejection of mainstream media narratives. In this, he expresses his audience's deep dissatisfaction with "the global elite" who want to control the narrative in an "information war." Like Trump (who appeared on *InfoWars* when he was a presidential candidate to praise Jones), Jones bucked the Corporate State, rejecting experts who detailed what was practical and realistic from above by making up his own reality.

This outlook often evokes the same themes as Herbert Marcuse in *One-Dimensional Man*. Ironic, since one of the conspiracy theories Jones rails against is "cultural Marxism," the idea that the Frankfurt School of philosophy, presumably including Marcuse, colluded in the 1950s to undermine the bedrock of American society with confusing subjectivity.

And though *InfoWars* is one of the fonts of the alt-right, its opening credits warn against the military-industrial complex and the very real conspiracies that once formed the bedrock of leftist counterculture philosophy—most notably, Robert McNamara lying about the Gulf of Tonkin incident to create a pretext for war with Vietnam.

The feeling of powerlessness that produced both the radical left and right has hardly changed since Marcuse and Reich were writing in the late 60s and early 70s. Many of their ideas were reexpressed on 4chan's radical political sections, for example, in this popular piece of "copypasta" that ricocheted around 4chan's /pol/ circa 2013:

There will be no "collapse" the way some of these people think it . . .

You'll notice that every day simple things will become a little more expensive. Everyone's homes and apartments will start to get smaller. Your work hours will get longer, but your pay will decrease. You'll see family and friends less and find that in time you care less about them. Every day you'll find yourself lowering your standards for everything: work, food, relationships, etc. Job security will no longer exist as a concept. You'll notice houses and apartments shrinking. People will start hanging on to clothing longer and longer. Less people will get married, even less will have children. People will engross themselves in technological distractions and fantasy while never truly experiencing the real world.

Whatever dream people used to have about what their lives were going to be will become for them a distant memory. The only thing left for them will be the reality of their debt and poverty. And every minute of every be day they will be told, "You are stupid, ugly, and weak, but together we are free, prosperous, and safe."

This is the collapse. The reduction of the American man into a feudal serf, incapable of feeling love or hate, incapable of seeing the pitiful nature of his situation for what it is or recognizing his own self worth.

This sentiment—in which people's natural independence and freedom is diminished by not only a power structure but ideology convincing them that their debased state is perfectly normal, inevitable, and a source of contentment—was the central complaint of the Beat and hippie counterculture, who held that power, wherever it could be found above the head of someone else, ought to be divided and diluted.

In 2016, this concept found its way into both the far left and right. When I asked long-term 4chan users and antifa what their political philosophy was, they often told me they were libertarian socialists in the style of Noam Chomsky, interested in shattering power structures. (There is a Marxist /leftypol/ on 8chan, which is nearly as popular as 4chan's /pol/.)

This is not to say their philosophies are the same or, as it was often expressed on 4chan, that there was a "horseshoe effect" where the two radical ends of the political spectrum looped around to meet. Rather, the causes were the same but the diagnoses of the problem and the proposed solutions were drastically different.

To those on the right, a profound sense of isolation and impotence led them to find camaraderie and power in race-based thinking. Similarly, de-socialized romantic failure led to cruel-minded power fantasies regarding women. And the confusion resulting from subjectivity and the freedom to choose led to grasping at the certainty of tradition.

The left, by contrast, found collectivity in a renewed interest in socialism and, somewhat contradictorily, a hyper-fascination with self and identity.

When I began this book, I wasn't quite sure how deep the roots of far-right thinking went on 4chan.

As I tracked down the original moderators and creators of the site, mostly Christopher Poole's friends from Raspberry Heaven, few had much to say about the creation of 4chan, except that it was an adolescent lark and something they didn't think all that much about. Poole himself, if he ever got my messages, refused to talk to me.

However, they did refer me to one moderator who was largely credited with defining the philosophy and direction of 4chan as an anonymous message board. At the very beginning, posters employed usernames and the site wasn't all that different from Something Awful's anime section. But in 2004, a moderator who went by the handle "Shii" wrote an influential essay arguing for Japanese-style anonymity.

At the time, he was fifteen years old and living in an upper-middle-class household in New England. From the age of twelve onward, he had spent much of his childhood isolated online, reading message boards, first on Pokémon and atheism, then Japanese sites like 2channel, and then Something Awful.

When I spoke with him, I found him to be urbane, articulate, and well read. He told me that a decade ago he had become deeply religious, and through his interest in religion he had moved to the right politically. For many years, his scholarly interests centered around his favorite philosophers, Julius Evola and René Guénon. He made the same journey as the rest of 4chan's userbase, from vacant commodity culture to a groping quest for transcendent meaning.

Unlike the other moderators, he was willing to answer my questions head-on. Though they were all essentially the same question: How did it feel to have left such a weird accidental stamp on history at fifteen? One that you did not even want associated with your real name?

We spoke right after the deaths in Charlottesville. He referred me to an obscure Italian cult novel from the 1970s titled *The Twenty Days of Turin*. He didn't really read the boards anymore, he explained, but confessed that he'd found out about the novel while browsing 4chan's /lit/ section some months prior.

In the book, a group of teenagers, clean-cut boys who appeared easy to trust, announce the opening of a unique library in Turin that would be composed entirely of anonymous entries, private diaries, notes, and musings. The idea, they claim, is to connect people for unique conversations.

Inevitably, like 4chan, the library attracts "people with no desire at all for regular human communication." It fills to the brim with bizarre confessions, nightmarish perversions, and sickly jibbering. "Masterpieces could appear by accident," the narrator describes as he attempts to piece together the documents, "but they were about as easy to track down as a particle of gold in a heap of gravel. There were manuscripts whose first hundred pages didn't reveal any oddity, which then crumbled little by little in the depths of bottomless madness, or works that seemed normal at the beginning and end, but were pitted with fearful abysses further inward. Others, meanwhile, were conceived of in the spirit of pure malice."[1]

Soon a significant portion of the city, mostly young people, are spilling their guts, scraping the deepest contents of their souls to be deposited in the library. And with this came awful nightmares, in which the kids, drained of their innermost desires, dreamed only of a dry lake.

Eventually, the patrons of the library, unable to sleep, began to congregate in a public square in the middle of the night, under the shadow of an immense statue. At moments, the pedestal appears to be empty. And it is at these times when a giant emerges unseen to dash one of the sleepwalkers' heads against the stone.

What does this mad myth mean? In the book, there is no explicit meaning, only a Kafkaesque shuffling down branching corridors. Everywhere we are nowhere. The clean-cut boys who introduced the library are never found. I found Shii, but he just told me the story again, nested recursively in the fiction of *The Twenty Days of Turin*, confessing that, though he knew the facts, their interpretation eluded him. What did 4chan mean? What does a heap of words without meaning mean? What is the value of this sort of accumulation? An unending, unedited stream of feelings, days, pictures, people, thoughts, desires, and confessions? All of it vulgar in the literal sense, meant for public consumption, profaned, no longer private, and so no longer special to anyone?

Does it mean that no one will ever know? Or, as the writer Milan Kundera put it, "one morning (and it will be soon), when everyone wakes up as a writer, the age of universal deafness and incomprehension will have arrived."[2]

Yet, here we are replicating the story, with 4chan and social media, with young people, congregating around statues and smashing each other's heads against the pedestals.

A few days after my conversation with Shii, I was riding my bike just after midnight in Baltimore when I came upon a peculiar sight.

It was our mayor. I was surprised to find her out in the middle of the night. But even more unusually, she was dressed in jeans and a T-shirt, as if she had just been roused from bed.

She was standing apart from a small crowd that had gathered under klieg lights, watching a massive statue of General Robert E. Lee drift off its pedestal. For the first time, I noticed Lee's badly hewn feet. The sculptor had assumed that no one would ever see them. Oddly enough, I had never bothered to look at any of him until that moment, just as he was disappearing. The piece was so similar to Charlottesville's it could have been cast in the same mold. Later I learned that the mayor had not announced her plans to move it to anyone but, presumably, the crane operators.

In *The Twenty Days of Turin*, the burden of history, disputed and willing to return, had killed the teens. In real life, the statues had become the center of so much psychic energy because they were also a representation of how the protesters felt about themselves, in the shadow of the supra-entities above us. Not just the forces of history, but the immortal figures of corporations and governments who, wrought in the inhuman scale of ages, seemed impossible to pry off their pedestals.

This was how students had regarded the statues on their campuses several years earlier: as stand-ins for the entities above the entities like Yale, the institutions everyone could beseech, despite the fact they were deaf to all but the most inconsequential pleas.

To outsiders, it had all appeared like nonsense and madness. But it was mania in the ancient sense, a holy disease. A message too big to be expressed so we only saw one incomprehensible facet of it as it collided with our smaller, human dimension. It seemed half that and half, as people said, a tantrum, like when children have no words to express their complaint and no power to change anything, so they act in a way that doesn't make any sense, that seems at first inexplicable to the parent.

I was shocked that Shii still checked 4chan. I have to admit, I stopped around 2013. Until, of course, I began to write this book. Though I had tried to describe the site for years, I had long ago abandoned the effort. I assumed that the disintegration of Anonymous was the last chapter in 4chan's story and that whatever young people were doing, whatever culture they were forming, and whatever sites they were visiting were something entirely different.

But instead, youth culture kept treading the same furrowed circle, unable to leave.

The last year I went to Otakon, in 2016, the convention center was completely full. I couldn't move. As with most of the suburbs along the East Coast, the vacant, breezy emptiness I recalled from my childhood had been replaced with a scrabbling, packed-in feeling. The next year, in search of a larger venue, Otakon moved to Washington, D.C. The night it kicked off, August 12, was the night the torch-lit protests in Charlottesville began. In Baltimore that weekend, a brony convention took Otakon's old place at the Baltimore Convention Center.

It wasn't the last time I would feel that weird symmetry of mouse clicks. In 2017, traditional conservatives had been so terrified of Steve Bannon's Trumpism taking over the party they had not only disinvited Yiannopoulos from the Conservative Political Action Conference (CPAC), they had destroyed his career. The next year, CPAC was dominated by Trump's brand of conservatism. Bannon wasn't there, but they'd invited Marion Maréchal-Le Pen, the granddaughter and self-described political heir of French fascist Jean-Marie Le Pen, to speak. When an anti-Trump conservative named Mona Charen criticized Republicans for inviting a fascist to speak, she was escorted out of the conference by security guards who were afraid she might be attacked.[3]

Milo Yiannopoulos too was going to come to the 2018 CPAC. But this time no one cared. What eventually drove him and Mike Cernovich to another venue was not the threats of conservatives, but the threats of antifa. I had come to witness the conflict. When I learned via Twitter they had fled, I stood in the vast lobby wasting my time, studying the sea of young cherubic faces in "Make America Great Again" hats. Norman Mailer had described the boys who had come out for Goldwater in '64 as "thrifty young men, hardworking young men, polite, slightly paralyzed before the variety of life, but ready to die for a cause." Not these boys. They had a softness about them, pinched and pink, ruddy in the cheeks, an air of breezy self-satisfaction, as if they had been freshly scrubbed and kissed, no longer by their mothers, but America's America, Trumpitos. The young women, by contrast, were skinny as poles, wrapped in uncomfortable-looking cocktail dresses, an elaborate binding ritual that involved stockings and high heels as if to say, fuck fuck the patriarchy.

When I had asked a 4chan source to connect me with friends of his who actually identified as alt-right, he told me, "Just go to CPAC, man. Wander around, make friends," as if CPAC were now an anime con.

The last time I had been in that room, I realized, was when I had attended an enormous nerd-themed convention larger than Otakon several months earlier. I had gone to meet a source for this book. He was a young African American who had also chronicled 4chan since the early days. Many of the videos of their first gatherings on YouTube were his. When we met up, he begged me to help him find a job. He had been unemployed for years, though he had a technical degree from the University of Maryland. Together we had watched as a procession of wizards moved by, an endless procession, it turned out, wizard after wizard with no end in sight.

At CPAC, looking at MAGA bros in baggy suits and their dates zipped into short dresses, I thought about the line of wizards that had once been there and it seemed to have still not yet ended. The whole world was appareled in the most ridiculous costume.

When I returned to reading 4chan, I found that I couldn't grow a new thick skin. Rather, I was hyper-sensitive to the bile. Drinking from a concentrated font of misery, it turned out, was vitiating. Who knew? Why had I read it for so long?

A long-dormant depression returned. I felt a little like the defeated protagonist in *The Twenty Days of Turin*, attempting to piece together the hideous fragments from the library. One day he blows on his recorder and finds that what emerges aren't the dulcet tones of the sublime, but a joyless, vacant puffing. The notes are unwilling to waft upward. Cruelly, they fall with a thud, artless and dull.

To many, the advent of the alt-right and Bannon's social media machinations meant that the utopian dreams of the early internet creators had been naive; that their efforts to connect people had instead created, as one writer put it recently, "a nightmare machine."[4]

But I think something different is going on.

If we're worried that our communications networks are becoming clogged with human misery, we might look to the misery rather than the networks.

This has been, by and large, I will admit, a pessimistic book. Which is unfortunate, because I consider myself an optimist. And I would like to end it by making an argument for optimism.

One of the few things both the left and right agree on is pessimism about the future. To everyone, it feels as though we are hurtling toward a cliff and try as we might to hit the eject button, nothing is happening. In a world of narrow-minded expertise, as Charles Reich wrote in 1971, it felt as if no one at the top was steering the ship. The apparatus of civilization appeared to be a labyrinth of hyper-detailed, rhizomatic subjectivity, perhaps best embodied by our social media feeds.

This was partially the impetus for electing the "wrecking ball" of Trump. Peter Thiel became an avid Trump supporter just a few years after he wrote that he was abandoning democracy because he believed that civilization itself was going wildly off course.

The most popular political meme of the election was not Pepe the Frog, but another symbol of helplessness: a dog sitting in a burning house insisting, "This is fine."

Both sides felt intuitively that the system was crumbling, but the only respite available was justifying our own paralysis as we waited for the inevitable collapse.

This common conception that we are doomed is often reflected in fiction. A spate of post-post-apocalyptic films in the last decade (*Cloud Atlas*, *After Earth*, *Oblivion*, *Interstellar*) all depicted a stable future full of unspoiled nature. But these possible worlds were only credible to audiences if they were preceded by a world catastrophe. Or as Slavoj Zizek pointed out in his speech at Occupy Wall Street, it's easy to imagine the end of the world, but we cannot imagine the end of capitalism.

In 2018, the writer Douglas Rushkoff described how tech millionaires had hired him for a private session, asking how best to prepare for the future, by which they meant total societal collapse.

Finally, the CEO of a brokerage house explained that he had nearly completed building his own underground bunker system and asked, "How do I maintain authority over my security force after the event? For all their wealth and power, they don't believe they can affect the future. . . .

They knew armed guards would be required to protect their compounds from the angry mobs. But how would they pay the guards once money was worthless? What would stop the guards from choosing their own leader? The billionaires considered using special combination locks on the food supply that only they knew. Or making guards wear disciplinary collars of some kind in return for their survival.[5]

Just as Peter Thiel is preparing to jet to New Zealand when civilization collapses, so too are other tech billionaires, Rushkoff wrote, following his lead. They did not see technology as an emancipator but as an imminent disaster.

In its first ad, Apple imagined it would prevent a *1984*-style totalitarian dystopia by empowering individuals. Of course, the dystopia did not come in the form of the grim, grand, tragic *1984*, but in the form of the minor screen comedy, the farce of the farce, the loops and whirls of absurdity as entertainment fiction passed in and out of tiny fake realities. Like the inscrutable, apocalyptic visions of the biblical Daniel, Trump appeared first as a reality TV star, then Pepe the Frog, then president of the United States. When the future was revealed to us, the procession was so bizarre and comical it was nearly impossible to decode.

The screen hadn't trapped people into a singular totalitarian viewpoint and invaded their privacy by sticking cameras in their bedrooms. Instead, people invaded their own privacy, filming themselves in their most intimate moments to become little reality TV stars.

Our "boring dystopia," as Mark Fisher called it, is a far cry from H. G. Wells' postwar utopia in *The World Set Free*. But it does resemble Aldous Huxley's parody of the book, *Brave New World*, in which instruments of liberation are freely available to future citizens. But, distracted by shallow entertainment, few care to employ them. For the first time in history, a better world seems out of reach not for technological reasons but for political ones. Absurdly, we all think we're going to die when civilization collapses because we can't imagine everyone acting better.

Unlike previous eras that could only anticipate a machine utopia, we actually have the technological capacity to replace workers with automation. It's estimated that nearly 40 percent of U.S. jobs will be performed by robots in the next fifteen years.[6] And we are once again debating where all that excess income from free labor will go: to a few privileged owners of factories or to everyone as a universal basic income?[7]

The technological barriers that once existed are largely gone. Only the far more insubstantial barriers—the psychological ones—remain, stubbornly enduring for longer than most imagined they would.

Reich thought they would be swept away in a decade or so when the new countercultural "consciousnesses" overtook the world. It did. But the old patterns of thought, behavior, and politics also remained in place.

Once again we are faced with the problem of finding a new way of understanding human nature, a new way of behaving to accompany the new technology. It now appears naive, even to far-right tech industrialists, to imagine that neoliberal capitalism will endure forever as the end of history, that it will survive a world of automation.

Technology is not an anti-democratic "nightmare machine." Rather, technology becomes nightmarish when it is distorted by the anti-democratic tendencies of capitalism. When Peter Thiel wrote that "capitalist democracy" was an "oxymoron" in 2009, he was right. Trump, the ultra-capitalist who views fellow autocrats like Vladimir Putin as competitors, is a living demonstration of Arendt's theories on how capitalism's mindset devolves into cruel-minded autocracies. In the past decades, we have seen capitalism coexist happily with nationalist authoritarian regimes in Russia and China. And it is these models that Trump emulates.

As a libertarian, Thiel was expressing that if faced with a choice between capitalism and democracy, he would jettison democracy. This is what he meant when he wrote, "I no longer believe freedom and democracy are compatible." By freedom, he meant the freedom to do business in laissez-faire-style capitalism. When he stated, "We are in a deadly race between politics and technology," he meant the world would have to choose between capitalism and the advances of technology. And indeed, the two are on a collision course.

New generations have noticed that climate change and automation challenge neoliberal economics in totally novel ways. Tumblr, Twitter, and even the chans have filled with socialist memes. The internet's earliest countercultural utopianism has returned. Young people have once again become obsessed with abandoning capitalism and replacing it with a radically different post-scarcity society that technology has always promised.

When I was speaking to another source for my book, a lifelong 4chan user who had migrated from TOTSE, he had recently converted to the left. He was an African American called "Warsie" who lived on Chicago's East Side and palled around with alt-right chan users. He had been sympathetic to gamergate and even to the beta uprising. But he was now a socialist. When I brought up the renewed interest in socialism online, he sang the meme to me. It was an old meme, experiencing something of a renaissance. "Fully! Automated! Gay! Luxury! Space! Communism!" Youth culture had come full circle, out of post-nihilist despair and back to the 60s' push toward a reinvented neo-techno-socialism.

Scratch underneath this culture war and one finds that much of youth culture shares similar sentiments about living on the bottom of an unjust and increasingly irrelevant power structure.

8chan's founder Fredrick Brennan had expressed very similar thoughts to Warsie's when I asked him about his post-chan political views.

"All of these old political systems, with the images of the factories in the nineteenth century, I just don't know if they fit anymore," he told me. "I entered the gig economy before it was called that and everyone became part of it. But each year automation is doing a better job. Obviously, the free-market approach is not going to work if a computer can do everyone's job better for pennies on the dollar."

This new youth culture doesn't imagine a nineteenth-century revolution of workers, but rather, people simply rearranging society in a way that makes sense and doesn't fill everyone with a dread that we're all doomed. Or, as the writer of the popular far-left Pokémon/socialist-themed webcomic *Existential Comics* put it on Twitter in 2018, "Can you imagine thinking capitalism will survive a fully automated society? Like everything is done by robots, but some asshole trillionaire owns it all and decides what the robots make, and the plebs are supposed to be happy to get enough scraps to not starve to death?"[8]

Indeed, technology, far from being a world-ending threat, is threatening to create a post-capitalist world. Once again, youth culture has returned to Marcuse's sentiment in *One-Dimensional Man*: "If the individual were no longer compelled to prove himself on the market, as a free economic subject, the disappearance of this [compulsion] would be one of the greatest achievements of civilization." And oddly enough, that is the sentiment now being built out of pop-culture meme snippets.

Of course, there are the same old pitfalls. If the last half century of counterculture has taught us anything, it's that how you dress and who you have sex with present little or no challenge to the power structure (if only!). In fact, fascination with sexual permission and personal image is capitalism's briar patch. The place where, like Br'er Rabbit, it feints at being beaten, though in fact, it delights in going there. Capitalism has trained successive generations of young people to center their thinking on personal gratification through media infused with the countercultures it has already consumed. Now that so many lead lives streaked with fears of a sudden catastrophic economic collapse, these small pleasures and affirmations appear doubly fascinating.

For example, in September 2018, the *New York Times*' Style section ran an article on how the youth trend of gender fluidity is selling like hotcakes. "Brands," it reported, "are now racing to capture the market of young people who strive to live gender identities that fit." Just like the older countercultures, the LGBT effort to shatter existing power structures was being pounded into a paste to shore up very ancient walls. "Corporations see in [gender nonconforming people] the future of consuming," the article declares, going on to profile a new generation of gender nonconforming models with "100,000 Instagram followers."[9]

What's remarkable about the piece is how stale it all sounds. The subtle art of marketing once lay in how such co-optation was coyly concealed. Now it was the title of the article ("For Capitalism, Every Social Leap Forward Is a Marketing Opportunity"). Though nonbinary theory was first utilized to smash the language of self-hatred developed to market gendered products like cosmetics, the piece celebrates "the Phluid Project, a NoHo store billing itself as the world's first nonbinary retail shop; to a booming trend in the cosmetics business for so-called genderless beauty." "One way," a source suggests, to "bust out of the gender constrictions [is to] . . . enjoy consuming a gender nonconforming experience." Thus, in the wink of an eye, the vast graveyard of LGBT activists who fought and died for societal parity was bottled into a trans-consuming experience, the infinite realm of personal choice enclosed in a nutshell, the horizon flattened into the dimensions of an ad. As everyone feels increasingly hemmed in, infinite personal choice is still the hottest commodity on the market.

But maybe that old spell can't harm us anymore.

The internet has provided a means by which nastiness can be excavated and collected in a reservoir. But the font of all that unhappiness is not human beings, but their context. 4chan is not the waste byproduct of some natural capacity of the mind to be weird and cruel. Rather, it's the byproduct of cruel societal artifices: our culture's emphasis on materialism, entertainment culture, and self-gratification.

If the rapid mutations of the internet demonstrate anything, it's not that there is a group of irredeemable nightmare kids lurking in the backwaters of the internet, but that human beings are intensely mutable and creative. And that even in the most intense anonymous isolation, they long to be defined in a community. Beyond the loopy journey into false realms, counterculture is still reinventing itself and trying to jettison the deeply flawed past.

Standing at CPAC, furiously checking Twitter to see where the planned anti-fascist street brawl would begin, I became fascinated by the Trumpitos clustering in the ballroom where I was accustomed to seeing wizards waving their magic wands. The scene reminded me of Stanislaw Lem's 1971 science-fiction novella *The Futurological Congress*. In this story, the protagonist, Ijon Tichy, finds himself standing in a luxurious hotel convention center in Costa Rica, attending a conference of academics who study the future. As the futurologists deliver their papers on what the future might hold (much of it bleak), they are dismayed to learn that the revolution is taking place around them. Tichy and his companions flee to the hotel's sewer, but not before they are gassed with psychedelics by both the revolutionaries and the local riot police. Thus begins a cascading set of misadventures that Tichy can never be sure are real or a product of the drugs. At one point, he finds himself frozen and revived in a far-flung future, which appears to be, in all respects, a utopia. Given a stipend and an apartment in Manhattan, where the air is brisk and fresh, he eventually becomes acclimated to his new life. Except for one niggling detail. Now and again, the otherwise lighthearted utopians pant uncontrollably. They always seem out of breath.

He soon learns the reason. The utopia is an illusion, brought on by the generous application of drugs in the air and water. Taking an antidote, he briefly glimpses the "real" world, where gray mobs climb like spiders up broken elevator shafts in bombed-out buildings, hence the residents' constant puffing and huffing.

At this point, he utters a sad cry. Perhaps he will awake yet, like he had after so many other bad dreams, in the sewer beneath the Hilton. "Could it be that even here somewhere there was a sewer," he hopes, "my guardian sewer, my only talisman and touchstone to reality?"[10]

It is this passage that I think of when I attempt to answer why I returned over and over to 4chan, and why I imagine other people did as well.

It was my guardian sewer.

The panting and clambering of the drugged utopians represent how we can be convinced that things are fine when in fact conditions are intolerable, when in fact we are suffering. Even if one doesn't have an alternative and doesn't know what to believe, he or she can retreat as far as despair, to the lowest level. It's really only the first step in a long journey, recognizing one's own misery when the world insists that you ought to be content. When it tells you that you are illogical, mad, stupid, or otherwise foolish not to be happy, where else can you retreat but your guardian sewer? Which, in its own cruel, inane unreality, insists on new possibilities.

At a certain point, a captain of industry in this panting dystopia explains to Tichy that he runs the world of the future by meting out "bites" to the populace.

"Surely you mean 'bits,'" Tichy protests. "The basic unit of information?" No, the man assures him, bites. The basic unit of human cruelty.

What could be more upside down than the way it is now? As the internet insists society should be composed of more bits than bites, not the other way around.

Acknowledgments

Great thanks to my agent William, without whom this book would not exist, Cricket, David, Paul, Sonya, Liz, Dr. Lou, Jordan, Quimby, Carlynn, BMKTPT, all those kind people who agreed to talk to me for the book, the scholars whose work I relied on to write it, and everyone from 4chan who sent me angry or otherwise bananas emails.

Notes

INTRODUCTION

1. David Neiwert, *Alt-America: The Rise of the Radical Right in the Age of Trump* (New York: Verso, 2017), 231–232.
2. George Eaton, "Francis Fukuyama interview: 'Socialism ought to come back,'" *New Statesman*, October 17, 2018, https://www.newstatesman.com/culture /observations/2018/10/francis-fukuyama-interview-socialism-ought-come-back.
3. Karl Marx, *The Eighteenth Brumaire of Louis Bonaparte* (First issue of *Die Revolution*, 1852, New York, republished Marx/Engels Internet Archive 1995), 5, https://www.marxists.org/archive/marx/works/1852/18th-brumaire.

CHAPTER 1

1. Barbara Ehrenreich, *The Hearts of Men: American Dreams and the Flight from Commitment* (New York: Doubleday, 1983).
2. Herbert Marcuse, *One-Dimensional Man: Studies in the Ideology of Advanced Industrial Society*, 2nd ed. (Boston: Beacon Press, 1991), 78–79.
3. *The Pervert's Guide to Ideology*, directed by Sophie Fiennes (Blinder Films, 2012).
4. See Dale Beran, "Occupy Batman," Tumblr, September 9, 2012, http://daleberan .tumblr.com/post/31966231768/occupy-batman.
5. Charles A. Reich, *The Greening of America* (New York: Bantam, 1970), 176; Reinhold Niebuhr, *On Progress in Technology and Morality* (America's Town Hall Meeting of the Air, broadcast February 16, 1939), https://www.oldtimeradio downloads.com/drama/americas-town-meeting-of-the-air/americas-town -hall-meeting-of-the-air-39-02-16-reinhold-niebuhr-on-progress-in-technology -and-morality-excerpt; John Kenneth Galbraith, *The New Industrial State* (Boston: Houghton Mifflin, 1967), 37–38.
6. Marcuse, *One-Dimensional Man*, 7.
7. See Dale Beran, "A Tale of Two Hipsters: A 10,000 word essay on what the term

hipster means," Tumblr, April 4, 2014, http://daleberan.tumblr.com/post/8300
2114449/a-tale-of-two-hipsters.

8. See Ehrenreich, *The Hearts of Men*, 114–115.

9. Mark Fisher, *Ghosts of My Life: Writings on Depression, Hauntology and Lost Futures* (Washington, DC: Zero Books, 2014).

10. Jacques Derrida, *Specters of Marx: The State of the Debt, the Work of Mourning and the New International* (Paris: Editions Galilée, 1993, New York: Routledge, 1994).

11. Jean Baudrillard, *The Illusion of the End* (Stanford, CA: Stanford University Press, 1994), 26.

12. Ibid., 9.

13. Thomas Piketty, *Capital in the Twenty-First Century* (Cambridge, MA: Harvard University Press, 2017), Introduction and chapter 8, Figure 8.5.

14. Slavoj Zizek, *Trouble in Paradise: From the End of History to the End of Capitalism* (London: Penguin Books, 2014), 51–52.

15. Milan Kundera, *The Unbearable Lightness of Being* (New York: Harper & Row, 1984), 2.

16. Fisher, *Ghosts of My Life*, chapter 1; Grafton Tanner, *Babbling Corpse: Vaporwave and the Commodification of Ghosts* (Washington, DC: Zero Books, 2016).

17. Baudrillard, *The Illusion of the End*, 9.

18. Bernie Sanders, "Democrats Need to Wake Up," *New York Times*, June 28, 2016, https://www.nytimes.com/2016/06/29/opinion/campaign-stops/bernie-sanders -democrats-need-to-wake-up.html; Slavoj Zizek, "Could Brexit Breathe New Life into Left-Wing Politics?" *Newsweek*, June 24, 2016, https://www.newsweek .com/brexit-eu-referendum-left-wing-politics-europe-zizek-474322.

19. Various posts on 4chan.org/pol/ in 2015–2016, archived at archive.4plebs.org, accessed January 29, 2019, http://archive.4plebs.org/pol/search/text/breaking %20the%20conditioning/start/2015-01-01/end/2017-01-01.

CHAPTER 2

1. "Milo Yiannopoulos, Steven Crowder and Christina Hoff Sommers at UMass," accessed January 29, 2019, https://www.youtube.com/watch?v=yCcp36n"2cDg.

2. Max Read, "The Whole World Is Now a Message Board," *New York*, April 30, 2017, http://nymag.com/intelligencer/2017/04/the-whole-world-is-now-a-message -board.html.

3. Baudrillard, *The Illusion of the End*, 7.

4. "Mario Savio," Wikipedia, accessed January 29, 2019, https://en.wikipedia.org /wiki/Mario_Savio.

5. Fred Turner, *From Counterculture to Cyberculture: Stewart Brand, the Whole Earth Network, and the Rise of Digital Utopianism* (Chicago: University of Chicago Press, 2006), 11–12.

6. *The Fog of War: Eleven Lessons from the Life of Robert S. McNamara*, directed by Errol Morris (Sony Pictures Entertainment, 2004), DVD.

7. Turner, *From Counterculture to Cyberculture*, 11–12.

8. Marcuse, *One-Dimensional Man*, 4.

9. H. G. Wells, *The World Set Free: A Story of Mankind* (New York: E. P. Dutton, 1914).

10. Tom Wolfe, *The Electric Kool-Aid Acid Test* (New York: Bantam, 1969), 147.

11. Reich, *The Greening of America*, 4–8, 91–100.
12. Ibid.
13. Rory Cellan-Jones, "Hackers and hippies: The origins of social networking," BBC, January 25, 2011, http://www.bbc.co.uk/news/mobile/technology-12224588.
14. Turner, *From Counterculture to Cyberculture*, 11–12.
15. Ibid., 38–39.
16. Ibid., chapters 2–4.
17. Michael Hauben and Ronda Hauben, "Netizens: On the History and Impact of Usenet and the Internet," *First Monday* 3, no. 8 (August 3, 1998), https://firstmonday.org/ojs/index.php/fm/article/view/613/534.
18. Cole Stryker, *Epic Win for Anonymous: How 4chan's Army Conquered the Web* (New York: Overlook Duckworth, 2011), 110–113; Turner, *From Counterculture to Cyberculture*, chapters 2–4.
19. "Is Computer Hacking a Crime?" *Harper's*, March 1990, https://harpers.org/archive/1990/03/is-computer-hacking-a-crime/; Turner, *From Counterculture to Cyberculture*, 162–174.
20. "Is Computer Hacking a Crime," *Harper's*; See also *HyperNormalisation*, directed by Adam Curtis (BBC, 2016).
21. "Is Computer Hacking a Crime," *Harper's*.
22. Mary B. W. Tabor with Anthony Ramirez, "Computer Savvy, with an Attitude: Young Working-Class Hackers Accused of High-Tech Crime," *New York Times*, July 23, 1992, http://www.nytimes.com/1992/07/23/nyregion/computer-savvy-with-attitude-young-working-class-hackers-accused-high-tech-crime.html?pagewanted=all.

CHAPTER 3

1. Michael Hauben, *The Net and Netizens: The Impact the Net Has on People's Lives*, chapter 1, unpublished draft, Columbia University, June 5, 1996, http://www.columbia.edu/~hauben/book/ch106.x01.
2. FATSEX, "Seriously though, sisterdeath is no reason . . . ," forum post, Something Awful, February 28, 2010, https://forums.somethingawful.com/showthread.php?threadid=3272627&userid=0&perpage=40&pagenumber=17.
3. Stewart Brand, "Scream of Consciousness," *Wired*, January 1, 1993, https://www.wired.com/1993/01/paglia/.
4. Karl Taro Greenfeld, "The Incredibly Strange Mutant Creatures Who Rule the Universe of Alienated Japanese Zombie Computer Nerds," *Wired*, January 1, 1993, https://www.wired.com/1993/01/otaku/.
5. Clyde Haberman, "Japan's Youth Seem Old Before Their Time," *New York Times*, March 11, 1984, https://www.nytimes.com/1984/03/11/weekinreview/japan-s-youth-seem-old-before-their-time.html.
6. Greenfeld, "Mutant Creatures"; "Tsutomu Miyazaki," Wikipedia, accessed January 29, 2019, https://en.wikipedia.org/wiki/Tsutomu_Miyazaki.
7. Ndee "Jkid" Okeh, "2ch History," accessed January 29, 2019, https://github.com/bibanon/bibanon/wiki/2ch-History.
8. "A small history of Ayashii World," February 9, 2013, http://ayashiiworldhistory.blogspot.com/; Stryker, *Epic Win for Anonymous*, 130.
9. "2ch Chronicle/2ch History Timeline," WikiBooks, https://en.wikibooks.org/wiki/2ch_Chronicle/2ch_History_Timeline; "The History of Ayashi Warudo," accessed January 29, 2019, http://f16.aaacafe.ne.jp/~stwalker/; Ndee "Jkid" Okeh,

"The Protochannel and the First Channel—Ayashii World and Amezou World—The Grandparents of the Western Imageboard Culture," accessed January 29, 2019, http://yotsubasociety.org/ayashii-and-amezou/; "Shii," email message with author, August 2017; Ndee "Jkid" Okeh, conversations with author, 2017.

10. Lisa Katayama, "Meet Hiroyuki Nishimura, the Bad Boy of the Japanese Internet," *Wired*, May 19, 2008, https://www.wired.com/2008/05/mf-hiroyuki/?currentPage=all.

11. Turner, *From Counterculture to Cyberculture*, 140.

12. Ibid., 214.

13. Ibid., 235.

14. Taylor Wofford, "Fuck You and Die: An Oral History of Something Awful," *Vice*, April 5, 2017, https://motherboard.vice.com/en_us/article/nzg4yw/fuck-you-and-die-an-oral-history-of-something-awful.

15. Antonizoon, "AOHell," GitHub, https://github.com/bibanon/bibanon/wiki/AOHell.

16. Rita Gunther McGrath, "5 Years Later, Lessons from the Failed AOL–Time Warner Merger," *Fortune*, January 10, 2015, http://fortune.com/2015/01/10/15-years-later-lessons-from-the-failed-aol-time-warner-merger/.

17. "The Great Scam," GitHub, https://github.com/bibanon/bibanon/wiki/American-Dream.

CHAPTER 4

1. Bibliotheca Anonoma, "Something Awful," https://wiki.bibanon.org/Something_Awful.

2. Christopher Poole, "Branching points," July 2, 2014, https://chrishateswriting.com.

3. Jonny, "4chan history," http://shii.bibanon.org/www.jonnydigital.com/4chan-history; Parmy Olson, *We Are Anonymous: Inside the Hacker World of LulzSec, Anonymous, and the Global Cyber Insurgency* (Boston: Back Bay Books, 2013), 27.

4. Richard "Lowtax" Kyanka, conversation with author, February 19, 2018.

5. Christopher Poole, "4chan.net," Something Awful forum thread, 2003–2004, December 8, 2003, https://forums.somethingawful.com//showthread.php?threadid=724028&userid=0&perpage=40&pagenumber=17.

6. Christopher Poole, "4chan.net," Something Awful forum thread, 2003–2004, June 2004, https://forums.somethingawful.com//showthread.php?threadid=724028&userid=0&perpage=40&pagenumber=1.

7. Jared Hodges and Lindsay Cibos, *Draw Furries: How to Create Anthropomorphic and Fantasy Animals* (Cincinnati: F+W Media, 2009).

8. Maureen Dowd, "This Is Why Uma Thurman Is Angry," *New York Times*, February 3, 2018, https://www.nytimes.com/2018/02/03/opinion/sunday/this-is-why-uma-thurman-is-angry.html.

CHAPTER 5

1. Lev Grossman, "The Master of Memes," *Time*, July 9, 2008, http://content.time.com/time/magazine/article/0,9171,1821656,00.html; David Smith, "The 20-Year-Old at Heart of Web's Most Anarchic and Influential Site," *Guardian*, July 20,

2008, https://www.theguardian.com/technology/2008/jul/20/internet.google; Jamin Brophy-Warren, "Modest Web Site Is Behind a Bevy of Memes," *Wall Street Journal*, July 9, 2009, https://www.wsj.com/articles/SB121564928060441097.

2. Richard Dawkins, *The Selfish Gene*, 3rd ed. (New York: Oxford University Press, 2006), chapter 12.

3. Ibid., chapter 11.

4. Brophy-Warren, "Modest Web Site Is Behind a Bevy of Memes."

5. Mattathias Schwartz, "The Trolls Among Us," *New York Times Magazine*, August 3, 2008.

6. Stryker, *Epic Win for Anonymous*, 94–96, 114.

7. Ibid., 110–113.

8. Brophy-Warren, "Modest Web Site Is Behind a Bevy of Memes."

9. Julian Dibbel, "Mutilated Furries, Flying Phalluses: Put the Blame on Griefers, the Sociopaths of the Virtual World," *Wired*, January 18, 2008, https://www.wired.com/2008/01/mf-goons/.

10. David Kushner, "We All Got Trolled," *Medium*, Matter, July 22, 2014, https://medium.com/matter/the-martyrdom-of-weev-9e72da8a133d; Adrian Chen, "The Internet's Best Terrible Person Goes to Jail," Gawker, November 11, 2012, https://gawker.com/5962159/the-internets-best-terrible-person-goes-to-jail-can-a-reviled-master-troll-become-a-geek-her.

11. Christopher Poole, "4chan.net," Something Awful forum thread, 2003–2004, June 21, 2004, https://forums.somethingawful.com//showthread.php?threadid=724028&userid=0&perpage=40&pagenumber=30.

12. Schwartz, "The Trolls Among Us."

13. Brophy-Warren, "Modest Web Site Is Behind a Bevy of Memes."

CHAPTER 6

1. Olson, *We Are Anonymous*, 60–62.

2. "Complete History of 4chan," Tanasinn.info, http://tanasinn.info/wiki/Complete_History_of_4chan.

3. Olson, *We Are Anonymous*, 72, 91.

4. Kevin Poulson, "Hackers Assault Epilepsy Patients via Computer," *Wired*, March 28, 2008, https://www.wired.com/2008/03/hackers-assault-epilepsy-patients-via-computer/.

CHAPTER 7

1. Andrew Sullivan, "Goodbye to All That: Why Obama Matters," *Atlantic*, December 2007, https://www.theatlantic.com/magazine/archive/2007/12/goodbye-to-all-that-why-obama-matters/306445/.

2. John M. Broder, "Shushing the Baby Boomers," *New York Times*, January 21, 2007, https://www.nytimes.com/2007/01/21/weekinreview/21broder.html. See also Damien Cave, "Generation O Gets Its Hopes Up," *New York Times*, November 9, 2008, https://www.nytimes.com/2008/11/09/fashion/09boomers.html.

3. Naomi Klein, *No Logo*, 10th anniversary edition (New York: Picador, 2009), xxix.

4. Rick Astley, "moot," *Time*, April 30, 2009, http://content.time.com/time/specials/packages/article/0,28804,1894410_1893837_1894180,00.html.

5. Gabriella Coleman, *Hacker, Hoaxer, Whistleblower, Spy: The Many Faces of Anonymous* (Brooklyn, NY: Verso, 2015), 82.
6. Institute for Public Accuracy and Daniel Ellsberg, news release, December 7, 2010, http://www.ellsberg.net/public-accuracy-press-release/; *Observer*, "Pentagon Papers' Daniel Ellsberg Says He Suffered Same Attacks as WikiLeaks and Assange," December 9, 2010, http://observer.com/2010/12/pentagon-papers-daniel-ellsberg -says-he-suffered-same-attacks-as-wikileaks-and-assange/.
7. Olson, *We Are Anonymous*, 119–120.
8. RoyalCourtTheatre, "The Big Idea: In Conversation with LulzSec," YouTube, September 29, 2014, https://youtu.be/KpGiLPF5BxQ.
9. "Complete History of 4chan," Tanasinn.info, http://tanasinn.info/wiki/Complete _History_of_4chan.
10. Olson, *We Are Anonymous*, 335.
11. Ibid., 49.
12. RoyalCourtTheatre, "The Big Idea: In Conversation with LulzSec."

CHAPTER 8

1. Shawn E. Tuma, "Yes, Case Law Says It Really Is a CFAA Violation to DDOS a Website," Business Cyber Risk, October 9, 2013, https://shawnetuma.com /2013/10/09/yes-case-law-says-it-really-is-a-cfaa-violation-to-ddos-a-website/; *Pulte Homes, Inc. v. Laborers' Intern. Union of North America*, 648 F.3d 295 (6th Cir. 2011).
2. Olson, *We Are Anonymous*, 86–89; David Kravets, "Anonymous Member Pleads Guilty to Scientology Web Attacks," *Wired*, May 11, 2009, https://www.wired .com/2009/05/teen-pleads-guilty-to-scientology-web-attacks/.
3. Anonymous posts on 4chan, read by the author during the attacks.
4. aaron@hbgary.com to greg@hbgary.com, "So I decided to privately," email, February 6, 2011, https://www.wikileaks.org/hbgary-emails/emailid/1604.
5. Nate Anderson, "How One Man Tracked Down Anonymous—and Paid a Heavy Price," *Wired*, February 10, 2011, https://www.wired.com/2011/02/ anonymous/.
6. Olson, *We Are Anonymous*, 1–25.
7. Eric Bangeman, "Colbert Report features Ars Anonymous/HBGary coverage," *Ars Technica*, February 25, 2011, https://arstechnica.com/staff/2011/02 /our-anonymous-hbgary-coverage-on-colbert-report/.
8. Nate Anderson, "Spy Games: Inside the Convoluted Plot to Bring Down WikiLeaks," *Wired*, February 14, 2011, https://www.wired.com/2011/02/spy/; Glenn Greenwald, "More Facts Emerge About the Leaked Smear Campaign," *Salon*, February 15, 2011, https://www.salon.com/2011/02/15/palantir/.
9. Joe Weisenthal, "Here's the Secret Document That Banks and Other Big Organizations Are Using to Prepare for WikiLeaks," *Business Insider*, February 9, 2011, http://www.businessinsider.com/palantir-wikileaks-2011-2#-13; Coleman, *Hacker, Hoaxer, Whistleblower, Spy*, 207.
10. Anderson, "Spy Games."
11. mark@hbgary.com to aaron@hbgary.com, "Data," email, January 8, 2011, 22:32, https://www.wikileaks.org/hbgary-emails/emailid/10894.
12. aaron@hbgary.com to mark@hbgary.com, "small side project," email, January 20, 2011, 10:32, https://www.wikileaks.org/hbgary-emails/emailid/2685.

13. msteckman@palantir.com to aaron@hbgary.com, "Eli and I had to run this way up the chain (as you can imagine). The short of it is that we got approval from Dr. Karp and the Board to go ahead with the modified 40/30/30 breakdown proposed." See also "Revisions to Palantir/Berico TA and proposals," email, November 18, 2010, 17:22, https://wikileaks.org/hbgary-emails/emailid/4717.

14. Nate Anderson, "Anonymous vs. HBGary: The Aftermath," *Ars Technica*, February 15, 2011, https://arstechnica.com/tech-policy/2011/02/anonymous-vs-hbgary-the-aftermath/2/; Greenwald, "More Facts Emerge About the Leaked Smear Campaign"; Andy Greenberg, "Palantir Apologizes for WikiLeaks Attack Proposal, Cuts Ties with HBGary," *Forbes*, February 11, 2011, https://www.forbes.com/sites/andygreenberg/2011/02/11/palantir-apologizes-for-wikileaks-attack-proposal-cuts-ties-with-hbgary/#320018345585.

15. Peter Waldman, Lizette Chapman, and Jordan Robertson, "Palantir Knows Everything About You," Bloomberg, April 19, 2018, https://www.bloomberg.com/features/2018-palantir-peter-thiel/.

16. Peter Thiel, "The Education of a Libertarian," *Cato Unbound*, April 13, 2009, https://www.cato-unbound.org/2009/04/13/peter-thiel/education-libertarian.

17. Maureen Dowd, "Confirm or Deny: Peter Thiel," *New York Times*, January 11, 2017, https://www.nytimes.com/2017/01/11/fashion/peter-thiel-confirm-or-deny.html.

18. Matt Burns, "Leaked Palantir Doc Reveals Uses, Specific Functions and Key Clients," January 11, 2015, https://techcrunch.com/2015/01/11/leaked-palantir-doc-reveals-uses-specific-functions-and-key-clients/.

19. *Griswold v. Connecticut*, 381 U.S. 479 (1965).

20. "Transcript of Mark Zuckerberg's Senate Hearing," *Washington Post*, April 10, 2018, https://www.washingtonpost.com/news/the-switch/wp/2018/04/10/transcript-of-mark-zuckerbergs-senate-hearing/?noredirect=on.

21. Barrett Brown, "NPR Says I'm Planning Global Chaos. This Is a Half-Truth," Noteworthy, July 12, 2018, https://blog.usejournal.com/npr-says-im-planning-global-chaos-this-is-a-half-truth-a38e50874456.

22. "Anonymous Hackers Have Their Say," *NBC Nightly News*, March 8, 2011, http://www.nbcnews.com/video/nightly-news/41977337; Olson, *We Are Anonymous*, 195–196.

23. Barrett Brown, phone conversation with author, April 12, 2018; Andy Isaacson, "Are You Following a Bot? How to Manipulate Social Movements by Hacking Twitter," *Atlantic*, May 2011, https://www.theatlantic.com/magazine/archive/2011/05/are-you-following-a-bot/308448/.

24. "Barrett Brown," Wikipedia, https://en.wikipedia.org/wiki/Barrett_Brown; Michael Hastings, "Exclusive: FBI Escalates War on Anonymous," *Buzzfeed*, https://www.buzzfeed.com/mhastings/exclusive-fbi-escalates-war-on-anonymous?utm_term=.sdN4yLjD3#.uuOWn3yQK.

25. Ben Makuch, "Barrett Brown Went to Prison Again for Talking to Me," *Motherboard*, May 1, 2017, https://motherboard.vice.com/en_us/article/ypya9x/barrett-brown-went-to-jail-again-for-talking-to-me.

26. Maureen Dowd, "'All Men Are Guilty,' Says Mega-Mogul Barry Diller," *New York Times*, March 24, 2018, https://www.nytimes.com/2018/03/24/style/barry-diller-iac.html.

27. Adrian Chen, "The Truth About Anonymous's Activism," *The Nation*, November 11, 2014, https://www.thenation.com/article/truth-about-anonymouss-activism/.

28. Coleman, *Hacker, Hoaxer, Whistleblower, Spy*, 33–35.
29. Adam L. Penenberg, "The Troll's Lawyer," *Wired*, January 5, 2015, https://www
.wired.com/2015/01/the-trolls-lawyer/.
30. TechCrunch, "Weev's Speech Before District Court Sentencing," YouTube,
March 19, 2013, https://youtu.be/-rycPq2P1-Y.
31. Becca Lewis, "Media Manipulation and Disinformation Online," Data & Society,
May 15, 2017, https://datasociety.net/output/media-manipulation-and-disinfo
-online/.
32. Schwartz, "The Trolls Among Us."
33. Penenberg, "The Troll's Lawyer."
34. Luke O'Brien, "The Making of an American Nazi," *Atlantic*, December 2017,
https://www.theatlantic.com/magazine/archive/2017/12/the-making-of-an
-american-nazi/544119/.

CHAPTER 9

1. "4chan—The Facebook Age," GitHub, https://github.com/bibanon/bibanon/wiki
/4chan—The-Facebook-Age.
2. 4chan post by Christopher Poole, "Why were /r9k/ and /new/ removed?" Archived
at https://www.webcitation.org/6159jR9pC?url=http://content.4chan.org/tmp
/r9knew.txt; 4chan post by Christopher Poole, "Welcome back, robots," archived
at https://www.webcitation.org/62dybAZ9z.
3. Fredrick Brennan, "Hotwheels: Why I Support Eugenics," *Daily Stormer*, December 30, 2014, https://archive.is/ftgkC.
4. "/b/ User's Suicide Attempt," Know Your Meme, http://knowyourmeme.com
/memes/events/b-users-suicide-attempt.
5. Whitney Phillips, *This Is Why We Can't Have Nice Things: Mapping the Relationship Between Online Trolling and Mainstream Culture* (Cambridge, MA: MIT
Press, 2016), 79–99.
6. Rick Anderson, "'Here I am, 26, with no friends, no job, no girlfriend': Shooter's
Manifesto Offers Clues to 2015 Oregon College Rampage," *Los Angeles Times*,
September 23, 2017, http://www.latimes.com/nation/la-na-school-shootings
-2017-story.html.
7. Mary Elizabeth Williams, "4chan and the Oregon Shooter: What the Suspicious
Thread Says About a Horrifying Subculture of Young Male Rage," *Salon*, October 3, 2015, https://www.salon.com/2015/10/02/4chan_and_the_oregon_shooter
_what_the_suspicious_thread_says_about_a_horrifying_subculture_of_young
_male_rage/.
8. Chris Harper-Mercer, "My Story," https://schoolshooters.info/sites/default/files
/Christopher-Sean-Harper-Mercer-My-Manifesto.pdf.

CHAPTER 10

1. Marcella Szablewicz, "The 'Losers' of China's Internet: Memes as 'Structures of
Feeling' for Disillusioned Young Netizens," *China Information* 28, no. 2 (2014):
259–275.
2. "Are Japanese Moe Otaku Right-Wing?" *Neojaponisme*, May 30, 2012, http://
neojaponisme.com/2012/05/30/are-japanese-moe-otaku-right-wing/.
3. See Neiwert, *Alt-America*, 355–361.

4. F. A. Hayek, *The Road to Serfdom* (New York: Routledge, 1944).

5. Ajay Singh Chaudhary and Raphaele Chappe, "The Supermanagerial Reich," *Los Angeles Review of Books*, November 7, 2016, https://lareviewofbooks.org /article/the-supermanagerial-reich/#!.

6. Howard Zinn, *A People's History of the United States* (New York: HarperPerennial, 2005), chapter 10.

7. Edward Bellamy, *Looking Backward* (New York: Houghton Mifflin, 1889), chapter 1.

8. Hannah Arendt, *The Origins of Totalitarianism* (Cleveland: World, 1962), 131.

9. Ibid., 317.

10. Ibid., 134.

11. Ibid., 146.

12. Ibid., 157.

CHAPTER 11

1. Leigh Alexander, "'Gamers' Don't Have to Be Your Audience. 'Gamers' Are Over," Gamasutra, August 24, 2014, https://www.gamasutra.com/view/news/224400 /Gamers_dont_have_to_be_your_audience_Gamers_are_over.php.

2. Fredrick Brennan, audio Skype conversation with author, September 26, 2018.

3. "Zoe Quinn," knowyourmeme.com, https://knowyourmeme.com/memes/people /zoe-quinn, https://i.kym-cdn.com/photos/images/original/000/814/180/8b4.jpg.

4. Ibid., https://i.kym-cdn.com/photos/images/original/000/814/179/5c6.jpg.

5. Zoe Quinn, *Crash Overdrive* (New York: Hachette Book Group, 2017), 12, chapter 11.

6. "Timeline of Gamergate," Rational Wiki, https://rationalwiki.org/wiki/Timeline _of_Gamergate.

7. David Kushner, "4chan's Overlord Christopher Poole Reveals Why He Walked Away," *Rolling Stone*, March 13, 2015, https://www.rollingstone.com/culture /features/4chans-overlord-christopher-poole-reveals-why-he-walked-away-2015 0313.

8. Sam Machkovech, "Ars Interviews 8chan Founder Fredrick Brennan," *Ars Technica*, March 17, 2015, https://arstechnica.com/information-technology/2015/03 /full-transcript-ars-interviews-8chan-founder-fredrick-brennan/.

9. World News, "Al Jazeera America: The Other America: Fredrick Brennan," YouTube, September 20, 2013, https://www.youtube.com/watch?v=REnlB3631Nw; Michael Wilson, "City Newcomer Is Let Down by a Stranger, Then the Police," *New York Times*, January 18, 2014, https://www.nytimes.com/2014/01/18/nyregion /city-newcomer-is-let-down-by-a-stranger-then-the-police.html.

10. Fredrick Brennan, audio Skype conversation with author, September 26, 2018.

11. Ben Dowell, "Milo Yiannopoulos—Meet the 'Pit Bull' of Tech Media," *Guardian*, July 8, 2012, https://www.theguardian.com/media/2012/jul/08/milo-yiannopoulos -kernel-technology-interview.

12. Milo Yiannopoulos, "Feminist Bullies Tearing the Video Game Industry Apart," *Breitbart News*, September 1, 2014, http://www.breitbart.com/london/2014 /09/01/lying-greedy-promiscuous-feminist-bullies-are-tearing-the-video-game -industry-apart/.

13. Chadwick Moore, "Send in the Clown: Internet Supervillain Milo Doesn't Care That You Hate Him," *Out*, September 21, 2016, https://www.out.com

/out-exclusives/2016/9/21/send-clown-internet-supervillain-milo-doesnt-care
-you-hate-him.

14. Milo Yiannopoulos, "I'm Writing a Book About Gamergate," *Breitbart News*,
December 15, 2014, http://www.breitbart.com/london/2014/12/15/i-m-writing-a
-book-about-gamergate/.

CHAPTER 12

1. "Dank Memes," https://knowyourmeme.com/memes/dank-memes.
2. @realDonaldTrump, "@codyave: @drudgereport @BreitbartNews @Writeintrump
'You Can't Stump the Trump,' https://www.youtube.com/watch?v=MKH6PAo
UuD0 . . . https://twitter.com/codyave/status/653848101120143360/photo
/1pic.twitter.com/iF6S05se2w," Twitter, October 13, 2015, https://twitter.com
/realdonaldtrump/status/653856168402681856?lang=en.
3. @CheriJacobus, "@JamieW1776 @TrumpForEmp16 @TheRickWilson the green
frog symbol is what white supremacists use in their propaganda. U don't want to
go there," Twitter, January 7, 2016, 16:51, https://twitter.com/cherijacobus/statu
s/685262398345867265?lang=en.
4. "Pepe is a white supremacist symbol," 4chan post archived at 4plebs.org, https://
archive.4plebs.org/pol/thread/60352092/#60352827; "The Year Where 4chan
Won," Neato Burrito Productions, January 4, 2017, https://youtu.be/m7Zuff
Brloo?t=961.

CHAPTER 13

1. Joshua Green, *The Devil's Bargain: Steve Bannon, Donald Trump, and the Nationalist Uprising* (New York: Penguin Books, 2017), 4.
2. *New York Times*, "Read Trump's Reaction to Steve Bannon's Comments," January 3, 2018, https://www.nytimes.com/2018/01/03/us/politics/trump-statement
-steve-bannon.html?hp&action=click&pgtype=Homepage&clickSource=story
-heading&module=first-column-region&region=top-news&WT.nav=top-news
&_r=0.
3. Green, *The Devil's Bargain*, x, 146.
4. Ibid., 81–83; Issie Lapowsky, "Trump's Campaign CEO's Little Known *World of Warcraft* Career," *Wired*, September 2, 2016, https://www.wired.com/2016
/09/trumps-campaign-ceos-little-known-world-warcraft-career/; Julian Dibbel,
"The Decline and Fall of an Ultra Rich Online Gaming Empire," *Wired*, November 24, 2008, https://www.wired.com/2008/11/ff-ige/.
5. Dibbel, "The Decline and Fall of an Ultra Rich Online Gaming Empire."
6. Green, *The Devil's Bargain*, 147.
7. Jason Horowitz, "Steve Bannon Cited Italian Thinker Who Inspired Fascists,"
New York Times, December 2, 2017, https://www.nytimes.com/2017/02/10
/world/europe/bannon-vatican-julius-evola-fascism.html.
8. "Julius Evola," Wikipedia, https://en.wikipedia.org/wiki/Julius_Evola.
9. Green, *The Devil's Bargain*, 74.
10. "Watch a Reading of Steve Bannon's Screenplay Which Attempted to Turn Shakespeare's Coriolanus into a Rap Musical," *Open Culture*, May 3, 2017, http://
www.openculture.com/2017/05/watch-a-reading-of-steve-bannons-screenplay
-which-attempted-to-turn-shakespeares-coriolanus-into-a-rap-musical.html.

11. Jeremy W. Peters, "Bannon's Views Can Be Traced to a Book That Warns, 'Winter Is Coming,'" *New York Times*, April 8, 2018, https://www.nytimes.com/2017 /04/08/us/politics/stephen-bannon-book-fourth-turning.html.

12. Arendt, *The Origins of Totalitarianism*, 165.

13. See Dale Beran, "Utopia Lost: The Case for Radical Technological Optimism," July 24, 2017, https://medium.com/@DaleBeran/utopia-lost-7be0603716a4.

14. Ian W. Toll, *Pacific Crucible: War at Sea in the Pacific, 1941–1942* (New York: W. W. Norton, 2011, Kindle ed.), 1773–1777.

15. "4chan at its best," Reddit, https://www.reddit.com/r/funny/comments/lpok6 /4chan_at_its_best/.

16. Paul Bond, "Milo Yiannopoulos Documentary in the Works as Outrageous Tour Demands Revealed (Exclusive)," *Hollywood Reporter*, August 30, 2016.

17. Jordan B. Peterson, *12 Rules for Life: An Antidote to Chaos* (New York: Penguin, 2018), chapter 1, "Overture."

18. Ibid., chapter 2, "Rule 1: 'Stand up straight with your shoulders back.'"

19. See Louis B. Rosenblatt, *Buckets from an English Sea: 1832 and the Making of Charles Darwin* (New York: Oxford University Press, 2018), 140–185.

CHAPTER 14

1. William D. Cohen, "How Stephen Miller Rode White Rage from Duke's Campus to Trump's West Wing," *Vanity Fair*, May 2017, https://www.vanityfair.com/news /2017/05/stephen-miller-duke-donald-trump.

2. "Richard B. Spencer," Wikipedia, https://en.wikipedia.org/wiki/Richard_B._Spencer.

3. Joseph Bernstein, "Alt-White: How the Breitbart Machine Laundered Hate," *Buzzfeed*, October 5, 2017, https://www.buzzfeed.com/josephbernstein/heres-how -breitbart-and-milo-smuggled-white-nationalism?utm_term=.bbNXJroZO#.svy 8AE560.

4. Ibid.

5. Ibid.

6. Zachary Mider, "Robert Mercer's Secret Adventure as a New Mexico Cop," Bloomberg, March 28, 2018, https://www.bloomberg.com/news/features/2018 -03-28/robert-mercer-s-secret-adventure-as-a-new-mexico-cop.

7. Jane Mayer, "The Reclusive Hedge-Fund Tycoon Behind the Trump Presidency," *New Yorker*, March 27, 2017, https://www.newyorker.com/magazine/2017/03 /27/the-reclusive-hedge-fund-tycoon-behind-the-trump-presidency.

8. "Exposed: Undercover secrets of Trump's data firm," Channel 4, March 20, 2018, https://www.channel4.com/news/exposed-undercover-secrets-of-donald-trump -data-firm-cambridge-analytica; "Cambridge Analytica," Wikipedia, https://en .wikipedia.org/wiki/Cambridge_Analytica.

9. Arjun Kharpal, "Palantir Worked with Cambridge Analytica on the Facebook Data It Acquired, Whistleblower Alleges," CNBC, March 27, 2018, https://www .cnbc.com/2018/03/27/palantir-worked-with-cambridge-analytica-on-the-facebook -data-whistleblower.html.

10. Kimberly Ricci, "Donald Trump and Kellyanne Conway Attended a 'Heroes and Villains' Ball in Perfect Costumes," UPROXX, December 3, 2016, https:// uproxx.com/viral/trump-conway-heroes-villains-costumes/.

11. Formerly located at "The Sea Owl," http://www.winchdesign.com/portfolio/sea -owl/, archived by author May 22, 2018.

CHAPTER 15

1. Reuters, "Yahoo Hints That $1 Billion Tumblr Acquisition Was Mostly Wasted Money," *Fortune*, February 29, 2016, http://fortune.com/2016/02/29/yahoo-hints-that-1-billion-tumblr-acquisition-was-mostly-wasted-money/.
2. Rachael Krishna, "The 'Asian Character Hair Streak' Is Real and a Huge Problem," *Buzzfeed*, August 21, 2017, https://www.buzzfeed.com/krishrach/people-want-to-know-why-asian-cartoon-characters-all-have?utm_term=.jtX8dLeBK#.xsR5n4beJ; "Asian Hair Streak," Know Your Meme, http://knowyourmeme.com/memes/asian-hair-streak#fn1.
3. Dani Fletcher, "Guys on Guys for Girls," *Sequential Tart*, http://www.sequentialtart.com/archive/may02/ao_0502_1.shtml.
4. "Hamilkin," Know Your Meme, http://knowyourmeme.com/memes/subcultures/hamilkin.
5. ContraPoints, "Incel," YouTube, August 17, 2018, https://www.youtube.com/watch?v=fD2briZ6fB0.
6. Trey Taylor, "Why 2015 Was the Year of Trans Visibility," *Vogue*, December 29, 2015, https://www.vogue.com/article/2015-year-of-trans-visibility.
7. Olson, *We Are Anonymous*, 100; Coleman, *Hacker, Hoaxer, Whistleblower, Spy*, 174–175.

CHAPTER 16

1. Klein, *No Logo*, 108.
2. Ibid., 123.
3. Ibid., 122.
4. Ibid.
5. Ben Calhoun, "It's My Party and I'll Try if I Want To," *This American Life*, June 22, 2018, https://www.thisamericanlife.org/649/its-my-party-and-ill-try-if-i-want-to.
6. Jessica Anderson, "Local Campaigns Aim to Help Baltimore Students See 'Black Panther,'" *Baltimore Sun*, February 22, 2018, http://www.baltimoresun.com/entertainment/movies/bs-md-ci-black-panther-fundraiser-20180222-story.html.
7. Jonah Engel Bromwich, "Disney to Donate $1 Million of 'Black Panther' Proceeds to Youth STEM Programs," *New York Times*, February 27, 2018, https://www.nytimes.com/2018/02/27/movies/disney-black-panther-stem.html.
8. Jackson McHenry, "Is the Ending of Black Mirror's 'San Junipero' Exactly as It Seems?" *Vulture*, October 24, 2016, http://www.vulture.com/2016/10/black-mirror-san-junipero-ending.html; Andrea Reiher, "Emmys: Why *Black Mirror*'s 'San Junipero' Is Such a Big F*cking Deal," PopSugar, September 19, 2017, https://www.popsugar.com/entertainment/What-Black-Mirror-San-Junipero-Episode-About-44039278.

CHAPTER 17

1. "4chumblr," Know Your Meme, http://knowyourmeme.com/memes/4chumblr.
2. Neiwert, *Alt-America*, 17.
3. Ibid., 18.
4. Liam Stack and Gabrielle Fisher, "Princeton Agrees to Consider Removing a

President's Name," *New York Times*, October 19, 2015, https://www.nytimes
.com/2015/11/20/nyregion/princeton-agrees-to-consider-removing-a-presidents
-name.html.

5. Rachel L. Swarns, "Yale College Dean Torn by Racial Protests," *New York Times*,
November 15, 2015, https://www.nytimes.com/2015/11/16/nyregion/yale-college
-dean-torn-by-racial-protests.html.

6. "In Nationwide Student Revolt over Campus Racism, NY's Ithaca College Is
Latest School to Erupt," Democracy Now, November 13, 2015, https://www
.democracynow.org/2015/11/13/in_nationwide_student_revolt_over_campus;
John Eligon and Richard Pérez-Peña, "University of Missouri Protests Spur a
Day of Change," *New York Times*, November 13, 2015, https://www.nytimes
.com/2015/11/10/us/university-of-missouri-system-president-resigns.html.

7. Swarns, "Yale College Dean Torn by Racial Protests."

8. Angela Nagle, *Kill All Normies: Online Culture Wars from 4Chan and Tumblr
to Trump and the Alt-Right* (Washington, DC: Zero Books, 2017), 61.

9. Arendt, *The Origins of Totalitarianism*, 177.

10. "Yale Students Protest Halloween Costume (part 3)," posted November 6,
2015, https://www.youtube.com/watch?v=9IEFD_JVYd0.

11. Ibid.

12. Justin Wm. Moyer, "Oberlin College sushi 'disprespectful' to Japanese," *Washington Post*, December 21, 2015, https://www.washingtonpost.com/news/morning
-mix/wp/2015/12/21/oberlin-college-sushi-disrespectful-to-japanese/?noredirect
=on&utm_term=.3f08fbc6b3cd.

13. Fisher, *Ghosts of My Life*, chapter 1.

14. See also James 'Grim' Desborough, *Inside Gamergate* (Postmortem Studios, 2017),
a self-published pro-gamergate account that details the author's struggles with
suicidal depression.

CHAPTER 18

1. Gavin McInnes, "The VICE Guide to Happiness," November 30, 2003, *Vice*,
https://www.vice.com/en_us/article/av7xm8/the-vice-v10n1.

2. Robert Culkin, "Proud Boys: Who Are They?" August 24, 2017, https://official
proudboys.com/proud-boys/whoaretheproudboys/.

3. Nicole Disser, "Gavin McInnes and His 'Proud Boys' Want to Make Men Great
Again," July 28, 2016, Bedford and Bowery, http://bedfordandbowery.
com/2016/07/gavin-mcinnes-and-his-proud-boys-want-to-make-white-men-
great-again/.

4. Ibid.

5. Lyrics to "Proud of Your Boy" for *Aladdin* by Alan Menken, https://genius.com
/Alan-menken-proud-of-your-boy-broadway-lyrics.

6. Jazmine Ulloa, John Myers, Emily Alpert Reyes, and Victoria Kim, "7 Stabbed
at Neo-Nazi Event Outside Capitol in Sacramento," *Los Angeles Times*, June 26,
2016, http://www.latimes.com/local/lanow/la-me-neo-nazi-stabbed-20160626
-snap-htmlstory.html; "2016 Sacramento Riot," Wikipedia, https://en.wikipedia
.org/wiki/2016_Sacramento_riot.

7. Sarah Posner, "How Donald Trump's New Campaign Chief Created an Online
Haven for White Nationalists," *Mother Jones*, August 22, 2016, https://www

.motherjones.com/politics/2016/08/stephen-bannon-donald-trump-alt-right
-breitbart-news/.

8. Bernstein, "Alt-White: How the Breitbart Machine Laundered Hate."
9. Michael Barbaro, "The Story of Roger Stone and WikiLeaks," *New York Times*, January 28, 2019, https://www.nytimes.com/2019/01/28/podcasts/the-daily/roger -stone-trump-mueller-wikileaks.html; "U.S. v. Roger Stone Jr.: The full indictment," *Washington Post*, February 1, 2019, https://www.washingtonpost.com/roger -stone-indictment/7cedd188-130a-4fa3-8736-904a46747c92_note.html?utm_term =.5e4c2a729571.
10. Andrew Marantz, "Trolls for Trump," *New Yorker*, October 31, 2016, https:// www.newyorker.com/magazine/2016/10/31/trolls-for-trump.
11. Ibid.
12. /pol/ archived thread, http://archive.is/RffAd; Luke O'Brien, "How Pizzagate Pusher Mike Cernovich Keeps Getting People Fired," *Huffington Post*, July 21, 2018, https://www.huffingtonpost.com/entry/mike-cernovich-james-gunn-fired_ us_5b5265cce4b0fd5c73c570ac.
13. O'Brien, "How Pizzagate Pusher Mike Cernovich Keeps Getting People Fired."
14. Justin Bank, Liam Stack, and Daniel Victor, "What Is QAnon: Explaining the Internet Conspiracy Theory That Showed Up at a Trump Rally," *New York Times*, August 1, 2018, https://www.nytimes.com/2018/08/01/us/politics/what -is-qanon.html?rref=collection%2Fbyline%2Fjustin-bank&action=click&content Collection=undefined&region=stream&module=stream_unit&version=latest& contentPlacement=1&pgtype=collection.
15. See Brandy Zadrozny and Ben Collins, "How three conspiracy theorists took 'Q' and sparked Qanon," NBC News, August 14, 2018, https://www.nbcnews .com/tech/tech-news/how-three-conspiracy-theorists-took-q-sparked-qanon-n 900531.

CHAPTER 19

1. Perry Stein, "Women's March on Washington Officially Has a Permit for Jan. 21," *Washington Post*, December 15, 2016, https://www.washingtonpost.com/news /local/wp/2016/12/15/the-womens-march-on-washington-officially-has-a-permit -for-jan-21/?utm_term=.db30991e45ef.
2. Elizabeth King, "J20, One Year Later: What It's Like to Face Decades in Prison for Protesting," *Rolling Stone*, January 20, 2018, https://www.rollingstone.com /culture/features/j20-one-year-later-what-happened-to-defendants-w515646.
3. Paul P. Murphy, "White Nationalist Richard Spencer Punched During Inter-view," CNN, January 20, 2017, https://edition.cnn.com/2017/01/20/politics/white -nationalist-richard-spencer-punched/index.html.
4. Casey McNerthney, "Charges filed after University of Washington shooting outside Milo Yiannopoulos event," KIRO7, April 24, 2017, https://www.kiro7.com/news /local/charges-filed-after-university-of-washington-shooting-outside-milo-yianno poulos-event/515656517.
5. Nagle, *Kill All Normies*, 120; Malini Ramaiyer, "How Violence Undermined the Berkeley Protest," *New York Times*, February 2, 2017, https://www.nytimes. com/2017/02/02/opinion/how-violence-undermined-the-berkeley-protest.html.
6. Laurie Penny, "On the Milo Bus with the Lost Boys of America's New Right," *Pacific Standard*, February 21, 2017, https://psmag.com/news/on-the-milo-bus -with-the-lost-boys-of-americas-new-right.

7. Milo Yiannopoulos, "A note for idiots (updated) . . . ," Facebook, February 19, 2017, https://www.facebook.com/myiannopoulos/posts/851263248344905.

8. Michelle Ye Hee Lee and Craig Timberg, "How Cambridge Analytica Broke into the U.S. Political Market Through Mercer-Allied Conservative Groups," *Washington Post*, March 23, 2018, https://www.washingtonpost.com/politics /how-cambridge-analytica-broke-into-the-us-political-market-through-mercer-allied -conservative-groups/2018/03/23/141adba8-2ead-11e8-b0b0-f706877db618 _story.html?utm_term=.fab4d1c0b915.

9. Brian Lamb, "Q&A with Allison Stanger," C-SPAN, October 10, 2017, https:// www.c-span.org/video/?435406-2/qa-allison-stanger.

10. Allison Stanger, "Understanding the Angry Mob at Middlebury That Gave Me a Concussion," *New York Times*, March 13, 2017, https://www.nytimes.com /2017/03/13/opinion/understanding-the-angry-mob-that-gave-me-a-concussion .html.

11. Jared Taylor, "For Whom the Bell Curves," *American Renaissance*, February 1995, https://www.amren.com/news/2017/09/charles-murray-bell-curve-race -and-iq-richard-herrnstein-jared-taylor/; https://www.amren.com/news/2014 /01/race-differences-in-intelligence-2/.

12. "Nathan Benjamin Damigo," Southern Poverty Law Center, https://www.splcenter .org/fighting-hate/extremist-files/individual/nathan-benjamin-damigo.

13. Speel, "Based stickman the greatest American of this generation," YouTube, March 5, 2017, https://www.youtube.com/watch?v=lfLoltHDpno; A. C. Thomp- son, Ali Winston, and Darwin BondGraham, "Racist, Violent, Unpunished: A White Hate Group's Campaign of Menace," *ProPublica*, October 19, 2017, https://www.propublica.org/article/white-hate-group-campaign-of-menace-rise -above-movement?utm_campaign=sprout&utm_medium=social&utm_source =facebook&utm_content=1508436861.

14. Jocelyn Gecker, "Ann Coulter Was a No-Show at a UC Berkeley Protest in Her Honor," *Business Insider*, April 28, 2017, https://www.businessinsider.com/ap-ann -coulter-a-no-show-at-raucous-but-peaceful-berkeley-rally-2017-4.

15. Doug Brown, "Suspect in Portland Hate Crime Murders Is a Known White Su- premacist," *Portland Mercury*, May 27, 2017, https://www.portlandmercury .com/blogtown/2017/05/27/19041594/suspect-in-portland-hate-crime-murders -is-a-known-white-supremacist.

16. Jason Wilson, "'Alt-Right Celebrities' Are Holding a Rally in Portland. Who Are They?" *Guardian*, June 2, 2017, https://www.theguardian.com/us-news/2017 /jun/02/alt-right-celebrities-rally-portland-train-stabbing.

17. KGW-TV, "14 Arrested During Competing Protests in Portland in Wake of Train Stabbing," *USA Today*, June 5, 2017, https://www.usatoday.com/story/news /nation/2017/06/05/portland-demonstrations-marked-arrests-clashes/102508926/.

18. Michael Barbaro, "A Year of Reckoning in Charlottesville," *New York Times*, August 13, 2018, https://www.nytimes.com/2018/08/13/podcasts/the-daily/charlot tesville-rally-anniversary.html.

19. Lisa Provence, "Paul Goodloe McIntire: Goodwill to all men?" *CVille*, March 30, 2016, http://www.c-ville.com/paul-goodloe-mcintire-goodwill-men/#.WvRW p4gvwzP.

20. Chris Suarez, "'Inappropriate' Tweets from Bellamy Cause Some to Call for His Removal," *Daily Progress*, November 27, 2016, http://www.dailyprogress.com /news/local/inappropriate-tweets-from-bellamy-cause-some-to-call-for-his/article _2c5a86fa-b514-11e6-88b1-878551ca38ab.html.

21. "Fraternal Order of Alt-Knights (FOAK)," Southern Poverty Law Center, https://www.splcenter.org/fighting-hate/extremist-files/group/fraternal-order-alt-knights-foak.

22. Charles Johnson, "Stupidest Man on the Internet Quietly Deletes Lucian Wintrich #PizzaGate Screed," Little Green Footballs, March 26, 2017, http://littlegreenfootballs.com/article/47017_Stupidest_Man_on_the_Internet_Quietly_Deletes_Lucian_Wintrich__PizzaGate_Screed; Media Matters Staff, "A Dangerous Troll Is Now Reporting from the White House," Media Matters, February 13, 2017, https://www.mediamatters.org/blog/2017/02/13/dangerous-troll-now-reporting-white-house/215320.

23. Andrew Marantz, "The Alt-Right Branding War Has Torn the Movement in Two," *New Yorker*, July 6, 2017, https://www.newyorker.com/news/news-desk/the-alt-right-branding-war-has-torn-the-movement-in-two.

24. Dave Davies, "In the Wake of Charlottesville, Journalist Begins 'Documenting Hate' in America," *Fresh Air*, August 8, 2018, https://www.npr.org/2018/08/02/634890750/in-the-wake-of-charlottesville-journalist-begins-documenting-hate-in-america.

25. Jason Kessler (@themaddimmension), "The VA Proud Boys that care about defending Western Civilization and the people who built it will be at #UniteTheRight, polo or no," Twitter, July 19, 2017, 8:57, https://twitter.com/TheMadDimension/status/887702979339571200; Based in Colorado, "Proud Boys Official Statement on the 'Unite the Right' Rally," *Proud Boy Magazine*, 2017, https://web.archive.org/web/20170720033405/http://officialproudboys.com/news/gavin-mcinnes-virginia-unite-the-right-rally-disavowed/.

26. Davies, "In the Wake of Charlottesville, Journalist Begins 'Documenting Hate' in America."

27. Justin Wm. Moyer and Lindsey Bever, "Vanguard America, a White Supremacist Group, Denies Charlottesville Ramming Suspect Was a Member," *Washington Post*, August 15, 2017, https://www.washingtonpost.com/local/vanguard-america-a-white-supremacist-group-deniecharlottesville-attacker-was-a-member/2017/08/15/2ec897c6-810e-11e7-8072-73e1718c524d_story.html?utm_term=.615f448f4ff3.

28. "James Alex Fields Jr.," Rational Wiki, https://rationalwiki.org/wiki/James_Alex_Fields_Jr.

29. Bob Strickley, Sarah Brookbank, Chris Graves, and Chris Mayhew, "911 Calls, Records Reveal Tumultuous Past for Accused Charlottesville Driver, Family," *Cincinnati*, August 14, 2017, https://www.cincinnati.com/story/news/local/northern-ky/2017/08/14/mom-previously-accused-charlottesville-driver-james-alex-fields-jr-beating-her/566078001/.

30. Linda Qiu, "Trump Asks, 'What About the Alt-Left?' Here's an Answer," *New York Times*, August 15, 2017, https://www.nytimes.com/2017/08/15/us/politics/trump-alt-left-fact-check.html.

31. Maggie Haberman, Michael D. Shear, and Glenn Thrush, "Stephen Bannon out at the White House After Turbulent Run," *New York Times*, August 18, 2017, https://www.nytimes.com/2017/08/18/us/politics/steve-bannon-trump-white-house.html.

32. Glenn Thrush, "New Outcry as Trump Rebukes Charlottesville Racists 2 Days Later," *New York Times*, August 14, 2017, https://www.nytimes.com/2017/08/14/us/politics/trump-charlottesville-protest.html.

33. Abigail Hausohner, Joe Heim, and Susan Svrluga, "'Go Home, Spencer!' Protesters Disrupt White Nationalist's Speech at the University of Florida," *Washington Post*, October 19, 2017, https://www.washingtonpost.com/news/grade-point/wp/2017/10/18/uf/?noredirect=on&utm_term=.48fa394268ac.
34. "Richard Spencer Hosted an Event at a Maryland Farm. Halfway Through, Everyone Was Kicked Out," *Washington Post*, November 21, 2017, https://www.washingtonpost.com/local/richard-spencer-hosted-an-event-at-a-maryland-farm-halfway-through-everyone-was-kicked-out/2017/11/21/1cd92dfe-9f33-40c4-b6f5-a271a8874c5d_story.html?utm_term=.6e7d6292fbaf.

CHAPTER 20

1. Giorgio de Maria, *The Twenty Days of Turin* (New York: Liveright, 2017), 38.
2. Milan Kundera, *The Book of Laughter and Forgetting* (New York: HarperCollins, 1996), 147.
3. Mona Charen, "I'm Glad I Got Booed at CPAC," *New York Times*, February 25, 2018, https://www.nytimes.com/2018/02/25/opinion/im-glad-i-got-booed-at-cpac.html.
4. Laura Hudson, "If you want to know how we ended up in a cyber dystopia, read Ready Player One," *The Verge*, April 19, 2018, https://www.theverge.com/2018/4/19/17250892/ready-player-one-book-facebook-internet-dystopia.
5. Douglas Rushkoff, "Survival of the Richest," *Medium*, July 5, 2018, https://medium.com/s/futurehuman/survival-of-the-richest-9ef6cddd0cc1.
6. Aric Jenkins, "Robots Could Steal 40% of U.S. Jobs by 2030," *Fortune*, March 24, 2017, http://fortune.com/2017/03/24/pwc-robots-jobs-study/.
7. See Peter Frase, *Four Futures: Visions of the World After Capitalism* (London: Verso, 2016).
8. @existentialcoms, https://twitter.com/existentialcoms/status/1005179265745182720.
9. Guy Trebay, "For Capitalism, Every Social Leap Forward Is a Marketing Opportunity," *New York Times*, https://www.nytimes.com/2018/09/18/style/gender-nonbinary-brand-marketing.html.
10. Stanislaw Lem, *The Futurological Congress* (New York: Mariner Books, 1985).

Index